Transforming Prejudice

Transforming Prejudice

Identity, Fear, and Transgender Rights

MELISSA R. MICHELSON AND
BRIAN F. HARRISON

OXFORD
UNIVERSITY PRESS

OXFORD
UNIVERSITY PRESS

Oxford University Press is a department of the University of Oxford. It furthers
the University's objective of excellence in research, scholarship, and education
by publishing worldwide. Oxford is a registered trade mark of Oxford University
Press in the UK and certain other countries.

Published in the United States of America by Oxford University Press
198 Madison Avenue, New York, NY 10016, United States of America.

Library of Congress Cataloging-in-Publication Data
Names: Michelson, Melissa R., 1969– author. | Harrison, Brian F., author.
Title: Transforming prejudice : identity, fear, and transgender rights /
Michelson and Harrison.
Description: New York, NY : Oxford University Press, [2020] |
Includes bibliographical references and index.
Identifiers: LCCN 2019056233 (print) | LCCN 2019056234 (ebook) |
ISBN 9780190068882 (hardback) | ISBN 9780190068899 (paperback) |
ISBN 9780190068912 (epub)
Subjects: LCSH: Transgender people—United States—Public opinion. |
Transphobia—United States. | Transgender people—Civil rights—United States.
Classification: LCC HQ77.965.U6 M53 2020 (print) | LCC HQ77.965.U6 (ebook) |
DDC 306.76/80973—dc23
LC record available at https://lccn.loc.gov/2019056233
LC ebook record available at https://lccn.loc.gov/2019056234

1 3 5 7 9 8 6 4 2

Paperback printed by Marquis, Canada
Hardback printed by Bridgeport National Bindery, Inc., United States of America

To the transgender women murdered 2019: We honor the strength it took to be yourselves. We dedicate our work to you in the hope that no more names will be added to this list.

Dana Martin
Ellie Marie Washtock
Jazzaline Ware
Johana Medina Leon
Ashanti Carmon
Claire Legato
Muhlaysia Booker
Michelle "Tamika" Washington
Paris Cameron
Chynal Lindsey
Johana Medina Leon
Chanel Scurlock
Zoe Spears
Brooklyn Lindsey
Denali Berries Stuckey
Tracy Single
Marquis "Kiki" Fantroy
Pebbles LaDime Doe
Bailey Reeves
Bee Love Slater
Elisha Chanel Stanley
Itali Marlowe
Brianna "BB" Hill
Nikki Kuhnhausen
Yahira Nesby

Contents

Tables, Figures, and Permissions

Tables

Figures

Permissions

1.3. From Jones, Philip Edward, and Paul R. Brewer. "Elite Cues and Public Polarization on Transgender Rights." *Politics, Groups, and Identities* (2018). doi:10.1080/21565503.2018.1441722. Reprinted with permission of the publisher (Taylor & Francis Ltd, http://www.tandfonline.com).

2.4. Published with permission from Senator Jack Reed.

2.5. Published with permission from NBCUniversal Archives.

4.5. Published with permission from Logan Ireland.

5.1. From Plutchik, Robert. "The Nature of Emotions: Human Emotions Have Deep Evolutionary Roots, a Fact That May Explain Their Complexity and Provide Tools for Clinical Practice." *American Scientist* 89, 4 (2001): 349, Figure 6. Reprinted with permission from *American Scientist*.

6.1. Photos of Brian and Melissa (photo credit for Brian: Pamela Einarsen Photography; photo credit for Melissa: Darcy Blake, Menlo College).

6.2. Published with permission from Kimberly Shappley.

6.3. Published with permission from Can Stock Photo Inc., © grebeshkovmaxim.

The epigraph in chapter 7 is from "A Litany for Survival." Copyright © 1978 by Audre Lorde, from The Collected Poems of Audre Lorde by Audre Lorde. Republished with permission from W. W. Norton & Company, Inc.

Some details of the framing experiment described in chapter 3 were published in Harrison, Brian F., and Melissa R. Michelson, "Using Experiments to Understand Public Attitudes Towards Transgender Rights." *Politics, Groups, and Identities* 5, 1 (2017): 152–160.

Some details of the laboratory experiment described in chapter 4 were published in Harrison, Brian F., and Melissa R. Michelson, "Gender, Masculinity Threat, and Support for Transgender Rights: An Experimental Study." *Sex Roles* 81, 1 (2019): 63–75.

Acknowledgments

A team of amazing, hard-working students collected data for the Jack Reed experiment described in chapter 1. They include Jairo Archila, Stephanie Duru, Devyn Gallagher, Emma Greene, Bastien Grunenwald, Tiffany Hac, Cecilia Logan, Megan Ma, Aracely Seminario, Amisha Sharma, Michael Stamatopoulos, Marina Suazo, and Lucy Webb. Thanks also go to Lowell High School APES teacher and knitting phenom Kathy Melvin for recruiting most of those fabulous assistants. Thanks also go to Melissa's parents, Mei and Arthur Michelson, for working for hours on Halloween night 2018 to recruit participants for the Journey Story experiment described in chapter 6. Menlo College students Giselle Martinez Collado and Esther Funez expertly entered the data from those paper surveys into spreadsheets.

Much of the work in this book was shared with friends and colleagues along the way, and we appreciate their feedback and support. Logan Casey was originally a coauthor for the book project and played a huge role in designing and conducting the acknowledgment experiment described in chapter 6. He also was crucial to our conversations early in the process about how changing minds about transgender people and rights differs from our earlier work on gay and lesbian rights, and what sort of strategies and messages might be effective at reducing reactance. Before the project was complete, Logan chose to separate from the project to focus on his important work at the Movement Advancement Project. We are grateful for his contributions and for his friendship.

We are also grateful to the LGBT politics colleagues who have shared feedback at conferences and in email conversations and whose work we build upon in our own. We are grateful to have such a supportive group of friends with whom we are working with as a subgroup in the discipline of political science to advance equality and justice for all LGBT people. This includes Jami Taylor, Ken Sherrill, Helma deVries-Jordan, Zein Murib, Andrew Flores, Barry Tadlock, Phil Jones, Pat Egan, Ellen Andersen, Jeremiah Garretson, Ben Bishin, Erin Mayo-Adam, Meg Osterbur, Shawn Schulenberg, R. G. Cravens, Gary Segura, Andrew Reynolds, Tony Smith, and Eric van der Vort. Other political science colleagues who are not part of the LGBT caucus but who also provided crucial support and feedback include Don Green, Alex Coppock, Marcela García-Castañon, and Jessica Lavariega Monforti.

The team at Oxford University Press was, as always, immensely encouraging and helpful. We are pretty sure that Angela Chnapko is the best book editor ever. Thanks also to the rest of the OUP team, especially Alexcee Bechthold.

We also thank the American Political Science Association, which provided funding for the acknowledgment experiment described in chapter 6.

Melissa is grateful for the amazing support she receives from folks at Menlo College and for their financial support of her research. She is also grateful for the love and support of her family, including her parents, Linda Bernstein and Mei and Arthur Michelson, and also her husband, Christopher Gardner, and her children: Colin Gardner, Jackson Gardner, Joshua Michelson, and Zachary Michelson. The older boys are crucial for keeping her tuned in to recent cultural knowledge, such as the introduction of new transgender characters on Netflix shows, and the younger ones for keeping her from spending too much time staring at computer screens working when she could be playing with them. Christopher, of course, is crucial in ways that cannot fit on this page. Thanks, schmoopie, for everything. Brian would like to thank Joshua and Vivian for being patient with Daddy when he was working when they'd rather be playing—and for asking good questions about what his book was about. I hope in the not-too-distant future, everyone will be as appreciative of how wonderful our differences are as these 7-year-olds are. And thank you to Shawn, as always, for your love and support. Love you.

About the Authors

Dr. Melissa R. Michelson (PhD, Yale University) is Professor of Political Science at Menlo College.

Dr. Brian F. Harrison (PhD, Northwestern University) is Lecturer at the Humphrey School of Public Affairs at the University of Minnesota. He is also Founder and President of Voters for Equality, an organization dedicated to mobilizing LGBT voters and allies to be more active and engaged participants in American political life.

Transforming Prejudice

1

Just a Little Bit of History Repeating

Definitions, Public Opinion, and the Issues

It's tempting to think that what has happened can predict what's to come, that we can learn from history and craft remedies by studying familiar processes and problems. This thought process makes new challenges less threatening because we can simply find the most similar case from before and do better this time around. The Propellerheads summarized this sentiment in their 1997 song *History Repeating*:

> The word is about, there's something evolving
> Whatever may come, the world keeps revolving
> They say the next big thing is here,
> That the revolution's near
>
> But to me it seems quite clear
> That's it's all just a little bit of history repeating.
> The newspapers shout a new style is growing,
> But it don't know if it's coming or going
>
> There is fashion, there is fad
> Some is good, some is bad
> And the joke rather sad,
> That it's all just a little bit of history repeating.

Does history truly repeat? Or do we just have an incentive to feel like it does?

In 1967, CBS News released a documentary called *The Homosexuals*, an hour-long broadcast anchored by Mike Wallace. The product of three years of preparation and research, the episode interviewed gay men, psychiatrists, legal experts, and police, giving the show the feel of a research-based account of what it meant to be gay in America at the time. However, the program simply perpetuated myths and stereotypes, portraying gay men as mentally

Transforming Prejudice. Melissa R. Michelson and Brian F. Harrison, Oxford University Press (2020) © Oxford University Press.
DOI: 10.1093/oso/9780190068882.001.0001

ill sexual predators, lecherous threats to children, and creepy loiterers in public bathrooms waiting for their next victims. Wallace described the average gay man this way:

> The average homosexual, if there be such, is promiscuous. He is not interested in nor capable of a lasting relationship like that of a heterosexual marriage. His sex life, his love life, consists of a series of one-chance encounters at the clubs and bars he inhabits. And even on the streets of the city—the pick-up, the one night stand, these are characteristics of the homosexual relationship. (Tropiano 2002: 11)

People often fear what they don't know or understand, particularly outgroups they perceive as different from them in some fundamental way. The CBS documentary was based on such fears and portrayed homosexuality as a mental illness, a pathological and fundamentally different, unfamiliar existence. These stereotypes endured for decades, even into the late 1990s and early 2000s, when surveys revealed that many Americans, repelled by the "ick factor" of same-sex intimacy, believed that same-sex relationships and marriage equality posed a threat to themselves and to society (Mucciaroni 2008). Mucciaroni argued that "whether gay rights advocates succeed in getting their policies adopted depends partly upon whether Americans view their demands as threatening" (p. 88).

It is true that attitudes toward gay people changed dramatically in the 50 years since the CBS documentary. They changed slowly at first and at times even moved backward (such as during the AIDS crisis) but after decades of struggle, discrimination, violence, and heartache, prejudice against gay men diminished and continues to do so. Gallup has tracked attitudes toward same-sex relationships since 1977, when only 43% of the American public believed that gay or lesbian relations between consenting adults should be legal (see Figure 1.1). In 2019, 73% of the public agreed—a shift of 30 percentage points over just a few decades. Over the same period, opposition to same-sex relations dropped from 43% to 26% and the proportion of respondents who report having no opinion on the issue dropped dramatically.

Attitudes have shifted dramatically on other issues as well: large majorities of the public now support the rights of same-sex couples to marry, to legally adopt children, and to be protected against discrimination in employment, housing, and public accommodations like parks, restrooms, and restaurants (Gallup 2019; Lang 2016). The seismic shift in attitudes toward gay and

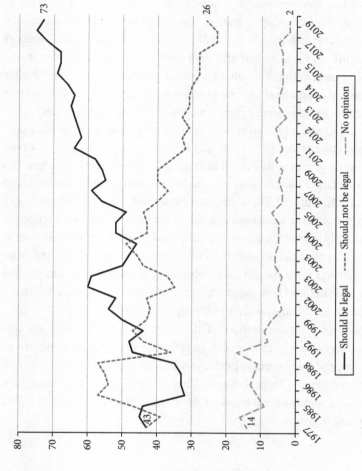

Figure 1.1. Support for gay and lesbian relations between consenting adults, Gallup polls 1977–2019.

Source: Gallup Trend Poll, https://news.gallup.com/poll/1651/gay-lesbian-rights.aspx.

Should be legal — — — Should not be legal — — — No opinion

lesbian people even includes shifts among Republicans and older Americans, groups that have historically been more opposed to gay rights.

Recent vocal and vociferous anti-transgender messages parallel historical attacks throughout the 20th century, particularly those aimed at gay men. Back then many people described gay and lesbian people as pedophiles, sexual deviants, unnatural, or mentally ill. Both historically and today, opponents to transgender equality often call into question the legitimacy of transgender identity, dismissing transgender people as predatory, deviant, a threat to the natural order, or mentally ill (Focus on the Family 2015; Jeffreys 2014; Raymond 1979). In recent and nationally reported fights over trans-gender people's access to bathrooms and other public spaces, these familiar arguments are once again taking center stage. In other words, in this narrow sense as it relates to transgender rights, it feels like history is repeating.

It's tempting to think that attitudes toward transgender people—in many ways, a newer stigmatized group—would follow a similar trajectory to how attitudes toward gay men and lesbians changed. After all, these identities are all part of a larger coalition we call the LGBT (lesbian, gay, bisexual, and transgender) community.[1] The somewhat rapid attitudinal shift toward gay and lesbian people and for issues like marriage equality is, however, quite unusual. Not only have attitudes shifted differently for lesbian and gay people but the attitudes themselves are different from those toward transgender people. That brings us to the aim of this book: to investigate the uniqueness of how people think and feel about transgender people and to craft distinc-tive strategies to encourage positive public opinion shifts.

There are three considerations that demonstrate how attitudes are dif-ferent when it comes to transgender people: the nature and structure of public opinion, the role of media portrayals, and the impact of interpersonal contact with outgroups. To follow, we address each in turn, describing how the past, present, and future of transgender rights differ from those of rights for gay men and lesbians.

Public Opinion Change

One of the most studied recent phenomena related to public opinion toward gay men and lesbians is the unusual and dramatic shift from opposition to support of marriage equality that took place between the mid-1990s and the mid-2010s. In 2015, political analyst Nate Silver wrote, "Probably one-half to two-thirds of the rise in support for gay marriage has been a result of people changing their minds on the issue" (Silver 2015). Scholars have identified three factors that contributed to that dramatic shift in opinions: (1) interpersonal proximity and visibility, (2) the message and tone of the conversations, and (3) the diverse set of voices encouraging support for same-sex marriage (Harrison 2020).

First, *interpersonal proximity and visibility*. In 1993, only 61% of Americans surveyed said they knew someone who was gay or lesbian; in 2015, the same Pew Research Poll found 88% of Americans now reported knowing someone who was gay or lesbian. Further, the data showed that three-quarters of respondents who said they knew someone gay or lesbian were also supportive of marriage equality. (In fact, 48% strongly supported it.) Almost 70% of respondents with gay or lesbian family members supported marriage equality. On the flip side, people with few or no friends who were gay or lesbian were far less supportive of marriage equality (Pew Research Center 2015). In 2017, Gallup reported that more than 10% of LGBT adults were married to their same-sex spouse, suggesting that more and more Americans were coming into contact with married same-sex couples; this matters because individuals who know a married same-sex couple are more likely to support marriage equality (J. M. Jones 2017; Egan 2013).

Second, the *message and tone* of the conversations. Rather than focusing on abstract rights and principles, advocates spoke about love, commitment, and family. They used personal stories and anecdotes to help people think about how marriage was about real people. One example comes from the work done in Massachusetts, when advocates crafted a campaign focused on families and inclusion to persuade lawmakers on some key marriage equality votes. Marc Solomon, national campaign director for Freedom to Marry, wrote about how that strategy worked to convince lawmakers in Massachusetts to change their vote:

> We knew that the one thing that could break through the fear was allowing lawmakers to get to know [same-sex] married couples and their families. When they did, they would understand viscerally that these families were not much different from their own and that they should treat gay families as they'd want their own family to be treated. (2014: 79)

Finally, having a *diverse set of voices*. Our theory of Dissonant Identity Priming, explored at length in our 2017 book *Listen, We Need to Talk*, showed that individuals could be motivated to change their minds about contentious issues like same-sex marriage when they received a message from someone they identified as a fellow ingroup member, particularly when that message was counter-stereotypical. Thus, for example, when President Barack Obama evolved his position on marriage equality, a surprising message given widespread Black opposition, many Black Americans were motivated to also change their minds on the issue. The varied and increasing number of opinion leaders, including politicians from both sides of the aisle, religious leaders, sports teams and prominent athletes, and celebrities, as well as friends and family members who publicly shared that they had changed their mind about marriage equality, encouraged others to reconsider their own opinions.

Motivating people to change their opinions about transgender people and rights is different because these three factors are not present: most Americans do not personally know anyone who is transgender; advocates have yet to find a message that widely resonates with existing values; and there are far fewer voices speaking out in their favor. In fact, there are very prominent voices speaking out *against* transgender rights, including that of the president of the United States.

In the aftermath of the November 2016 election and in the context of the Trump administration, attacks on transgender rights intensified both at the national and at the state and local levels. The Trump administration in its first year moved to reverse Obama-era protections for transgender students, transgender patients, transgender prison inmates, and transgender troops. Perhaps most visible of Trump's attacks on transgender rights was his decision in 2017 to move to block transgender people from serving openly in the U.S. military. According to the Human Rights Campaign, 2017 was the deadliest year on record for transgender people, with at least 29 transgender people killed; the spike in violence continued in 2018, when 26 murders were reported. Overall, at least 128 transgender people were killed between 2013 and 2018, of whom 80% were people of color (Christensen 2019). As a result of this climate of discrimination and violence against transgender people, transgender rights have become a more prominent part of public debate. The right of transgender people to use public restrooms and other public spaces that match their gender identity has become a particularly contentious issue of public discussion and votes. We return to an in-depth discussion of these two issues (bathroom access and military service) in chapter 3.

Discriminatory attitudes and behaviors toward transgender people stem from a variety of sources, including a lack of (factually correct) information; deeply held beliefs about the presence of a gender binary; lack of contact, either interpersonally or via media, with transgender people; ideological and political conservatism; strength of attachment to one's own gender identity; and others. Men, on average, have more negative views of transgender people compared to women, and attitudes toward transgender women (women assigned or identified as male at birth) tend to be more negative than attitudes toward transgender men (men assigned or identified as female at birth).

Support for transgender people lags far behind support for gay men and lesbians. Increasingly, in line with the current era's partisan polarization, Democrats are generally supportive of the rights of transgender people while Republicans are opposed. Most Republicans (80%) believe that gender is what you are assigned at birth while most Democrats (64%) believe that a person's gender can be different from what they were assigned at birth (A. Brown 2017). There are also partisan divides on issues related to gay men and lesbians but support is much stronger for members of those groups among both Democrats and Republicans. Overall, 70% of Americans now say that homosexuality should be accepted, including a majority (54%) of Republicans and 83% of Democrats (Figure 1.2).

The ongoing opposition to transgender rights, despite relatively widespread support for gay and lesbian rights, belies the neat packaging of these groups together into a simple, familiar acronym: while the public is increasingly familiar with the concept of LGBT rights and with the definition of the word *transgender*, most of the shift in public attitudes and public policy changes that we have observed over the past few decades are focused on the L and G segments of the community (Taylor et al. 2018). Transgender advocates have often taken advantage of this grouping to slip gender identity protections into bills focused on protecting the rights of gay men and lesbians. While this strategy has the advantage of advancing the rights of transgender and gender nonconforming people and allows advocates to sidestep the hard work of building up public support, it also means that significant public unease and opposition are left intact.[2]

In contrast to the advances made in improving attitudes toward and increasing support for the rights of other groups, significant resistance and hostility to transgender people persists in the United States.[3] Many remain uncomfortable with the idea that gender exists on a continuum and

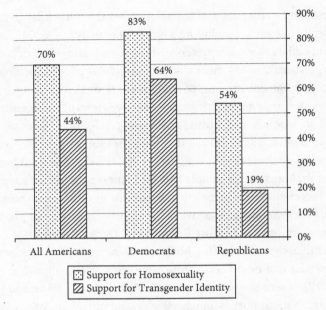

Figure 1.2. Support for homosexuality and transgender identity, by partisanship, 2017 surveys.

Source: Pew Research Center. Data on transgender identity collected August 8–21 and September 14–28, 2017 (see Brown 2017). Data on support for homosexuality collected June 8–18 and June 27–July 9, 2017 (see Pew Research Center 2017).

violence against transgender people is disturbingly frequent (N. Adams et al. 2018). If information and coming into contact with transgender people have been found to be ineffective, it begs fundamental and more complex questions: what *will* change hearts and minds about transgender people and rights? How can people be motivated to rethink their anti-transgender attitudes and persuaded to support transgender rights?

Opinion toward transgender people is a complicated minefield of informational, ideological, and psychological frameworks: lack of knowledge, emotion and affect, values, personality characteristics, and interpersonal experience and exposure to transgender people themselves all influence political attitudes. Overall, there are relatively few studies attempting to explain attitudes toward transgender people. One study found that while a majority of Americans support some transgender rights in the abstract, there is considerable negativity when asking more specific questions about transgender people and candidates, with substantial numbers of people reporting negative stereotypes about transgender people's morality and trustworthiness (P. E. Jones et al. 2018).

The challenges facing transgender people and their allies are readily apparent; what to do to enact change is less immediately clear. Simply put, there are more questions than answers. What can you do or say to someone who does not identify as transgender to get them to care about transgender rights, even if they are already a self-identified liberal or progressive? Some demographic groups tend to be more likely to oppose transgender rights, including people who identify as conservatives, who identify as strongly religious, or who live in rural areas. How can they be persuaded to be more supportive? Are some people simply unmovable on these sets of issues and if so, who are they and why are they so resistant? And what are the implications for advocates of transgender people who seek to reduce prejudice and violence against members of this vulnerable community?

In today's political environment, persuading others to rethink their prejudices is exceedingly difficult. Our various identities have become increasingly sorted, leaving us less likely to be tolerant of outgroup members (Mason 2018). We are more likely to feel threatened and angered by opponents and less likely to perceive them as reasonable people. The American public views political contests largely as opportunities for their side to win or lose. People seem to care less about actual policies or belief systems that underlie elections and debates with outgroups. Changing minds about the transgender community—a much smaller community than the gay and lesbian community and thus less able to fight for acceptance through contact, particularly in today's polarized and sorted political contexts—will require a different approach. We illustrate this point in chapter 2 with results from a randomized experiment testing the power of the sort of primed, shared identities that proved so powerful in our prior work on marriage equality.

The burden of attitudinal shift of the majority should not fall on the marginalized groups; we are not privileging the feelings and insecurities of those who oppose transgender people and rights. At the same time, however, it is important to acknowledge the challenges of encouraging people who have little to no stake in the well-being of transgender people to be more supportive. Our approach is to find a middle ground by putting forth a set of strategies to bolster and to reaffirm the identities of groups in need of persuasion while acknowledging that they should reconsider their prejudices. In other words, we hypothesize that the most effective messaging on this set of issues meets people where they are, acknowledges their discomfort and fear without judgment or criticism, and helps them think about transgender people and rights with links to their existing values and feelings. It lifts them up and appeals to their better angels while helping them tamper down their prejudices. These existing attitudes and identities are not what supporters of transgender people and rights wish they were; we think it is important to begin a discussion of attitude change, however, with realistic assessments of the status of thoughts and feelings toward transgender people and rights. We in no way endorse those prejudices.

We begin with a broad discussion of persuasion and the reasons it tends to be difficult to change people's minds. Resistance to sociopolitical issues is often deeply rooted in individual identity, making persuasion particularly difficult. It *is* possible, of course, and we identify a few recent examples of how hearts and minds can be changed before turning our focus to transgender rights; specifically, we discuss theories and explanations about why attitudes about transgender rights have not moved as quickly as on gay and lesbian rights like marriage equality. As we detail in chapter 2, we found that messaging based on Dissonant Identity Priming, the theory introduced in our 2017 book *Listen, We Need to Talk*, was not a productive method of reducing prejudice against transgender people or of increasing support for transgender rights, emphasizing our need to find a different approach. We close this chapter with our new theory and its key elements, outlining the remainder of the book.

Identity and Attitude Change

Intergroup discrimination is sometimes explained as a reasonable, realistic conflict of interests (Campbell 1965). For example, there may be limited resources or a finite amount of political capital for different identity groups (e.g., religious, ideological, or partisan) that might lead to legitimate feelings of intergroup discrimination. However, that is often not the case. Multiple studies of intergroup behavior and social identity theory (Brewer and Brown 1998; Hewstone, Rubin, and Willis 2002; Hogg and Abrams 1988; Sachdev and Bourhis 1987; Tajfel 1979, 1981; Tajfel and Turner 1979) posit that both salient social categorization and ingroup identification are necessary and sufficient characteristics for intergroup discrimination, providing a broader view that includes relatively irrational discrimination (e.g., minimal group identity). Oaks, Haslam, and Turner (1994: 83) summarize five variables that social identity theory deems relevant to intergroup discrimination measured in the minimal group paradigm: (1) the degree to which subjects identified with the relevant ingroup, (2) the salience of the relevant social categorization in the setting, (3) the importance and relevance of the comparative dimension to ingroup identity, (4) the degree to which the groups were comparable on that dimension (similar, close, ambiguously different), and (5) the ingroup's relative status and the character of the perceived status differences between the groups.

In other words, intergroup discrimination is based on comparing ingroups to outgroups on a known, distinguishable, comparable dimension but only if that ingroup identity is salient and if status differences between the groups are taken into account. Tajfel and Turner (1986) and Rubin and Hewstone (1998) claim that one crucial variable is excluded from this list: self-esteem. Social identity theory suggests that minimal group members discriminate in favor of their group to imbue it with a "positive distinctiveness" (Hogg and Abrams 1988: 23) to achieve, maintain, or enhance a positive social identity. It follows that "by establishing positive distinctiveness for the in-group as a whole, in-group members are establishing a positive social identity for themselves and hence positive self-esteem" (Rubin and Hewstone 1998: 41). Hogg and Abrams (1990) expand upon this principle with corollaries of their self-esteem hypothesis: that successful intergroup discrimination enhances social identity and thus elevates self-esteem. Self-esteem is a dependent variable, a product of specific forms of intergroup behavior. Relatedly, low self-esteem or threats to self-esteem can motivate intergroup discrimination aimed at boosting one's self-esteem. This also means that boosts to self-esteem should make individuals more open to persuasive communication about members of outgroups.

In this book, we advance a theory of how to change attitudes toward stigmatized groups (using transgender people as the focal example) through a focus on bolstering the self-esteem of the recipients of persuasive messages. Extensive psychological research finds that people do not like to be lectured or condescended to, that you can create a connection by appealing to shared values, and that you can generate prosocial attitudes and behaviors by appealing to positive attributes. You are unlikely to create openness to persuasion by attacking someone's existing beliefs as backward or wrong; you will, in such cases, trigger them to react emotionally and dig in their heels instead. You can create connections through appeals to shared values such as patriotism, belief in God, or other shared identities (see Harrison and Michelson 2015, 2016, 2017a). You can also appeal to the version of people that they want to believe is true (even if it is not) to motivate prosocial behaviors; for example, you could thank a person for being a voter to induce future civic engagement (Panagopoulos 2011) or appeal to an individual's sense of moral elevation to increase their likelihood of supporting social justice (Schnall and Roper 2012).

Marketing scholars have conducted extensive research on indirect techniques of persuasion. Indirect methods reduce the psychological barriers that can undermine persuasion efforts, making them more likely to succeed. These methods include framing, foot-in-the-door, low-balling, door-in-the-face, disrupt-then-reframe, and self-persuasion (see Bernritter, van Ooijen, and Müller 2017 for a review). For our purposes, the most important take-away from this extensive literature is that direct methods are less effective because of reactance. Similarly, and particularly because of the top-of-the-head negative affect that many people have toward transgender people, we posit that indirect methods will be more likely to persuade recipients of messages to be more supportive of transgender people and rights. We want to gently guide people to be more supportive or even to convince themselves that being supportive of transgender rights is a choice they are making on their own rather than one that is being demanded of them.

Backlash can emerge when prejudices are confronted directly and harshly. Similarly, self-affirmation that focuses on values that highlight intergroup contrasts (e.g., affirming family values prior to seeking to reduce prejudice against gay men) only strengthens dislike for gay men (Lehmiller et al. 2010). In contrast, self-affirmation strategies that focus people on egalitarian goals and values (e.g., fairness) or on bias-unrelated positive attributes (e.g., creativity) can provide "the self-integrity buffer that permits people to recognize [bias] and be more open-minded" (Stone et al. 2011: 597).

This is where we come in. We don't want to confront people too directly about their anti-transgender prejudices because we don't want to provoke anger or backlash. Instead, we seek to disarm and reassure people about their own values in a way that will generate open-mindedness and tolerance. We don't seek to convince people to feel completely comfortable with transgender people or to deny their discomfort; we seek to reassure them, to lower their defenses, and to transform their attitudes and behaviors gradually and indirectly.

Cohen and Sherman (2014: 352), reviewing a set of studies of the power of self-affirmation to reduce conflict, note: "When people are affirmed in valued domains unrelated to a dispute, they are more open to otherwise identity-threatening political information and less intransigent in negotiations." Stone et al. (2011) find that when Arab American men first asked prejudiced people self-affirming questions, they were then less defensive when confronted about their biases. Using self-affirmation to remind recipients of messages of their own self-worth has been found in numerous experiments to reduce extremism and closed-mindedness, including in experiments aimed at reducing prejudice against stigmatized groups (gay men and Arab Americans). We extend that literature to the stigmatized community of transgender people, while also providing mechanisms for harnessing the power of self-affirmation theory in ways that work outside of the (student) laboratory and in relatively brief face-to-face and Internet-based interactions.

The prior generation's minds were changed about marriage equality thanks to increased contact (both interpersonal and parasocial) and elite leadership (Rimmerman 2015; Ayoub 2016; Garretson 2018; Harrison and Michelson 2017a). Our 2017 book, *Listen, We Need to Talk*, tackled questions about how to persuade people to be more supportive of same-sex marriage, often called marriage equality. The Theory of Dissonant Identity Priming introduced in that book posits that people are more likely to be persuaded if you can find the right mix of message and messenger to focus on identities in common. Black people were more likely to be persuaded when a pro-marriage equality message was delivered by a Black messenger; fans of the Green Bay Packers football team were more likely to be supportive of marriage equality when the messenger was a prominent former Packers player. These effects were particularly strong if there was an element of dissonance or surprise, providing a cognitive speed bump that nudged recipients of messages to process the information and possibly to change their attitude. Our experiments were conducted during a time when attitudes were in flux and there was a widespread perception that the trajectory was moving toward support for marriage equality for more and more Americans all over the country. Even opponents were telling survey researchers that they expected same-sex marriage advocates to prevail. It became easier, in some senses, for opponents to become supportive because there were signs of support from all walks of life and many different identity groups. The perceived arc of history encouraged some people to push aside their misgivings and hop on the bandwagon of support for marriage equality.

Most of these recent shifts in attitudes and most public imagining of the community they relate to, however, are about gay men and lesbians. Bisexual people are often forgotten; transgender people are often deliberately excluded from both public debate and the public imagination. Starting just a few years ago, however, as the national conversation on same-sex marriage drew to a (legal) close, attention shifted to the rights of members of the transgender community. We know much less about public attitudes toward transgender people because until recently, public opinion surveys did not differentiate between attitudes toward transgender people specifically and the broader LGBT community.

Interpersonal and Mediated Contact

We argue that attitudes toward transgender people do not follow the same thought structure as attitudes toward gay and lesbian people and rights, the focus of our previous book. As a result, theories of attitude *change* must be different as well. As noted earlier, we believe most Americans will require a different approach to change their minds about transgender rights. We explored this assumption with a randomized experiment conducted over Memorial Day weekend in 2019, focused on the issue of transgender people serving openly in the U.S. military. Results from that experiment, shared in chapter 2, confirmed that Dissonant Identity Priming is not as powerful a method of persuasive messaging for transgender rights as it is for persuasive messaging on gay and lesbian rights. Throughout this book we provide evidence that persuasive messaging consistent with our new Theory of Identity Reassurance is a more productive avenue for shifting attitudes about transgender people and transgender rights.

Mirroring the rise in news stories and public opinion polls, there has been increased interest in recent years in academic work examining predictors and consequences of public attitudes toward transgender people. Some of this scholarship explores the impact of exposure and contact with transgender people or images as a means of reducing prejudice and increasing support for transgender rights. The work stems from Allport's (1954) Theory of Interpersonal Contact. Allport's main hypothesis is that interpersonal contact can reduce antagonism by the majority toward members of unpopular subgroups, possibly leading to reduced prejudice and bias. While originally and most frequently understood as a means of reducing racial and ethnic stereotypes, contact theory has also been used to predict attitudes toward gay and lesbian people and toward behaviors that may help or hinder the advancement of gay rights. However, there has been fairly heated debate about whether contact theory applies to transgender people given the negative reactions that many have toward transgender people, including disgust and fear, and the difficulty that few people have contact with transgender people (relative to contact with gay and lesbian people), which muddies the statistical waters.

While many studies have shown that reported contact with gay and lesbian individuals has positive effects on support for gay and lesbian rights and on attitudes toward transgender people, studies also show that reported contact with transgender people does not have the same positive effect on attitudes toward transgender people, controlling for other factors (Casey 2016; Flores 2015; Norton and Herek 2013; Tee and Hegarty 2006). Flores (2015) posits that this is because most people who know a transgender person also know a gay or lesbian person; multicollinearity between contact with gay and lesbian people and contact with transgender people is artificially minimizing the estimated effect of contact with transgender people. In other words, because people who know transgender people are also likely to know gay and lesbian people, it is difficult to statistically separate the effect of each form of interpersonal contact on attitudes. A weaker effect for interpersonal contact may also be due to the increased discomfort that people feel around transgender people compared to around gay men and lesbians (Taylor et al. 2018). Finally, of course, there is the limitation of the small size of the transgender population (0.6% of the U.S. population; see Flores et al. 2016), which means fewer Americans have the opportunity for interpersonal contact; this reality is compounded by the effort of many transgender people to pass rather than reveal their gender identity and risk becoming the victim of a violent assault (Hoffarth and Hodson 2018).[4]

Interpersonal contact was crucial to the success of the gay rights movement in changing attitudes and support for gay and lesbian rights. In 1978, Harvey Milk issued a call to his gay brothers and sisters that they must come out but cautioned that they should "come out only to the people you know, and who know you."

> Gay brothers and sisters, you must come out. Come out to your parents. I know that it is hard and will hurt them, but think about how they will hurt you in the voting booth! Come out to your relatives. Come out to your friends, if indeed they are your friends. Come out to your neighbors, to

your fellow workers, to the people who work where you eat and shop. Come out only to the people you know, and who know you, not to anyone else. But once and for all, break down the myths. Destroy the lies and distortions. For your sake. For their sake. (Milk 1978)

Milk understood that the power of interpersonal contact was based on the existing relationships that people had with closeted gay men and lesbians and that many people would respond positively to those coming out stories from people that they knew and loved. For transgender people, this is often not a viable strategy.

One study found evidence that knowing a transgender person reduces prejudice toward transgender people (King, Winter, and Webster 2009) while Flores (2015), examining data from a 2011 survey of American adults, found no evidence that contact improves attitudes toward transgender people. More recently, surveys from July and October 2015 found that mere exposure to images of transgender people is enough to reduce prejudice and increase support for transgender rights (Flores et al. 2017, 2018; Tadlock et al. 2017) while a national survey from November 2015 found no effect of contact (P. E. Jones et al. 2018).

These disparate results beg the question of whether contact with transgender people has a significant, across-the-board effect or whether effects are more nuanced, likely to have an effect on some but not on others. A clearer causal picture may emerge as more transgender people come out to their friends and family, with the limitation that, at only 0.6% of the population, most Americans have never met a transgender person face-to-face. In the July 2015 survey, 6.7% of respondents reported that they had a close friend or family member who is transgender. In the October 2015 study, 2.8% of respondents said they had a transgender family member and 3.5% reported that a close friend was transgender. A much higher (but still fairly small) number of respondents to the November 2015 study, 11%, reported a transgender close friend or family member. Asked in a much broader way—whether they "personally know anyone who is transgender"—an August–September 2016 Pew Research Survey found that 30% of respondents said that they knew someone who was transgender while 87% reported that they knew someone who was gay or lesbian (Pew Research Center 2016). Taylor et al. (2018) report very similar results in their October 2015 and June 2016 surveys.

Until the early 1990s, only 20% to 30% of Americans reported that they personally knew someone who was gay or lesbian. G. P. Lewis (2007) examines the 27 surveys between 1983 and 1994 that asked respondents about their contact with gay men and lesbians. Survey wording varies; limiting our focus here to those asking about close friends and family, the proportion reporting contact with gay men and lesbians was only 22% in February 1993, increasing to 32% by June 1993 and then 41% in October 1998. Starting in the mid-1990s, increasing numbers of gay men and lesbians came out to their families and friends (Garretson 2018). By March 2004, almost half of American adults were telling pollsters that they had a close friend or family member who was gay or lesbian; that proportion has remained fairly stable since then (G. P. Lewis 2007; Rosentiel 2007; Doherty, Kiley, and Weisel 2015).

As noted earlier, the contact hypothesis describes the idea that under certain conditions, interpersonal contact can reduce antagonism by the majority toward members of unpopular subgroups, possibly leading to reduced prejudice and bias (Allport 1954). However, contact with transgender people has *not* been found to be effective at producing positive attitude change or reducing anti-transgender bias when controlling for other factors, and it seems unlikely, given the small size of the transgender population, that this is a reliable method of moving attitudes for most Americans.

Media Portrayals

Interpersonal contact, while most closely hewing to Allport's Contact Theory, is not the only way in which contact with members of the LGBT community has been shown to reduce prejudice. A number of studies have found that exposure to characters in the mass media, including actors, celebrities, and public figures, also generates more positive attitudes (Ayoub and Garretson 2017; Garretson 2018; Schiappa et al. 2005; Gillig and Murphy 2016; Gillig et al. 2018). Survey respondents sometimes report contact with transgender people when they *know* a transgender celebrity or public figure, such as Laverne Cox or Caitlyn Jenner (Casey 2016). This measurement error may dilute the estimated power of interpersonal contact with transgender people but supports the idea that parasocial contact can also change beliefs about members of outgroups to which minority characters belong. Individuals who do not otherwise have interpersonal contact with members of the LGBT community but are able to form positive impressions of LGBT people portrayed in the mass media are likely to be less prejudiced against members of that community. Most relevant to our work, Schiappa et al. (2005) found that exposure to a comedy routine by Eddie Izzard, who at the time identified as a transvestite, reduced prejudice against transvestites. (Izzard now publicly identifies as transgender.)

More personal contact likely has a stronger effect: work by Pat Egan and Ken Sherrill finds that having a gay or lesbian family member leads to greater support for same-sex marriage when compared to the effect of other interpersonal contact (Egan 2013). Barth, Overby and Huffmon (2009) find in a study of residents of South Carolina that the effect of interpersonal contact varies among different types and levels of contact: Support for same-sex marriage was most strongly affected by having close personal friends and knowing couples in long-term homosexual relationships, and most modestly by those with gay family members or coworkers. But parasocial contact can still reduce prejudice, even if it is less powerful than interpersonal contact.

The power of parasocial contact is limited by the available supply of transgender celebrities and public figures who are well known and liked by the mass public, and by the availability of positively portrayed transgender characters in film and television shows. As Garretson (2018) notes, the ability of gay and lesbian characters in television and media to create positive affect toward gay men and lesbians more broadly is predicated on positive, reinforced exposure to those characters: "Fictional characters that are recurring and positive are more likely to result in successful contact, as these factors foster an emotional attachment to the character in the viewer" (p. 155). Transgender characters, however, tend to be portrayed less positively than gay men and lesbians, resulting in less positive (and less accurate) media exposure.

In fact, until fairly recently, it was unlikely that Americans would experience any parasocial contact with a transgender person or that that exposure would include transgender characters in film and television who were portrayed positively. Until a few years ago, transgender characters portrayed in media were frequently cartoonish in nature, often depicted as deviant, predatory, and/or mentally ill.

In 2012, GLAAD documented 102 episodes and nonrecurring storylines of scripted television from the previous decade that contained transgender characters and investigated trends in their depictions. Among their findings, they characterized 54% of the storylines as "containing negative representations at the time of their airing," with an additional 35% ranging from problematic to good. Only 12% were considered fair and accurate (GLAAD 2012). They also found that 40% of transgender characters were cast in a "victim role"; 21% of transgender characters were either killers or villains, and the most common profession of transgender characters was sex workers (20% of the sample). Anti-transgender slights, language, and dialogue were present in roughly 60% of the episodes and storylines. In 2014, GLAAD issued an updated report, finding that while depictions of transgender characters had improved, nearly half (45%) were based on negative, damaging stereotypes (Townsend 2014).

Also, the media tend to include transgender portrayals of transgender women while largely ignoring transgender men (Serano 2013). Media depictions of transgender women usually fall under one of two main archetypes: the "deceptive transsexual" or the "pathetic transsexual," both of whom "are designed to validate the popular assumption that trans women are truly men" (Serano 2013: 228). This trope dates back to long before the term *transgender* existed: in a 1917 silent movie, actor Fatty Arbuckle was shown "ogling women in the restroom while he's disguised in a dress and wig" (Berg 2017). This "persistent stereotype of transpeople as deceivers" plays a significant role in the recurrent violence against transgender people, especially transgender women of color (Bettcher 2013: 280). This "fear of fraud" is also used in arguments against allowing transgender people to update their government identity documents. As Currah and Moore note, "it is precisely because some transsexual women and men can pass in their new gender, can traverse many social, economic, even intimate landscapes as 'the other sex,' that authorities believe 'the public' must be protected from fraud" (2013: 611).

Another limitation of parasocial contact with transgender people is that transgender characters have historically been played by cisgender actors. For example, in one of the earliest portrayals, Tim Curry (a cisgender man) famously played the character Dr. Frank N. Furter in *The Rocky Horror Picture Show* (1975), an over-the-top, self-proclaimed "sweet transvestite from Transsexual, Transylvania." In 1992, Jaye Davidson (also a cisgender male) played the character Dil, a transgender woman who hid her gender identity in the film *The Crying Game*. Even contemporary portrayals that attempted to accurately tell the stories of transgender people have fallen short. For example, the 1999 movie *Boys Don't Cry* was a dramatization of real-life events surrounding the murder of Brandon Teena, a transgender man who was sexually assaulted and murdered. Teena was portrayed by Hilary Swank, a cisgender female. Similarly, cisgender actors like Jared Leto in *The Dallas Buyers Club* and Jeffrey Tambor in *Transparent* have increased visibility of the transgender population, though with backlash by those who would have preferred casting of transgender actors.

There has been some progress, however, as some transgender characters have become more multidimensional and, at least in some ways, more realistic. For example, Laverne Cox depicted Sophia Burset, a transgender woman of color, on the Netflix series *Orange Is The New Black* from 2013 to 2019. Cox earned a 2014 Emmy award nomination for the role, recognizing the complexity and depth of her portrayal. GLAAD has recognized episodes of shows like *Grey's Anatomy* (ABC), *Cold Case* (CBS), and *Two and a Half Men* (CBS) with GLAAD Media Award nominations for their realistic and positive depictions of transgender people, also mentioning groundbreaking storylines on shows like *The Education of Max Bickford* (CBS), *Degrassi* (Teen Nick), *The Riches* (FX), and *Ugly Betty* (ABC) for their "fully-formed and complex representations of transgender people" (GLAAD 2012). In 2018, this list expanded even further, including the FX series *Pose*, which includes five transgender actors of color cast in regular roles, setting a record for a scripted series (Goldberg 2017). The third episode was directed by Janet Mock, marking the first time an openly transgender woman of color had written and directed any episode of television (Gemmill 2018). Other additions, in 2019, included characters on *Supergirl* (on the CW), where transgender actor Nicole Maines plays a transgender superhero named Dreamer, and on *The Chilling Adventures of Sabrina* (Netflix), which includes as a storyline the transition of nonbinary actor Lachlan Wilson from Susie to Theo. As more positive transgender characters are portrayed in the media, particularly on shows that attract a widespread audience, opinion might continue to improve as well. Additional scholarship is necessary to test whether parasocial contact is changing minds in a durable way.

It is possible that the effect of contact, both interpersonal and parasocial, will decrease prejudice against transgender people over time as more Americans know that they are in contact with members of the community and as understanding of the term *transgender* increases. D. C. Lewis et al. (2017) note, however, that contact has a weaker effect for transgender people than for gay and lesbian people, and that many people do not feel a need to be ideologically consistent in their support for rights for different subsets of the LGBT community (especially Republicans, who have become more supportive of gay and lesbian rights over the past decade). This meshes well with work by Garretson (2018), who notes that contact works differently based on prior attitudes and political ideology: those with set negative opinions, or who are strongly conservative, sometimes become even less supportive of transgender people as reported contact increases, even if that contact is with close friends or family members.

Why Transgender Rights Are Different

Attitudes toward gay men and lesbians have shifted quickly in recent years, while discrimination against transgender people persists and in some instances has become more severe. In part, this reflects the hardened polarization of the Trump era and the accompanying atmosphere of emboldened bigotry. When the U.S. Supreme Court ruled in *Masterpiece Cakeshop* in 2018 that a baker could legally refuse to bake a cake for a same-sex wedding based on their religious beliefs, other Americans were encouraged to wear their anti-gay biases on their sleeves, including a Tennessee hardware store owner who posted a "No Gays Allowed" sign in his shop's front window (Robinson 2018). When President Trump rolled back protections for transgender students, transgender patients seeking healthcare, and transgender prison inmates—and when he announced his plan to reverse the policy of allowing transgender people to serve openly in the U.S. military—he sent messages to the public encouraging and endorsing discrimination.

It's not just the actions of the Trump administration that underlie bias against transgender people: discrimination against the transgender community was widespread long before he was elected. Studies show that public attitudes toward transgender people are rooted in feelings of threat, fear, disgust, and discomfort. Many Americans, particularly men, consider the idea of changing one's gender to be threatening to their own gender identity. Gender theorist Judith Butler roots anti-transgender violence in the threat to masculinity that the existence of transgender women poses to non-transgender (cisgender) men: "Trans women have relinquished masculinity, showing that it can be, and that is very threatening to a man who wants to see his power as an intrinsic feature of who he is" (quoted in Tourjée 2015). Opposition rhetoric about the alleged danger of transgender women in public restrooms has undermined efforts in multiple states to extend anti-discrimination protections to the transgender community (D. C. Lewis et al. 2015). Taylor and Lewis (2015: 122) note that legislators, particularly Republicans, are known to be "sometimes repulsed" by transgender people and are often "not comfortable with transgender persons unless they pass well." These visceral reactions are often shared by members of the mass public, limiting their openness to interacting with transgender people and their support for transgender rights (Casey 2016). Even when less rooted in fear and disgust, it is still difficult to persuade people to change their opinions. Persuasion is hard.

This book utilizes a variety of social science experiments to test the power of various messages meant to generate support for transgender people and rights.[5] These include experiments conducted using paper surveys collected from passersby on public sidewalks, online experiments conducted using various Internet platforms, and a laboratory experiment using undergraduate students. These are listed in Table 1.1.

Table 1.1. List of Experiments in This Book

Chapter	Theme	Target Population	Method	Location
2	Dissonant Identity Priming (the Jack Reed experiment)	Adults	Face-to-face	Redwood City and Fremont, California
3	Values framing (bathrooms)	Adults	Internet (MTurk)	National
	Values framing (transgender troops)	Adults	Internet (MTurk)	National
4	Gender identity threat	Undergraduate students	Laboratory	Midwest
	Gender identity bolstering	Adults	Internet (Lucid)	National
5	Emotions (the puppies and spiders experiment)	Adults	Internet (Lucid)	National
	Emotions (moral elevation)	Adults	Internet (Lucid)	National
6	Acknowledgment	Adults	Internet (MTurk)	National
	Acknowledgment and journey story (the journey story experiment)	Adults	Face-to-face	San Jose, California

Discussion and Conclusion

Overall, more attention needs to be paid to how the public forms their views of transgender people and rights and how those views might be changed. In part, the current lack of information on the topic is due to a lack of available survey data. Prior to April 2016, only six national surveys had ever asked respondents their attitudes about transgender people or rights, and one of these was a poll limited to LGBT respondents. Those early polls are also limited in that they only asked perceptions of discrimination toward transgender people and whether transgender people should be protected from discrimination. Only when the bathroom issue hit the national stage in spring 2016 did surveys begin to measure public attitudes toward specific rights and policies.

Taylor, Lewis, and Haider-Markel (2018) conducted three large nationally representative surveys about transgender rights for their book: one in June 2015, one in October 2015, and one in June 2016. While their focus is on policy changes in domains relevant to transgender people, they recognize that public opinion often shapes public policies and is used by advocacy groups to lobby for change. More importantly, they find considerable evidence that there is an opportunity to change public opinion on transgender rights: "Many of the survey items showed evidence of ambivalence and nonattitudes. . . . [M]any people's opinions on these issues do not seem to be fully formed. There is clearly an opportunity for the transgender movement, as well as opponents of transgender rights, to sway public opinion" (2018: 86).

Despite these fairly limited data, polls clearly indicate that support for specific transgender rights is limited, even as Americans acknowledge that transgender people are often discriminated against and should be protected against discrimination. General support for American values like the right to be treated equally and opposition to discrimination of any kind notwithstanding, large portions of the public are not ready to share public restrooms with transgender people, and they are even more opposed to transgender bathroom and locker room access rights in public schools. Understanding the predictors and determinants of attitudes toward transgender people is the first step toward developing tactics and messages aimed at shifting those attitudes. Transgender rights activists see other issues such as discrimination in employment and housing, hate crimes and violence, and health care as more pressing. Since the fights for transgender bathroom access rights and transgender military service are so closely linked to public opinion about transgender rights more broadly, however, we use those issues in some of the experiments in this book. More broadly, our experiments explore how to decrease bias against transgender people and open minds to persuasion on the issue of transgender rights.

Fifty years after the CBS documentary about homosexuality and almost 70 years after the Lavender Scare, an attempted purge of gay men working in the federal government (Johnson 2004), we see a similar narrative being built about transgender people: not just a denial of their identities but perpetuating the harmful falsehood that transgender people are inherently threatening and are all sexual predators and pedophiles. It took decades for gay and lesbian people to shift public opinion against these same characterizations and in many cases, they continue to persist. It feels like history is repeating. Does that mean it will take half a century to ease unsubstantiated fears about transgender people and generate widespread support for transgender rights? Or can we learn from history and from the science of randomized experiments to generate more rapid attitudinal change? In this book, we explore public opinion toward transgender people and share results from a variety of randomized experiments intended to shift public opinion and to help speed up the proverbial moral arc of the universe to more quickly bend toward justice.

2

Identity Reassurance Theory

Encouragement, Acknowledgment, and Values

A few years ago, Melissa showed up to work at her kid's Little League bat-a-thon fundraiser and started chatting with the other parent assigned to work at the prize table. The other parent introduced herself as Janet[1] and Melissa admired her bedazzled jeans and beautiful earrings. They shared stories about their children and organized the piles of socks and shirts. It was Melissa's first year with Little League but Janet had clearly done this all before and already knew what needed to be done. A short while later, Mark, the lead organizer of the event, came over to make sure they were okay. "You and James have everything under control over here?" Without missing a beat, Janet replied that they were good to go and Mark walked away.

The conversation happened so quickly that it took Melissa a moment to fully process what had just happened.

When she had first arrived, Melissa spoke to Janet about the mundane details of Little League without thinking twice. The clothes Janet was wearing were consistent with her persona; when she introduced herself as Janet, it was no different than any of the thousands of introductions Melissa had made when meeting someone new. She didn't know at the time, of course, that this interaction was different than most: Janet was transgender. Mark refused to acknowledge it and even went the extra step of referring to her by her "dead name." Mark's very public repudiation of Janet's identity was jarring but it was, at the same time, extraordinarily subtle and passive-aggressive. In the liberal bastion that is the San Francisco Bay Area, such a flippant dismissal of Janet and her identity felt very out of place. Why was he so threatened? Why couldn't he just respect her identity?

It's not only Mark: many Americans are uncomfortable with transgender people and rights. Some are outright hostile and violent. Even self-identified liberals and proponents of lesbian, gay, and bisexual rights, including gay, lesbian, and bisexual people themselves, are sometimes reluctant to fully embrace transgender people and rights. Outdated information and poorly

Transforming Prejudice. Melissa R. Michelson and Brian F. Harrison, Oxford University Press (2020) © Oxford University Press.
DOI: 10.1093/oso/9780190068882.001.0001

informed perceptions that transgender people are not real or are mentally ill persist. Further, several social groups cling to the idea that extending rights to transgender people will come at the expense of their values, of their own rights, or of the rights of other vulnerable groups (e.g., women and children). Since the history and content of LGB attitudes are different from those about transgender people and rights (as were the catalysts for attitude change), so too must our thinking be different to find the optimal strategy or strategies to change hearts and minds about transgender people.

This book offers that different approach, what we term Identity Reassurance Theory, which we show is a powerful tool for creating openness to persuasion on transgender rights. We posit that Identity Reassurance can increase support for transgender rights even if the targets of persuasive messages are uncomfortable with the underlying concept of gender as mutable and nonbinary. The key, per our theory, is shifting focus to existing core values that are central to a person's self-identity. In other words, rather than focusing on the identities of the transgender community, we focus on the targets of persuasion and on shifting their attitudes to better align with their preexisting senses of themselves as moral human beings.

In the next sections, we provide a basic introduction to relevant terms, including transgender and cisgender. We then explore current levels of public opinion about various sexual orientations and gender identities, including data from a large, national survey we conducted in early 2019. We then turn to our new theory. As we detailed in chapter 1, the history of public attitudes toward transgender people—one starkly different than the history of LGB people—requires a different approach to shifting those attitudes than those employed for other issues.

The Basics: Gender Identity and Transgender People

The National Center for Transgender Equality (NCTE) defines gender identity as a person's "internal knowledge of [their] own gender—for example, your knowledge that you're a man, a woman, or another gender" (NCTE 2016a). As they note, everyone—not just transgender people—has a gender identity. When we're born, a doctor usually says that we're male or female based on what our bodies look like. Many people never think about what their gender identity is because it matches their sex at birth (NCTE 2016a): most people who were labeled male at birth grow up to identify as men and most people who were labeled female at birth grow up to identify as women. These people are cisgender: people whose gender identity is consistent with the gender they were thought to be at birth.

But some people's gender identity—their innate knowledge of who they are—is different from how they were labeled when they were born. Most of these people describe themselves as transgender (or trans). NCTE (2016a) defines transgender people as "people whose gender identity is different from the gender they were thought to be at birth." For example, a transgender woman lives as a woman today but was thought to be male when she was born; a transgender man lives as a man today but was thought to be female when he was born. Scholars estimate that roughly 0.6% of the American population identifies as transgender (Flores et al. 2016). Some transgender people identify as neither male nor female or as a combination of male and female. There are a variety of terms that people who aren't entirely male or entirely female use to describe their gender identity, like nonbinary or genderqueer.

Feminist scholars have long argued that society constructs specific expectations for people according to the sex they are thought to be (Butler 1990), including norms about proper dress or attire, behavior, speech patterns, and more. Behavior that is consistent with cultural expectations is referred to as gender normative; behavior that is viewed as incompatible with these expectations is referred to as gender nonconforming.

When people deviate from long-standing gender norms and expectations (including transgender and gender nonconforming people), it tends to increase discomfort and negative affect among cisgender people. Support for this assertion empirically comes from a variety of data sources. For example, in the May 2016 Vox-Morning Consult poll, respondents were asked whether they hold favorable or unfavorable attitudes toward a variety of groups. Negative attitudes were more frequent for transgender people than for heterosexual and gay and lesbian people: 30% of people reported feeling unfavorably toward transgender people, 22% reported feeling unfavorably toward gay or lesbian people, and only 4% reported feeling unfavorably toward straight people (see Table 2.1). Just over half of respondents felt favorably toward transgender people, while 62% reported favorable attitudes toward gay and lesbian people and 86% said the same about straight people. (Note that the Vox survey asked for attitudes toward a variety of terms, even ones that are technically the same [e.g., heterosexual and straight; gay or lesbian and homosexual] to measure impressions based on terminology used.)

Table 2.1. Percentage Favorable and Unfavorable Attitudes Toward Sexuality and Gender Identity Groups, Vox Morning Consult May 2016 Survey

	Heterosexual People	Straight People	Gay or Lesbian People	Homosexual People	Transgender People
Favorable	80	86	62	63	55
Unfavorable	7	4	22	24	30

Note: N = 2,000, registered voters only. Data collected May 18–19, 2016. Table does not include "don't know/no opinion" responses.

https://cdn2.vox-cdn.com/uploads/chorus_asset/file/6532225/Vox_MC_poll_transgender_topline.0.pdf

Table 2.2. Thermometer Scores, 2016 American National Election Study

	Average (Mean) Score (SE)
Transgender people (N = 3,575)	54.97 (.46)
Gay and lesbian people (N = 3,598)	60.12 (.47)
Muslims (N = 3,579)	54.43 (.43)
Black Lives Matter (N = 3,590)	49.26 (.54)
Feminists (N = 3,579)	55.36 (.44)

Note: Data are weighted to be nationally representative. SE = standard errors.

Further evidence comes from the 2016 American National Election Study (ANES), which asks respondents to rate groups on a 0–100 thermometer in terms of their feelings of closeness. The ANES has asked thermometer rating questions about different groups since 1964, adding and removing groups as relevant to ongoing public debates. Gay and lesbian people were added in 1984. Transgender people were added for the first time in 2016, evidence of the increased salience of public debate about transgender rights. Those feelings are notably cooler than toward gay and lesbian people. The average (mean) thermometer rating for gay and lesbian people among respondents to the 2016 ANES was 60.12 compared to 54.97 for transgender people (Table

2.2). Unfortunately, the ANES does not include a feeling thermometer rating toward non-LGBT people as a discreet group for a valid category of comparison. However, feelings toward transgender people are near those of other groups most often disliked by conservatives, including Muslims, Black Lives Matter activists, and feminists. Taylor et al. (2018: 63) report similarly low thermometer ratings for transgender people in their national surveys from 2015 and 2016.

More detailed attitudinal data are available from a 2017 survey of New Zealand adults conducted by Gender Equal NZ to clarify attitudes about gender in New Zealand (Gender Equal NZ 2018). Their logic was that to best understand what a gender-equal New Zealand would look like and to improve the well-being of New Zealanders regardless of gender, more data were needed to understand the attitudes, norms, stereotypes, and expectations that belie gender inequality in the first place. Among the questions asked was how comfortable New Zealanders are with heterosexual and LGBT people in a variety of different scenarios and environments. For example, questions asked how comfortable respondents were having a transgender man as one of their work colleagues; having a heterosexual person as the MP (member of Parliament) for their electorate; or having a lesbian become a parent.

Overall, unsurprisingly, respondents were far more comfortable with heterosexual people in the contexts provided compared to LGBT people. There was, however, another clear trend: reduced levels of comfort with transgender people compared to LGB people. In early 2019, we replicated and expanded upon the New Zealand study with a survey in the United States, asking similar questions about attitudes toward sexual orientation and gender identity groups.

The 2019 Gender Attitudes Survey

As noted earlier, public opinion surveys show that attitudes toward members of the LGBT community have become increasingly positive over time, particularly toward gay men and lesbians. The question remains, however, whether support is evenly distributed throughout each identity group or whether attitudes differ between specific subsets of the LGBT population. In early 2019, we collected data on these questions from a national sample of U.S. adults, mirroring the 2017 gender attitudes survey exploring attitudes among New Zealanders.

Data were collected using the online platform Lucid between February 8, 2019, and March 5, 2019.[2] Lucid uses online opt-in panels that produce national panels that are close to nationally representative (Coppock and McClellan 2019). Among our 1,430 respondents, 47.9% (n = 685) identified as male, 51.5% (n = 737) as female, 0.4% (n = 6) as transgender female, and 0.1% (n = 2) as nonbinary. No respondents identified as transgender male. Most identified their sexual orientation as heterosexual (89.7%, n = 1,283), with another 3.8% (n = 54) identifying as gay or lesbian, 5.8% (n = 83) identifying as bisexual, and the remaining 0.7% (n = 10) identifying as other. A majority of respondents (69.7%, n = 996) identified as Anglo (White non-Latinx), 12.9% (n = 184) as Black, 7.3% (n = 105) as Latinx/Hispanic, 4.4% (n = 63) as Asian, and the remainder as mixed or another race. Their average age was 46. Just over 25% (n = 368) had a high school degree or less education, another 28.4% (n = 406) had some college, 12.9% (n = 185) had an associate's degree, 21.7% (n = 311) had a bachelor's degree, and the remaining 11.2% (n = 160) had a graduate degree.

We first asked respondents their degree of familiarity with a variety of gender terms, including heterosexual, gay, lesbian, bisexual, cisgender, transgender, and nonbinary. We expected the highest level of familiarity with the terms *heterosexual, gay, lesbian*, and *bisexual* but not uniform familiarity. For reference, in the 2017 New Zealand survey, only 79% of respondents said they definitely knew what *heterosexual* meant, 91% said they definitely knew what *gay man* and *lesbian woman* meant, and 87% said they definitely knew what *bisexual* meant. Among our U.S. respondents, familiarity was slightly higher for *heterosexual* but slightly lower for the other three gender terms: 95% definitely knew *heterosexual*, 83% definitely knew *gay* and *lesbian*, and 82% definitely knew *bisexual* (Figure 2.1). Familiarity with additional terms like *nonbinary gender* and *cisgender* was much lower, again similar to what was found in the 2017 New Zealand gender equality survey. Among New Zealanders, 71% said they definitely knew what *transgender* meant, compared to only 67% of Americans; 18% of New Zealanders said they definitely knew what *nonbinary gender* meant and 13% said they definitely knew what *cisgender* meant; familiarity among Americans on these two identities is similar, at 20% for *nonbinary gender* and 13% for *cisgender*.

Moving on to level of comfort with members of each of these sexual orientation and gender identity groups, respondents reported their level of comfort with people from each group they recognized in a variety of situations, ranging from more intimate situations such as a personal friend or

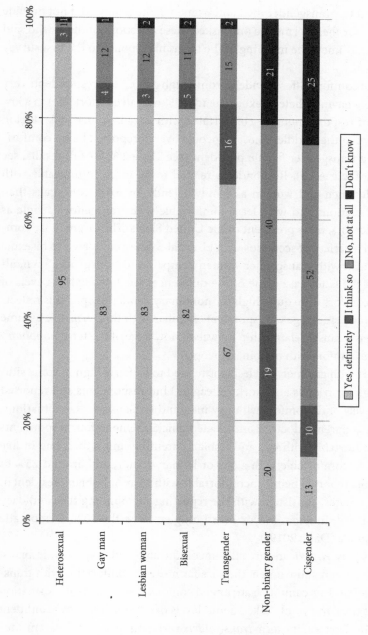

Figure 2.1. Familiarity with sexual orientation and gender identity terms, 2019 U.S. gender equality survey.

Note: Data collected February 8–March 5, 2019. *N* = 1,430. Question wording: *Do you know the meaning of each of the following terms?*

one's doctor to less intimate situations such as colleagues at work and elected officials. We asked separate questions about comfort for bisexual men and women and for transgender men and women. Note that we did not provide definitions for these terms; we only asked these questions of those who said they *definitely* knew the meaning of the terms in response to the first survey question.

Levels of comfort differed widely, from a high of 90.7% of respondents very comfortable having a heterosexual friend (97% overall comfortable) to a low of 41.6% of respondents very comfortable with a transgender male doctor. Somewhere in the middle, 57.8% of people overall reported being comfortable with a transgender female president (see Table 2.3; for full results, see Appendix Table A2.2). Respondents tended to be more comfortable with transgender men and women as family, friends, or work colleagues than in other situations and were least comfortable with transgender people as parents, doctors, or as president of the United States. They were more comfortable in a variety of scenarios with bisexual women compared to bisexual men and also with transgender women compared to transgender men, although in the latter case some of the differences were negligible. Levels of reported comfort were quite high for nonbinary gender people; this reflects the very low percentage of respondents familiar with this term. We assume that there is a causal relationship between knowledge of the term *nonbinary gender* and comfort with nonbinary people.

Comfort with gay men and lesbians tended to be fairly high in some situations (e.g., for friends and work colleagues) but respondents still reported notable levels of discomfort with gay men and lesbians in other situations, including as parents, doctors, and elected officials. One in four respondents was uncomfortable with gay and lesbian parenting; more than one in five would be uncomfortable with a gay or lesbian doctor; and around 25% of respondents reported being uncomfortable with a gay or lesbian president of the United States, consistent with the reporting surrounding the candidacy of South Bend, Indiana, Mayor Pete Buttigieg to be the 2020 Democratic Party nominee (Dann 2019).

While many Americans are still uncomfortable with gay men, lesbians, and bisexual men and women, they are far more uncomfortable with transgender people. This cannot be attributed completely to a lack of information given that the survey only asked about levels of comfort for those confident that they understood the term *transgender*. Variations between different situations suggest that some of this discomfort is based on levels of intimacy.

Table 2.3. Comfort With Transgender Men and Women, by Situation, 2019 Gender Attitudes Survey

	% Very Comfortable	% Somewhat Comfortable	% Comfortable (Sum)
As part of your family			
Transgender male	51.5	14.1	65.7
Transgender female	51.0	17.0	68.1
As one of your friends			
Transgender male	52.4	17.3	69.6
Transgender female	53.5	16.9	70.4
As one of your work colleagues			
Transgender male	53.1	17.6	70.7
Transgender female	53.3	19.0	72.3
As someone you play sports with			
Transgender male	49.7	17.7	67.4
Transgender female	49.8	17.5	67.3
Becoming parents			
Transgender male	44.2	16.1	60.3
Transgender female	45.8	16.3	62.1
As your doctor			
Transgender male	41.6	16.3	57.9
Transgender female	44.6	16.8	61.4
As your representative in Congress			
Transgender male	46.2	16.5	62.6
Transgender female	47.0	17.3	64.3
As the star of your favorite sports team			
Transgender male	49.7	16.9	66.6
Transgender female	49.0	18.5	67.5
As president of the United States			
Transgender male	42.0	16.1	58.1
Transgender female	42.5	15.3	57.8

Note: Comfort items were only asked of respondents who said they definitely knew what the term *transgender* meant. $N = 995$. Data collected February 8–March 5, 2019. Question wording: *"Would you be comfortable with transgender people in each of the following situations?"*

A (slight) majority reported they would be very comfortable with transgender men and women as members of their families, as friends, or as work colleagues. While these are fairly close relationships, they are not intimate. In contrast, only 42% to 45% were very comfortable with the idea of seeing a transgender doctor and only 44% to 46% were comfortable with transgender people being parents. Levels of comfort playing a sport with a transgender person—again, a situation that could lead to intimate contact depending on the sport—was only 50%. While we did not ask respondents to explain their reported attitudes, we noted lower levels of support reported for these more intimate situations.

Lower levels of support for transgender people in non-intimate public offices such as a transgender president (42%) or member of Congress (46% to 47%) are likely based on a different concern, possibly including higher levels of disgust (Haider-Markel et al. 2017) or on imputed political ideology (P. E. Jones and Brewer 2019). Low levels of comfort with a transgender professional athlete (49% to 50%), however, are probably not based on either perceived intimacy or political ideology. The variation in attitudes across different situations suggests that public opinion on issues of transgender people and rights is likely due to a variety of factors that are not necessarily consistent or applied the same way in every context.

The 2019 gender attitudes survey also collected some demographic information about respondents, allowing us to model predictors of responses to the comfort items, including their age, level of education, gender, sexual orientation, race, and whether they have any family members or close friends who are gay or lesbian, transgender, or nonbinary. Respondents who are older, have less education, are cisgender men, and do not have personal contact with LGBT people tend to report lower levels of comfort with members of sexual and gender minorities in these various roles. Race is not a consistent predictor of attitudes. We explore those findings in more detail in chapter 4. Overall, the survey confirms that U.S. adults are not nearly as comfortable with transgender people as they are with gay and lesbian people. There is plenty of room for improvement.

Determinants of Attitudes Toward Transgender People

Previous scholarship has identified multiple factors related to beliefs about transgender people and transgender rights including values, beliefs, and personal knowledge of or interpersonal contact with transgender people. Because anti-transgender bias is often rooted in a lack of information or contact (Norton and Herek 2013), providing basic information about transgender people can have positive effects on attitudes. Andrew Flores and his colleagues find that merely exposing people to basic information and pictures of transgender people slightly reduces overall discomfort and transphobia although it has no effect on support for transgender *rights*, suggesting that a lack of information at least partially motivates negative feelings and attitudes toward transgender people (Flores 2015; Flores et al. 2017).

Emotion and affect also play a role in public attitudes (Brader 2006; Marcus, Neuman, and MacKuen 2000). A lack of knowledge may generate emotions such as fear or discomfort about transgender people, particularly in vulnerable or intimate contexts such as bathrooms or schools. Cavanagh (2013: 427) argues that resistance to transgender bathroom rights in particular is linked to gut-level concerns about the danger it poses to cisgender people:

> This is not because one gender can infect the other but because gender disorder is sometimes *felt* to be a matter of life and death. Gender incoherence, or, rather, what is taken to be an incongruence between gender identity, the sex of the body, and the insignia on the bathroom door, is metonymically associated with disease. Sodomy is also associated with disease, HIV and AIDS in particular. There is never enough soap and disinfectant to kill whatever it is people are afraid of catching.

Values and personality characteristics also inform public opinion and some recent research explores these influences on transgender-related attitudes. Authoritarianism (Norton and Herek 2013), beliefs in traditional gender roles (Nagoshi et al. 2008), political conservatism (Norton and Herek 2013), and identifying as Republican (Flores 2015) are all associated with more negative beliefs toward transgender people.

Gender identity and gender roles also predict attitudes toward transgender people. The 2016 ANES included questions about perceived discrimination toward transgender people and attitudes toward transgender bathroom access rights. The survey had 4,271 respondents, including pre- and post-election waves, with data collected between September 2016 and January 2017. When asked how much discrimination there is in the United States against transgender people, women were more likely to say that transgender people experience *a great deal* of discrimination (27%) compared to men (17.5%).

There is more than simply gender driving these attitudes. Beliefs in traditional gender roles (Nagoshi et al. 2008) or a binary conception of gender (Norton and Herek 2013) also contribute to negative attitudes toward transgender people, consistent with research on attitudes toward gay men and lesbians (Vincent, Parrott, and Peterson 2011). Attitudes toward traditional gender roles also strongly correlate with attitudes toward transgender people, including thermometer ratings and perceptions of discrimination (Harrison and Michelson 2019). People who oppose equal pay for men and women have cooler feelings toward transgender people and report seeing less discrimination; respondents who oppose parental leave also have cooler feelings toward transgender people and report seeing less discrimination. These attitudes are more consistent predictors than respondent gender identity alone. In other words, beliefs about gender roles are a stronger predictor of attitudes toward transgender people and support for transgender rights than is gender identity.

The 2016 ANES also provides consistent results regarding attitudes about transgender bathroom access. Men perceive less discrimination against transgender people and are less supportive of access rights than women. Only 27.3% of men think there is a great deal of discrimination against transgender people compared to 35.8% of women (Figure 2.2). Only 44.3% of men support transgender bathroom access rights compared to 52.1% of women (Figure 2.3). These differences are statistically significant.

Moving beyond gender identity, our work led us to believe that beliefs about gender roles are even stronger predictors of attitudes toward transgender people and rights. Several items in the 2016 ANES measure gender role attitudes, including questions about equal pay for women and whether it is better for the man of the house to work and the woman to stay at home. Among women who oppose equal pay, only 28% support transgender bathroom access rights, but support nearly doubles (to 55%) among women who support equal pay. The difference among men follows the same pattern, with 36% of men who oppose equal pay supporting bathroom rights compared to 46% who support equal pay. Among women who think it is better for a man to work and a woman to stay at home, only a third (35%) support transgender bathroom access rights; support nearly doubles, to 61%, among women who disagree with that statement about traditional gender roles. Again, the

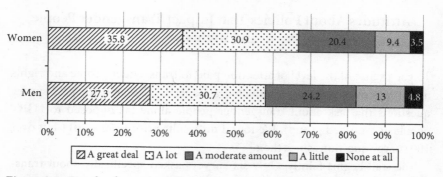

Figure 2.2. Levels of perceived discrimination against transgender people, by gender, 2016 American National Election Study.

Note: N = 4,219. Data are weighted to be nationally representative. Question wording: *How much discrimination in the United States is there against transgender people?*

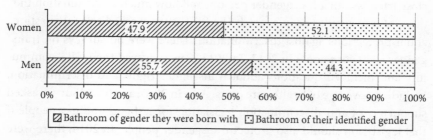

Figure 2.3. Attitudes toward transgender bathroom access rights, by gender, 2016 American National Election Study.

Note: N = 4,219. Data are weighted to be nationally representative. Question wording: *Should transgender people have to use the bathrooms of the gender they were born with, or should they be allowed to use the bathrooms of their identified gender?*

difference among men follows the same pattern: among those supporting traditional gender roles, 32% support bathroom access, compared to 52% of men who disagree with that statement. Regression models confirm that these attitudes are powerful predictors of both attitudes, particularly on attitudes about bathroom access rights (see Appendix Table A2.1).

These data indicate that while gender is a predictor of attitudes about transgender people and rights, it is not gender per se that determines those attitudes but rather the way in which people understand gender roles. Those with more traditional attitudes about men and women are less likely to be supportive of transgender people while those more supportive of gender equality are also more supportive of equality for transgender people.

Attitudes About Policies That Impact Transgender People and Rights

To get a sense of the level of attention paid to transgender people and rights in surveys over time, we conducted a Roper iPoll search for past survey questions that ask about transgender people alone (as opposed to LGBT people as a unified group). We found no results prior to July 2011 but over 100 survey questions since then.[3]

The trail begins faintly. Only six surveys asked specifically about transgender people prior to 2016, including two in 2011: one by the Human Rights Campaign (HRC) and one by PRRI (formerly known as the Public Religion Research Institute). The HRC survey included three items: a thermometer scale question, whether the respondent thought they could be close friends with a transgender person, and how much discrimination they thought transgender people faced. The PRRI survey asked several questions about protections against discrimination. There were no surveys on transgender rights or people in 2012. In 2013, Pew surveyed the LGBT community and included questions about transgender rights and discrimination, including coverage of health care costs. Also in 2013, a national survey asked supporters of anti-discrimination legislation for lesbians and gay people if that legislation should also protect transgender people. In 2014, there were no survey questions on any topic relating to transgender people or rights. In 2015, two publicly available surveys included questions about discrimination against transgender people (but several more were conducted by other scholars, which we detail later).

And then, in 2016, the floodgates opened. There were 47 surveys that included questions about discrimination against transgender people or about support for transgender rights in 2016 and another 12 in 2017. While most only asked about discrimination, occasional surveys measured public support for transgender bathroom access rights or the right to serve openly in the military.

P. E. Jones and Brewer (2018) documented the rapid increase in media coverage of transgender issues over this same period. They found that newspapers published roughly twice as many stories about transgender people and issues in 2016 than they did in 2014—increasing from about 100 per month to nearly 250 per month (see Figure 2.4).

Overall, majorities of the public consistently report that they think transgender people face *a lot* of discrimination, although it is difficult to

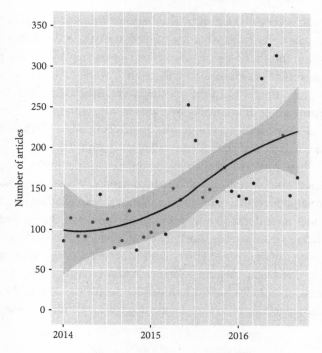

Figure 2.4. News stories about transgender issues, January 2014–September 2016.

Note: Number of news stories containing the term *transgender* or *transsexual* by month, for sample of major newspapers, January 2014–September 2016. Locally weighted regression line with 95% confidence intervals superimposed. *Data source*: Lexis-Nexis. Reprinted with permission from Jones and Brewer (2018).

determine whether attitudes are changing over time due to inconsistent question wording from different surveys. For example, a June 2019 CBS News poll found that 56% of respondents thought there was *a lot* of discrimination against "transgender people in society today," and other 21% said there was *some* discrimination. Six years earlier, a November 2013 PRRI survey found that 71% of adults agreed that *yes, there is a lot of discrimination against transgender people*. Majorities of the public also consistently support protections for transgender people against job discrimination: in polls conducted from 2011 to 2019, at least 70% of respondents said they support such laws. Support for more specific policies, including transgender access to public restrooms and the ability to serve openly in the U.S. military, is more divided, and also relatively consistent over time; we explore these data in depth in chapter 3.

The public is very divided over whether they think gender is determined at birth or can differ from what is assigned at birth. A 2017 Pew Research Center poll found that 54% of U.S. adults believe that whether a person is a man or a woman is determined only at birth while 44% believe a person's gender can be different from the sex they were assigned at birth (A. Brown 2017). Results differ dramatically by partisanship, with 80% of Republicans and 34% of Democrats saying gender is determined at birth and 19% of Republicans and 64% of Democrats saying it can differ.

Overall, these surveys reveal a striking difference in attitudes toward transgender people compared to gay and lesbian people. While the public has become more supportive of gay and lesbian relationships, including marriage, over time, attitudes toward transgender people show much less change over time. In part, this reflects the relatively short period of time for which data are available (and the passage of time needed for attitude shifts to occur and to be measured). That said, the increasing partisan polarization of attitudes in the modern era and the stickiness of attitudes toward transgender people over the past eight years suggests that something different is happening. History isn't repeating; it's stuck.

The Jack Reed Experiment

To test the effectiveness of the Theory of Dissonant Identity Priming from our first book when it comes to shifting attitudes about transgender rights, we conducted a survey experiment—what we call the Jack Reed experiment[4]— in two cities in the San Francisco Bay Area. Surveys were collected in Redwood City on Friday, May 24, 2019 from 5:30 to 8 p.m. and in Fremont on Saturday, May 25, 2019 from 11:30 a.m. to 4:30 p.m. Surveys were collected from passersby in proximity to local public events using paper surveys and pens. Participants were incentivized with Starbucks and Dunkin' gift cards. Data were collected by a team of student assistants from local colleges and high schools who were paid for their time.

Respondents were randomly assigned to one of three conditions: one with a description of Rhode Island Senator Jack Reed as a Republican (inaccurate), a Democrat (accurate), or a veteran (also accurate). In the two partisan conditions, participants were first asked their own partisan identification. They then were told that "**Democratic/Republican** U.S. Senator Jack Reed recently cosponsored legislation in favor of transgender Americans serving in the U.S. Armed Forces. He also tweeted about the bill." Underneath this statement was a photo of Senator Reed and a screenshot of his supportive tweet (Figure 2.5). We then asked a series of 10 questions about support for transgender rights, starting with a question about transgender Americans serving openly in the U.S. armed forces: "What about you? Do you support or oppose transgender Americans serving openly in the U.S. Armed Forces?"

In the third (veteran) condition, the initial survey question about the respondent's partisanship was replaced with a question about whether the respondent has an affiliation with the military. In addition, the photo of Reed was replaced with a screenshot of the senator speaking on television where he is clearly identified as a U.S. Army veteran (Figure 2.6); the veteran condition of the survey included Reed's same supportive tweet.

At the end of each survey, we asked participants their gender, sexual orientation, and whether they had any close friends or family members who are transgender or gender nonconforming. In the two partisan treatment conditions, we asked whether they were active or former military; in the veteran condition, we asked their partisanship and whether they thought Senator Reed was a Republican or a Democrat. After completing their survey, participants who were given false information were debriefed.

We had several expectations and hypotheses going into the experiment. As noted previously, these hypotheses are based on the Theory of Dissonant Identity Priming from our previous book which predicts attitude change will be most likely for those in a condition where a shared identity with the messenger is primed, especially when the message is dissonant. In this instance, the theory would suggest that the strongest messages would be those that match the identity of the receiver of communication with the sender: veterans would be most persuaded by the veteran condition; Republicans would

Figure 2.5. Jack Reed experiment, Democrat/Republican condition photo and tweet.

Figure 2.6. Jack Reed experiment, veteran condition photo.

be most persuaded by the Republican condition; and Democrats would be most persuaded by the Democratic condition.

Consistent with previous research, we expected support for transgender rights to be stronger among women, members of the LGBT community, and people with interpersonal contact with transgender or gender nonconforming friends or relatives. We also expected that participants assigned to the veteran treatment would be more likely to assume that Reed was a member of their own party if they supported transgender rights but would be more likely to assume he was a member of the opposing party if they did not.

The federal government added an unexpected additional piece of context to our experiment that should be noted. The day we began collecting data (Friday of Memorial Day weekend 2019), the Trump administration's Department of Health and Human Services proposed to roll back Obama-era protections of transgender people in the Affordable Care Act. Specifically, the proposed regulation would replace a rule that had defined discrimination "on the basis of sex" to include gender identity, allowing health care workers and insurance to deny care and coverage for transgender medical patients and health insurance customers. While not the focus of our experiment, our list of dependent variables did include an item about health care: "Transgender people deserve health insurance that covers all transgender-related health issues." Results from the experiment should be interpreted with the understanding that some very politically attentive respondents may have been affected by this news when considering their responses.

Results

Overall, we collected 473 completed surveys: 151 in the Republican condition, 152 in the Democrat condition, and 170 in the veteran condition. A majority of respondents (54%) were Democrats while 11% were Republicans and the rest either indicated that they were independents or declined to state their partisanship. A slight majority (53%) were female and most respondents were straight (88%) and not affiliated with the military (92%).

Results are shown in Table 2.4. Overall, people who were assigned to the condition where Senator Reed was referred to as a U.S. Army veteran were the most supportive of transgender troops. Differences between this condition and each of the other conditions (Democratic and Republican) were statistically significant. In other words, when people had it in their mind that the source of the information was a veteran, they were far more supportive of transgender military service compared to when they thought the source was a political partisan.

Recall that the Theory of Dissonant Identity Priming hypothesizes that the most persuasive messages would be those that matched the identity of the sender and receiver of communication. If that theory applied to transgender rights, we would see the highest levels of support for transgender rights among Democrats in the Democratic condition, Republicans in the Republican condition, and veterans in the veteran condition. While veterans were most supportive when they were randomly assigned to the veteran condition, they were a very small sample size and therefore we can't generalize about those results. As shown in Table 2.4, among people who identify as a Democrat, support for transgender rights is actually *weakest* in the condition where Senator Reed is referred to as a Democrat. Instead, support is strongest in the veteran condition, followed by the Republican condition.[5] Among Republicans, support is stronger for those in the Republican condition than those in the Democratic condition but only slightly; again, support is strongest among those assigned to the veteran condition. Other findings from the experiment are consistent with previous studies of public opinion toward transgender rights: support for transgender troops is stronger among respondents who reported knowing someone who is transgender or gender nonconforming, women, people who identify as LGBT, and Democrats. Overall support is weaker among those who report an affiliation with the military and Republicans.

Table 2.4. Support for Transgender Americans Serving Openly in the U.S. Armed Forces, Jack Reed Experiment

	Republican Condition	Democrat Condition	Veteran Condition
All respondents (*N* = 467)			
Strongly support	62.7%	62.9%	77.7%
Somewhat support	22.7%	25.8%	15.1%
Somewhat oppose	6.7%	6.6%	3.0%
Strongly oppose	8.0%	4.6%	4.2%
Democrats (*N* = 245)			
Strongly support	80.7%	73.1%	92.9%
Somewhat support	12.1%	20.5%	6.0%
Somewhat oppose	3.6%	3.9%	1.2%
Strongly oppose	3.6%	2.6%	0
Republicans (*N* = 50)			
Strongly support	26.7%	23.5%	50.0%
Somewhat support	40.0%	35.3%	27.8%
Somewhat oppose	13.3%	17.7%	5.6%
Strongly oppose	20.0%	23.5%	16.7%
Veterans (*N* = 35)			
Strongly support	46.7%	15.8%	57.1%
Somewhat support	26.7%	53.9%	28.6%
Somewhat oppose	0	23.1%	0
Strongly oppose	26.7%	7.7%	14.3%

Note: Data collected May 24–25, 2019.

Our Theory of Dissonant Identity Priming, which had proved so effective at changing attitudes about marriage equality, was not effective at changing attitudes about transgender rights. A new approach was needed and this is where our new Identity Reassurance Theory comes in, which we explain in more detail later in this chapter. In the chapters that follow, we explore the power of Identity Reassurance Theory as a method of motivating attitude change on transgender rights.

There is not widespread support for transgender issues and the nature of opposition is significantly different from historical opposition to marriage equality. Support is highly polarized along expected social, political, and ideological boundaries, and conversations about transgender rights are often framed in "us vs. them" terms (Green 2019; Steinmetz 2019). The Equality

Act, a congressional measure that would prohibit discrimination based on sex, sexual orientation, or gender identity in public accommodations or facilities, passed the U.S. House of Representatives on a highly polarized vote on May 17, 2019: all 173 nay votes came from Republicans, compared to only 8 of 236 aye votes; all of the voting Democrats supported the bill.

We do not seek to convince skeptics or opponents of the similarities between transgender people and themselves: many people will simply not believe it. The notion of changing one's gender identity is simply too divergent, too radical, and too uncomfortable for many people. It is a bridge too far. In the history of attitude change on LGBT rights, attitude change for lesbian and gay people occurred very slowly and through stages of fear, misunderstanding, disgust, disdain, a desire to live completely separate lives, and views of people as harbingers of disease and immorality. There were some who wanted to eliminate gay and lesbian people from American life completely. It took many decades to reach the point where gay and lesbian people could be accepted as members of communities, neighbors, friends, and family members. There is still work to be done, of course, but hard work by countless people led to the embrace of lesbian and gay people into everyday, mainstream life in many ways.

We are, to be frank, not yet to that place for transgender people. Not by a long shot.

Convincing people to reconsider their attitudes toward transgender people and rights, therefore, requires breaking through sometimes very rigid existing silos of identity in ways that have the potential to fuel emotional reactance. As we will discuss, there are several very strongly held beliefs that often belie quick and easy attitude change. Opening minds to persuasion requires a rhetorical flanking maneuver in one of two ways: (1) making an indirect appeal and evading direct attack on existing attitudes (since that will likely evoke reactance) or (2) generating reduced barriers and thus an increased willingness to receive and process persuasive messages. In this book, we seek a better understanding of the causes of widespread discomfort and opposition to transgender people and rights and ultimately, the best ways to convince others to be more respectful and supportive given the very real constraints of contemporary public opinion.

While more difficult in the face of stronger opposition to transgender issues, there *are* several possibilities for how to break down these increasingly large divides. Advocates can encourage people to rethink their existing attitudes toward transgender rights in ways that move them away from thinking of transgender people as an outgroup they must be wary of. This includes not just Republicans who are adopting the party line on transgender rights but other ingroup identities and imagined threats such as the concern among both men and women that transgender bathroom access poses a risk of harassment or even violence against women and girls (despite the well-documented fact that this never occurs). These methods encourage targets of persuasive messages to lower their defenses against members of outgroups and be their best imagined selves.

In the later chapters of this book, we identify challenges as well as routes for opening minds to persuasion on transgender rights, including appeals to values such as equality, freedom, and integrity (chapter 3); gender identities and threatening or reassuring the masculinity or femininity of recipients of messages (chapter 4); priming positive emotions and feelings of moral elevation (chapter 5); and acknowledging and addressing discomfort regarding transgender people (chapter 6). Broadly speaking, all of these tactics stem from an underlying need for people to feel confident in their own identity before they are able to branch out and embrace a threatening or stigmatized outgroup. We find that openness to respecting and supporting the rights of members of this outgroup can be encouraged through these routes of self-affirmation.

Cohen et al. (2007) have found that self-affirmation through reflecting on overarching personal values or a prized skill can create greater open-mindedness in situations where there is a focus on identity. Broockman and Kalla (2016) found that residents of Los Angeles were more open to trans-gender rights after first being asked to remember a time when they were discriminated against. This supports the idea of perspective taking as a method of reducing prejudice. However, Stone et al. (2011) note that perspective taking can generate anger and backlash, especially among highly prejudiced individuals. Similarly, Mooijman and Stern (2016) find that perspective taking can also induce *negative* attitudes and discomfort when the perspective taken threatens the individual's values or motivations.

Our New Theory: Identity Reassurance

In short, we have a lot more to learn about attitudes toward transgender people and rights. After multiple experiments and explorations of the predictors and facets of attitudes toward transgender people and rights including attitudes about gender roles, we developed a new theory about how to shift those attitudes and reduce prejudice: Identity Reassurance Theory. Identity Reassurance Theory is about softening the ground and creating fertile soil in which to plant seeds of positivity toward members of a stigmatized group about whom they feel uncomfortable: for example, transgender people, Arab Americans, Muslims, or members of the disability community. The key is reassuring recipients of persuasive messages about their own identities and their own self-esteem so that their gut reactions to members of these marginalized communities are softened and their reactance is minimized. It's about making them feel better about themselves so that they can be more open to accepting others. The path diagram for Identity Reassurance Theory is shown in Figure 2.7.

Attitudes are closely linked to our identities; as Lazarsfeld, Berelson, and Gaudet note, "a person thinks, politically, as he is socially" (1948: 27). The groups that people identify with as members affect their political attitudes and behaviors (Citrin and Wright 2009; Jackson 2011; Scheve and Stasavage 2006). Thus, attempts to change attitudes are often received as threats to those identities. Resistance to persuasive messages is often a reaction to protect self-esteem. Methods of reducing that resistance and opening minds to persuasion has been the topic of considerable scholarship, most notably Zaller's (1992) Receive-Accept-Sample (RAS) model, Petty and Cacioppo's (1981, 1986) Elaboration Likelihood Model (ELM), and Sherif, Sherif, and Nebergall's (1965) Social Judgment Theory (SJT).

According to Zaller's RAS model, citizens resist views that are inconsistent with their predispositions. When an issue is polarized (as is true for the issue of transgender rights), people will be likely to reflect that polarization in their own attitudes, especially if they are politically aware. Generating changed attitudes requires recipients of persuasive messages to accept and consider new ideas which will be less likely if the source is not seen as credible. If the new information comes from outside one's set of ingroups and is

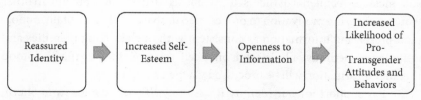

Figure 2.7. Identity Reassurance Theory path diagram.

seen as inconsistent with one's identity as a member of those ingroups, the information is unlikely to be accepted and considered. Thus, opening minds to persuasion requires as a first step that recipients of the messages be willing to consider them, to not see those messages as threats, or to see them as consistent with their existing identities.

Petty and Cacioppo's (1986) ELM is similarly based on the willingness of a recipient of a persuasive message to receive and process the information. Persuasive messaging, however, is about more than getting folks to listen. The very first step after a person receives what they perceive to be persuasive communication involves the motivation to process the information: is it personally relevant? Is there some kind of need or desire to better understand the information? The response to this step determines not only the likelihood of attitude change but also whether that change is meaningful, enduring, and predictive of future behavior or whether it will be ephemeral and relatively temporary. These two outcomes are what Petty and Cacioppo term a *central attitude change* or a *peripheral attitude change*. For a central attitude change (i.e., longer lasting, somewhat resistant) to occur, people will need to be motivated and able to process the information; further, the new considerations offered by the information will need to be more salient and more positive (for positive change) or more negative (for negative change) than previous ones. If there is any breakdown in this process at any stage—in motivation or ability to process information or if the new considerations are too weak or neutral—the receiver of communication is likely to fall into the peripheral route. If attitude change occurs at all, it is unpredictable, temporary, and unpredictive of future behavior.

ELM predicts that a person will be more likely to accept persuasive information if it is perceived as consistent with their existing beliefs and values. Our Identity Reassurance Theory builds on this work to note that people will be more likely to receive and process persuasive messages that are not seen as threats to their existing values and identities. This is particularly true when using the strategy of appealing to moral elevation to reassure message recipients of their self-esteem, as we detail in chapter 5. In other words, triggering motivation to process persuasive messages is vitally important; presenting information as consistent with one's existing identities and attitudes as methods of bolstering one's self-esteem increases the likelihood that that information will be processed via the central route.

Similar support for our Identity Reassurance Theory comes from Sherif, Sherif, and Nebergall's SJT. According to SJT, motivation to process information depends on whether it falls into a person's latitude of acceptance: "If a message does not fall appreciably beyond the individual's latitude of acceptance, the position of the message is likely to be assimilated" (Sarup, Suchner, and Gaylord 1991: 364). In other words, persuasion depends on creating a message that falls within a person's range of acceptable outcomes. Thus, persuasive messages about a stigmatized group, which might otherwise fall outside of that theoretical window, must be framed as nonthreatening and as consistent with existing values and identities.

Overall, existing studies of persuasion agree that messaging that is perceived as an attack on attitudes is more likely to generate resistance and reactance than attitudinal change. Making a lateral attack on prejudices rather than a head-on assault is more likely to allow a persuasive message to slip through cognitive defenses. Lowering those defenses and allowing a persuasive message to be received and processed can be achieved by appealing to a message recipient's existing moral values and desires to boost their self-esteem via moral elevation, and by reassuring them that openness to a message does not threaten their existing strongly held identities.

This is the kernel of Identity Reassurance Theory: we posit that when people feel reassured that their identities are secure, they can open their minds to persuasion about stigmatized groups they might otherwise perceive as threatening. If one's identities and self-esteem are secure, they are more open to protecting the rights of members of other groups and can revise their attitudes and behaviors in ways that further bolster those previously held identities. They can support transgender people and transgender rights even if they don't consider transgender people to be members of their existing ingroups because they are instead cementing their membership in other identity groups—as moral people, as people committed to justice and equality, as people who do not discriminate. Many Americans want to think of themselves as members of those groups. They do not want to think of themselves as bigoted, racist, or prejudiced but they often act in ways that are discriminatory to protect their self-esteem. Identity Reassurance Theory is all about flipping that script to encourage them to protect their self-esteem by being tolerant of transgender people and supportive of their rights.

Theory of Identity Reassurance

Public animosity toward transgender people and transgender rights is well documented in academic research. Scholars focused on social psychology, political communication, identity, and prejudice have developed many explanations of attitudes toward marginalized groups and efforts to change these attitudes. One of the most common strategies to combat intolerance and prejudice involves coming into contact with a member of an outgroup (Allport 1954; Festinger 1957; Harrison and Michelson 2017a; Petty and Cacioppo 1986; Zaller 1992). The contact hypothesis has proved especially central to attitudes toward gay and lesbian people (Herek and Capitanio 1996; Herek and Glunt 1993; Skipworth et al. 2010; Smith et al. 2009) but inconsistent so far toward transgender people, as detailed in chapter 1.

People have any number of reactions to transgender people that lead them to negative affect, including discomfort, threat, anger, fear, uncertainty, and disgust. These reactions are triggered not necessarily by transgender people or any attributes about transgender people but rather because of the lack of confidence in an individual's own identity membership(s) and the need to bolster self-esteem in their own, most salient identities. A person can reject transgender people because of a need to feel good about their gender identity; for example, as Judith Butler noted (quoted in Tourjée 2015), some men react very negatively to transgender women because of insecurities about their own masculinity and the concept that being a man is somehow not permanent or unchangeable. Thus, the key to attitude change toward transgender people, a relatively new and sometimes confusing concept for people, is identity reassurance and self-esteem boosting. This strategy lessens the negative reactions that many have while encouraging them to respect transgender rights, even if they remain somewhat uncomfortable. In other words, the key is to allow people to be their best and strongest selves, to jump across the chasm separating their core values from individual policy attitudes (even if that chasm remains wide and deep) by reassuring them that they won't fall. Reassurance that who a person is remains valid while reminding them that others who are different are *also* valid should help to mitigate negative reactions to outgroups.

Experiments described in later chapters of this book test our Identity Reassurance Theory. In a variety of geographic contexts and with a variety of different subgroups of the public and different presentations of transgender identities, we work to (1) *reassure* people's self-esteem and sense of self, (2) *acknowledge* rather than dismiss or denigrate their feelings and fears about transgender people, and (3) guide people to look to their own preexisting *values* as sources of support for transgender rights. Elevating self-esteem and their own existing social identities should increase the likelihood of people seeing themselves as good, moral people well grounded in who they are. Connecting the concept of transgender to positive self-esteem and self-image should help to mitigate and to possibly overcome prejudices and opposition to the rights the transgender community seeks.

Identity Reassurance Theory builds on work by multiple other scholars and strands of research and particularly on work that has examined how to shift attitudes about gay rights. While this work sometimes finds that efforts to move attitudes about gay men and lesbians can generate similar effects on attitudes about transgender people, not all of the findings from the former arena are effective in the latter. For example, there is a strong body of work that looks at the power of threats and affirmations of masculinity on the degree to which men support gay and transgender rights. Anti-gay prejudice among men often stems from a desire to affirm their masculinity and avoid appearing feminine (Martínez et al. 2015; Wilkinson 2004). In experimental manipulations that threaten their masculinity, men are more likely to express anti-gay prejudice, particularly against effeminate gay men (Rivera and Dasgupta 2018; Glick et al. 2007). This led us to theorize that threats to masculinity would cause men to express increased prejudice against transgender people, while affirmations of masculinity would cause them to express greater support for transgender rights. In chapter 4, we describe results from our experiments testing these hypotheses.

Identity Reassurance Theory builds on multiple threads of research in political and social psychology and political science. This leads to four key aspects of the theory:

1. People are unlikely to change their orientation toward a group or policy if they are uncomfortable, fearful, or disgusted by it. Shaming or telling people why their attitudes are wrong is more likely to cause attitude entrenchment, not persuasion. The first key is to acknowledge discomfort and reassure people that they are not bad people or under threat for thinking a certain way.
2. Everyone wants to believe that they are a good person. Appealing to their sense of moral elevation allows them to adopt attitudes and behaviors that they might otherwise resist.
3. People have a strong need for positive self-esteem and social identities. Threats to self-esteem and identity can trigger emotional and defensive responses. Thus, appeals that threaten one ingroup identity need to simultaneously boost a different one. Appeals that trigger positive emotions and/or disarm defensive responses will be more effective.

4. Attitudes are best moved incrementally so as to not trigger concerns about consistency. Moving individuals on one attitude (support for transgender rights) can be accomplished without necessarily moving them on others (rejection of the gender binary), even if the issues are related. People go through life with idiosyncratic and inconsistent belief systems.

In the remaining chapters of this book, we describe our experimental tests of various aspects of Identity Reassurance Theory. These tests include various approaches to bolstering the self-esteem of recipients of our pro-transgender rights messages, including moral elevation, reinforcing values, and acknowledgment of discomfort. Chapter 3 describes our initial studies using appeals to core values such as freedom, equality, and integrity; those experiments helped us refine our thinking and theory. Chapter 4 turns to the power of gender identity, including threats to and reassurances of participant masculinity and femininity. Chapter 5 explores the power of positive emotions, including happiness and moral elevation. Chapter 6 takes a more direct approach, with experiments that acknowledge the discomfort that people may have about transgender people and the additional impact of addressing those specific concerns or how they can be overcome in a journey of attitudinal change. Chapter 7 summarizes our findings and provides a guide for how advocates and allies can use Identity Reassurance Theory in their own work to open minds to persuasion on transgender rights.

Discussion and Conclusion

While in recent years lesbian, gay, and bisexual Americans have seen legal victories and declining explicit discrimination, transgender people remain astoundingly vulnerable, though increasingly visible. Though transgender people's experiences of precarity and discrimination are not new, public attention to them is. As this visibility and attention grow, the experiences and issues of transgender people are also moving into mainstream politics, as is particularly evident in recent years' debates around, for example, transgender people's access to bathrooms and public spaces and whether transgender people should be allowed to serve openly in the U.S. military. But despite this growing public and political attention to transgender people, many Americans know very little about them. Many people do not know what the term *transgender* means and few believe that they know a transgender person; attitudes are thus relatively unstable, and potentially malleable. A growing body of scholarship examines how the public forms their views of transgender people and rights and how to change those attitudes, but there are still many unanswered questions in this area and much work to be done.

Scholars in social psychology, political communication, identity, and prejudice have developed many explanations of attitudes toward marginalized groups and efforts to change these attitudes. One of the most common strategies to combat intolerance and prejudice involves coming into contact with a member of an outgroup. The theory of interpersonal contact has proved especially central to attitudes toward gay and lesbian people but so far not toward transgender people, both because there are fewer transgender people in the population, making contact less likely or possible, and because it does not seem to work as effectively. However, that contact theory doesn't appear to be effective for transgender attitudes begs a larger and more fundamental question: what *will* change hearts and minds about transgender people and rights?

The reality is, many people are simply not comfortable with the idea of transgender identity, let alone physically being near a transgender person. Moving attitudes on transgender rights requires acknowledgments of these predispositions and the use of strategies that avoid triggering reactance. Our Identity Reassurance Theory does just that, providing targets of persuasive messages with the necessary comfort and state of mind to reconsider their attitudes about transgender rights and be more supportive of transgender people. It does not require them to deny their discomfort; it acknowledges their discomfort and need to preserve their self-esteem. It reinforces existing core values and links them to ongoing debates about transgender rights in a way that does not threaten their gender identity or their need to feel safe and comfortable. It meets them where they are and encourages them to be their own best self. In other words, our theory suggests that to persuade people to support transgender rights, the most effective messaging will lead people to voice support for transgender rights because it confirms and bolsters their self-esteem as a morally virtuous person. Even if they are not entirely sure of that support, our expectation is that those lingering internal doubts will eventually dissipate as more people come to fully integrate support for transgender people and rights into their concepts of self.

3

Finding the Path to Attitude Change on Transgender Rights

In the fall of 2014, Brian taught an LGBT politics and identity course at a small liberal arts college in New England. The students were uniformly liberals and progressives and the conversations from the beginning were less about whether and how LGBT people deserved rights and legal protections and more about how the current Democratic Party was not committed to the progressive changes that needed to be made. At the same time, there was an ongoing debate about whether to make all campus bathrooms gender neutral, with student-led protests advocating for the policy change to benefit transgender and gender nonconforming students. One of Brian's students who identified as transgender described their uncomfortable experiences with bathroom use, ranging from enduring verbal harassment, dealing with anxiety over the possibility of being physically assaulted using the bathroom, and nearly having accidents because of uncertainty about having easy access to a bathroom that was safe for them. A cisgender male student let out an audible laugh. "I'm sorry but that's ridiculous," he said. "Just go. No one cares where you pee."

History shows us that's simply not true: People do care where other people pee and they especially care about where transgender people pee. In this instance—as is often the case—the cisgender person is simply discounting and dismissing the transgender person's feelings and experiences rather than listening and processing that first-hand information. As noted in chapter 1, while strong majorities believe that transgender people should be protected against discrimination, they don't tend to support their right to choose to use the public restroom that corresponds with their gender identity.

In this chapter, we first provide details about the fight over transgender public restroom and locker room access. Next we share results from an experiment aimed at increasing support for transgender bathroom access rights. Data come from an online survey experiment conducted in early 2016 that tested different framings of the issue, with a focus on frames of freedom and

Transforming Prejudice. Melissa R. Michelson and Brian F. Harrison, Oxford University Press (2020) © Oxford University Press.
DOI: 10.1093/oso/9780190068882.001.0001

safety. We then move on to the second most well-known public policy debate related to transgender rights: serving in the U.S. armed forces. The two issues balance each other well in terms of exploring differences in attitudes toward transgender men and transgender women. Most of the public debate about bathroom access focuses on perceptions of transgender women, while debates about the military are more likely to bring transgender men to mind. As noted in chapter 1, the military service issue came onto the national agenda early in the Trump administration as he moved to reverse an Obama-era ruling allowing transgender people to serve openly. After introducing the topic, we share results from an online survey experiment conducted in May 2018. We close the chapter with a review of how these two experiments helped us clarify how moving attitudes about transgender people and rights would require a different approach than most public policy issue areas and helped us develop Identity Reassurance Theory.

Transgender Access to Locker Rooms and Bathrooms

While transgender equality includes battles on a variety of issues, the one most clearly visible to the general public in recent years is that of access to bathrooms and locker rooms as evidenced by the flood of public opinion polls conducted on the issue in 2016 and 2017. These issues were not necessarily the priority of the transgender community but were brought to the forefront due to legal battles and rhetoric determined by the opposition.

We conducted a Roper iPoll search for publicly available polls of attitudes of U.S. adults toward transgender bathroom access. We found just nine, including five from 2016, three from 2017, and one in 2019. Some findings from these surveys as well as the 2016 American National Election Study (ANES) are shown in Figure 3.1. Support for the right of transgender people to use restrooms that correspond to their gender identity varies from 40% to 53% while opposition varies from 35% to 50%. More notable is the trend: while precise levels of support vary slightly, the public has been fairly evenly divided on the issue for several years, with volatility over time but no consistent increases or decreases in support for transgender bathroom access rights over time. The same trend is seen in polls conducted in 2015 and 2016 by Taylor et al. (2018).

Attitudes on this issue illustrate the divide between general statements about civil liberties and specific policies that have been a feature of

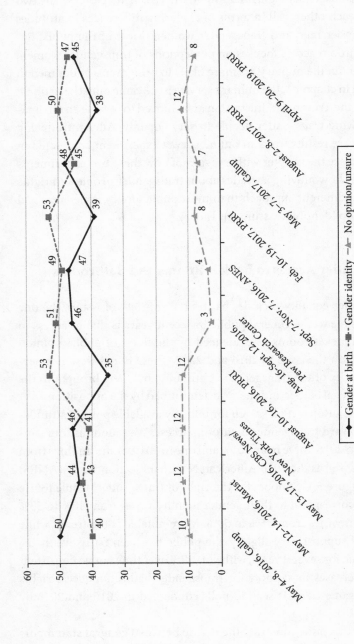

Figure 3.1. Public opinion about transgender bathroom rights, 2016–2019.

Source: Roper iPoll archive and 2016 ANES. *Note:* Taylor et al. (2018) include a bathroom access item in their national poll conducted in June 2016. They find that when respondents are forced to take a position (when there is no *don't know/no answer* option), 45% support transgender bathroom access rights and 55% are opposed. Among Democrats, this shifts to 62% in favor and 38% opposed; among Republicans, it shifts to 23% in favor and 77% opposed.

American politics for decades (McClosky and Brill 1983). As they note, most Americans are strong supporters of the rights of free expression and behavior when couched in general terms but less supportive when it comes to specific instances of people engaging in what they consider to be deviant or objectionable behavior. Consistent with this understanding of public opinion, while many Americans claim to support laws against discrimination in public accommodations (which would include public restrooms), they are much less likely to support the right of transgender people to use the restroom that they prefer. The most recent example at the time of publication, the April 2019 PRRI poll, found that 71% of respondents supported a law against discrimination in public accommodations while only 47% supported transgender bathroom access rights.

Attitudes about transgender bathroom access are deeply divided by political party. These partisan splits reflect what Mason (2018) calls identity-based democracy: elections and policy battles are now waged between two highly sorted megaparties. Her work focuses on the growing social gulf between Democrats and Republicans along social identities of race, religion, and other cultural groups. LGBT issues are also part of the political environment with sharp delineations by political affiliation (Michelson and Schmitt 2019). Support for transgender bathroom access is a good example of that phenomenon. Overall, 49% of respondents to the 2016 ANES think that transgender people should use the public restroom that corresponds to the gender they were assigned at birth while 47% think that they should be able to use the restroom that corresponds to their gender identity. Among Democrats, 65% support transgender bathroom access while 33% are opposed; among Republicans, 27% support bathroom access rights and 69% are opposed. P. E. Jones and Brewer (2018) find that elite cues are driving these partisan divisions, particularly among the most politically aware citizens.

After 2017, the issue of bathroom access mostly faded from the headlines, with no major polling data about it until the PRRI April 2019 survey. Instead, the polling focus shifted to other transgender issues, including levels of support for laws to protect transgender people against discrimination in jobs, public accommodations, and housing; transgender troops; and whether voters would support a transgender candidate for public office.

Freedom, Safety, and Bathroom Access Rights

As detailed in chapter 2, the battle over transgender bathroom access rights is extremely polarized. In part, this is due to "the irrational fears attached to transgender people" (Levi and Klein 2006: 89). Opponents on the right see access as indecent, as incompatible with privacy rights, and as giving sexual predators access to children, while some feminist scholars argue that transgender bathroom access rights deny the reality of male domination and forget that women's toilets are "essential to women's equality" (Jeffreys 2014: 46). Cavanaugh (2010: 30) claimed this opposition is rooted in transphobia and homophobia: "There seems to be a fetishistic quality to the obsessive interest in the gender of bathroom users. Separating bodies by urinary capacities— real and imagined—is a way to ensure sexual difference when our bodies do not always lend themselves to absolute and exacting divisions by gender." Murib (2019) argued that the debate is at its core about the right of transgender people to exist in public spaces and that denying transgender and gender nonconforming individuals the right to safely use public restrooms contributes to their social and political marginalization.

Conservatives used marriage equality as a wedge issue for many years (Camp 2008; Stone 2012). In 2004, Republicans placed several propositions banning same-sex marriage onto ballots in multiple states, hoping that those opposed to same-sex marriage would come out to vote on those propositions and then stay to vote in favor of Republican candidates, including incumbent President George W. Bush. Polls conducted in 2004 found that nearly half (49%) of Republican voters said that gay marriage was very important to their vote and 78% of Republicans opposed gay marriage (Pew Research Center 2012). Overall, exit polls found that large numbers of 2004 voters claimed that "moral values" were the most important determinant of their vote but analyses disagree as to whether the same-sex marriage issue motivated the Republican base to turn out (Lewis 2005; Hillygus and Shields 2005; Smith et al. 2006; Campbell and Monson 2008). Further research has shown that legislation and judicial decisions that advanced marriage equality *increased* consensus and support for those policies as legitimate rather than motivating increased disapproval or backlash (Flores and Barclay 2016).

Regardless of the actual effects, Republicans believed that it worked. Thus, as public opinion on marriage equality shifted, party strategists needed a new divisive cultural issue to mobilize voters. In multiple states, they turned to ballot measures focused on the right of transgender people to access public restrooms that conform to their gender identities, perpetuating and encouraging the longstanding stereotype of transgender women as secret sexual predators (Halberstam 1998; Juang 2006).

One of the first of these battles was in Gainesville, Florida in 2008. After the city commission added transgender-inclusive language to its nondiscrimination ordinance, opponents collected signatures to challenge the policy using a proposed charter amendment to be voted on by the city's voters. Proponents of the amendment stoked fear of transgender people as predators. As Taylor et al. (2014: 135) note:

> As the vote approached, amendment supporters aired a controversial TV commercial in which a little girl at a playground walks into a bathroom and is followed by a suspicious-looking man. Subsequently, a black screen flashed the words, "Your City Commission made this legal."

Gainesville voters killed the amendment with a 58%-to-42% vote, but the tactic lived on.

In 2011, the advocacy organization One Anchorage moved to put a measure on the ballot to extend city nondiscrimination protections to include members of the LGBT community. Leading up to the April 2012 vote, proponents framed the issue as one of fairness, while opponents aired inflammatory advertisements claiming the measure "would require day care centers to hire transvestites or face jail time." In the television advertisement, "a cartoon transvestite who wants to work at a day care is drawn as a man with a jutting jaw and body hair, wearing a short pink dress, red high heels and lipstick" (Taylor et al. 2014: 148). While not focused on the issues of public bathrooms, the Anchorage advertisement perpetuated the two messages used by opponents of transgender rights: that transgender people are men in drag and that they should be considered dangerous to children.[1] This time, the tactic was effective: the people of Anchorage defeated the initiative by a margin of 58% to 42%.

In April 2018, the issue came back to Anchorage, with voters asked to weigh in on a proposition to repeal the city's protections of transgender bathroom and locker room access rights which had been passed by legislators (without a public vote) in 2015. Proponents of the repeal centered their arguments on the usual themes: that the policy gave men access to spaces supposed to be for women only, endangering women and girls. Their website, safebathrooms.org, featured a video of a mom sharing her shock and fear at finding a "biological male" wearing a women's bathing suit in her health club pool locker room. The website's FAQ page (falsely) claimed, "Across the country cases exist where predators have used these harmful policies and ordinances to gain access to their victims when they are at their most vulnerable." Reversing their 2012 position, the voters of Anchorage rejected the repeal by a 54%-to-46% margin.

One of the most famous of these so-called bathroom bill battles is from Houston, Texas, where in November 2015, voters weighed in on the Houston Equal Rights Ordinance (HERO), which opponents claimed would give male sexual predators access to women's public restrooms. One television advertisement against the ordinance featured the following voiceover:

> Houston's Proposition 1 bathroom ordinance—what does it mean to you? Any man at any time could enter a woman's bathroom, simply by claiming to be a woman that day. No one is exempt. Even registered sex offenders could follow women or young girls into the bathroom. If a business tried to stop them, they'd be fined. Protect women's privacy. Prevent danger. Vote no on the Proposition 1 bathroom ordinance. It goes too far.[2]

Most of the advertisement video is innocuous scenes of the limbs of an unidentified person in the bathroom washing their hands but as the voiceover turns to the issue of danger, we see a young girl enter a stall and the person, who visually appears to be a man, come out of his stall and follow the girl into hers. The clear implication, of course, is that she is in danger. Another widely distributed opposition advertisement claimed that Proposition 1 "would allow troubled men to enter women's public bathrooms, showers, and locker rooms," putting women in harm's way (Moyer 2015). The fear-mongering campaign was effective; HERO was repealed by a 69%-to-31% vote.

In February 2016, the city of Charlotte, North Carolina passed a sweeping LGBT civil rights ordinance that included the right of transgender people to use the bathroom of their choice. Republican Governor Pat McCrory spoke out against the ordinance even before it was approved by the city council, claiming the policy would "create major public safety issues." Speaking to a reporter on local television (WBTV), McCrory said, "I was stunned that the city of Charlotte was even considering an ordinance in which a person with a male anatomy could use a women's restroom or locker room. . . . It basically breaks the basic standards and expectations of privacy" (*Charlotte Observer* 2016).

A month later, McCrory called a special session of the state legislature that approved a bill (HB2) overturning the Charlotte ordinance. This victory for opponents of transgender bathroom rights, however, was fleeting; national backlash against HB2 was strong and swift, including boycotts; reduced tourism; cancelled events by entertainers, the National Basketball Association, and the National Collegiate Athletic Association; and the cancellation of planned expansions in the state by PayPal, Deutsche Bank, and other companies. The Associated Press estimated that the bathroom bill could cost the state $3.8 billion in lost revenue over the next 12 years (Associated Press 2017). In November 2016, McCrory narrowly lost his reelection bid, losing to Democratic opponent Roy Cooper; a few months later, Cooper signed a deal he said would repeal HB2.[3]

In 2011, the Massachusetts state legislature approved a bill to extend nondiscrimination protections to the transgender community. Opponents denounced the legislation as "a 'bathroom bill' that would allow cross-dressing males access to women's restrooms and locker rooms," stoking fears of sexual assault on women and girls (Lewis et al. 2015: 176). The issue headed to the Massachusetts ballot in November 2018, with voters asked to weigh in on whether to repeal the bill, presented as Question 3. Proponents of the repeal, Keep MA Safe, made the usual arguments about the danger posed by transgender men:

> In other words, the bill relegates a person's sex to their state-of-mind or a mental choice, instead of basing it in biological reality. Those advocating for this bill do not believe that men are necessarily men and women are necessarily women. Rather, they believe that biology is an inconvenient fact when it comes to matters of identifying one's sex.
>
> This bill would endanger the privacy and safety of women and children in public bathrooms, locker rooms, dressing rooms, and other intimate places (such as common showers), opening them to whomever wants to be there at any given time, and also to sexual predators who claim "confusion" about their gender as a cover for their evil intentions.[4]

A video released by Keep MA Safe features a frightened young girl encountering a transgender man in a public restroom and ends with a list of headlines about biological men attacking or videotaping people in women's bathrooms, including six that mention that the offender is transgender.

Opponents of the repeal, organized as Freedom for All Massachusetts, denounced the video as deceitful hate mongering. Consistent with public opinion polls throughout the election season, the repeal was roundly rejected by Massachusetts voters, by a more than two-to-one margin (68% vs. 32%).

As these examples make clear, legislative and ballot initiative battles over bathroom access bills have been waged with rhetoric and imagery meant to use framing and priming as persuasive tools. Opponents of access rights, in particular, have consistently presented the issue as one of safety for women and girls and have portrayed transgender people as either confused men in dresses or deceitful predators, consistent with stereotypes perpetuated about both real and fictional transgender women (Serano 2013). We hypothesized that effective reframing of the issue might help to diffuse opposition to bathroom access rights and to reduce prejudice against transgender people. We turn now to a description of our experiment testing that theory.

The Framing Experiment

For this experiment, we framed the issue of transgender bathroom access rights as about either safety or freedom (for full details, see Harrison and Michelson 2017b). Respondents were randomly assigned to view a persuasive statement about the issue, framing it either as an issue of transgender rights and important for the safety of transgender people (including children) or as an issue of protecting the privacy and safety of women and girls; in each case, half of the messages were supportive of transgender bathroom access rights while the other half opposed those rights. These messages echoed those being used by advocates on both sides of the issue in real-world debates such as over the ballot measure battles reviewed earlier. A placebo treatment condition exposed participants to a persuasive message about using fewer paper towels in the bathroom.

Framing effects occur when differences in the presentation of an issue or event change one's opinion about that issue or object; it is a process by which people orient their thinking toward an object (Chong and Druckman 2007; Druckman 2004). For example, Sniderman and Theriault (2004) showed that 85% of respondents supported allowing a hate group rally when a free-speech frame was emphasized whereas support dropped to 45% when the issue was framed in terms of the potential for violence. Rasinki (1989) showed that support for government expenditures on welfare drops markedly when framed as "assistance to the poor" versus "welfare." Chong and Druckman (2007) presented frames in an expectancy model in which different considerations toward an object are weighted by the set of dimensions that affect an individual's evaluation, leading to what is known as a *frame in thought*. Frames in thought are often influenced by *frames in communication*, defined as information that attempts to change the emphasis on different considerations toward an object. As a result, a framing effect is defined as the instance where a frame in communication influences a frame in thought, ultimately changing an evaluation toward the attitude object.

Our study tested how framing effects impact public opinion toward transgender people accessing bathrooms that correspond to their gender identity. We recruited participants through Amazon.com's Mechanical Turk (MTurk). This online tool matches employers with workers who are paid to complete tasks, often including online surveys and experiments.[5] We posted our survey experiment job to MTurk on February 24, 2016, offering payment of $0.50 for a completed survey, consistent with fair wages and best practices on the site. MTurk workers who agreed to complete the job were randomly assigned to one of five conditions. All participants were then asked a set of questions about bathroom access (our dependent variables) and a few demographic questions. The experiment tested our hypothesis that framing could affect support for transgender bathroom access rights.

The experimental conditions framed bathroom access as about either safety or freedom compared to a placebo condition that exposed participants to a statement about reducing their use of paper towels. For the safety and freedom frames, participants were further split into conditions that framed the issue either negatively (that bathroom access for transgender people would reduce safety/freedom for cisgender people) or positively (that bathroom access would increase safety/freedom for transgender people). In sum, the purpose of the experiment was to examine how respondents answered questions about transgender bathroom choice differently depending on their random assignment to statements framing the issue in different ways.

In the safety frame in the supportive condition (Condition A), the text read:

> Keeping kids safe means allowing them to use the restroom without worrying about getting attacked or harassed. To do this, we need to allow transgender youth to use the restroom of their choice.

Keep kids safe. Allow kids to use the restroom they prefer.

In the safety frame in the opposition condition (Condition B), the text read:

Keeping kids safe means allowing them to use the restroom without worrying about getting attacked or harassed. To do this, we need to keep men who say they are transgender out of women's restrooms.

Keep kids safe. Keep men out of the ladies room.

In the freedom frame in the supportive condition (Condition C), the text read:

Transgender people should have the freedom to use the bathroom of their choice. No one should be forced to go into a bathroom they don't want to use.

It's all about freedom. Allow everyone to choose the restroom they prefer.

In the freedom frame in the opposition condition (Condition D), the text read:

Men and women should have the freedom to use a bathroom just for them, just for men or just for women.

It's all about freedom. Allow everyone to choose the restroom that is just for them.

The placebo condition (Condition E) encouraged respondents to use fewer paper towels when using the bathroom; the text read:

Using fewer paper towels when you use the restroom helps save trees and protect our planet.

Protect our trees. Protect the world. Use fewer paper towels.

Hypotheses

We hypothesized that the positive frames would increase support for transgender rights while the negative frames would decrease support. We also hypothesized that because the public debate about bathrooms has often focused on safety, messages using safety frames would be more powerful than messages using freedom frames. Specifically:

H_1: Support for transgender bathroom rights will be higher among participants exposed to a message in support of transgender bathroom rights compared to participants exposed to the placebo message.

H_2: Support for transgender bathroom rights will be lower among participants exposed to a message opposed to transgender bathroom rights compared to participants exposed to the placebo message.

H_3: Support for transgender rights will be higher among participants exposed to a message that frames support for transgender bathroom rights in terms of safety compared to participants exposed to a message that frames support for transgender bathroom rights in terms of freedom.

H_4: Support for transgender rights will be lower among participants exposed to a message that frames opposition to transgender bathroom rights in terms of safety compared to participants exposed to a message that frames opposition to transgender bathroom rights in terms of freedom.

Results

Overall, 443 MTurk workers completed the survey, including 282 men, 158 women, and 3 respondents who identified as genderqueer, genderfluid, or nonbinary. Between 84 and 94 participants were randomly assigned to each of the five conditions. Overall, support for transgender bathroom access rights was stronger among women, Democrats, younger respondents, respondents without children, and those with a friend or family member who is transgender or gender nonconforming. We also asked respondents if their gender (among other identities) was essential, important, not too important, or not important at all to their identities. Support for transgender bathroom access rights was weaker among those who said gender was essential to their identity (53.9% support) compared to respondents who said that their gender was not essential to their identity (68.6%).

Support for transgender rights in the placebo condition (Condition E) is strong, at 68.3% of respondents. Participants randomly assigned to the negative safety frame (Condition B) were the least supportive, with only 55.4% in favor of transgender bathroom access rights. This difference of nearly 18 percentage points is both substantively large and statistically significant. The effect persists in a multivariate regression (not shown) controlling for gender, age, partisan identification, education, whether one has children, race, whether one's gender is an essential part of one's identity, and interpersonal contact with a transgender or gender nonconforming person. Assignment to other frames, however, did not produce meaningful differences from the placebo, as shown in Table 3.1.

The results confirm that attitudes toward transgender people can be influenced by framing effects but also suggest that moving attitudes toward a stigmatized group in a positive direction may be more difficult than reinforcing negative attitudes. The statistically significant differences in responses between the two conditions persist when looking separately at theoretically interesting subsets of our respondents, by gender identity and strength of gender identity, as shown in Table 3.2.

Respondents who identified as women were much more supportive in the placebo condition (77.1%) but much less supportive when exposed to the negative safety frame condition (50%), a large and statistically significant difference of over 27 percentage points. Responses from men were less different in the two conditions and the difference is not statistically significant. As with the overall results, other differences by gender are small and not statistically significant. Among those claiming their gender is essential to their

Table 3.1. Support for Transgender Bathroom Access, by Condition, 2016 Values Framing Experiment

Condition	Percent Supportive (N)	Percentage-Point Difference From Placebo (SE)
(A) Safety, Pro	68.2 (60/88)	0.1 (6.9)
(B) Safety, Anti	55.4 (51/92)	−12.7* (7.1)
(C) Freedom, Pro	65.9 (56/85)	−2.2 (7.1)
(D) Freedom, Anti	60.7 (51/84)	−7.4 (7.2)
(E) Placebo	68.1 (51/94)	n/a

Note: $N = 443$. Data collected February 24, 2016. * = statistically significant at $p \leq .05$, two-tailed. SE = standard errors.

Table 3.2. Support for Transgender Bathroom Access, by Gender Identity and Strength of Gender Identity, 2016 Values Framing Experiment

	Placebo Condition	Negative Safety Condition	Difference (SE)
All respondents	68.1%	55.4%	−12.7*
	(51/94)	(51/92)	(7.1)
Women	77.1	50.0	−27.1*
	(27/35)	(13/26)	(12.0)
Men	62.7	55.6	−7.2
	(37/59)	(35/63)	(9.0)
Gender essential to identity	61.8	40.8	−20.9*
	(21/34)	(20/49)	(11.1)
Gender not essential to identity	72.1	71.7	0.4
	(31/43)	(43/60)	(9.1)

Note: $N = 443$. Data collected February 24, 2016. * = statistically significant at $p \leq .05$, two-tailed. SE = standard errors.

identity, 61.8% of participants assigned to the placebo condition support transgender bathroom access rights compared to only 38.3% of participants in the negative safety frame condition, a statistically significant drop of more than 20 percentage points. Differences for those who report that their gender is not essential to their identity, and across other conditions, are small and not statistically significant.

In sum, without framing, people (at least, liberal-leaning MTurk workers) are open to the idea of transgender bathroom access but anti-choice framing of the issue can easily erode that support, particularly among those most likely to feel threatened by a threatening frame (women) or those for whom gender is an essential component of their identity. The results support our contention that framing can affect attitudes toward transgender bathroom rights. However, the supportive frames failed to increase support.

We concluded from this experiment that while another frame might have been more effective, the strategy was probably not likely to be particularly successful because it did not address the underlying discomfort that many Americans feel toward transgender people. We needed to develop a theory of persuasion that took into consideration the gender identities and perceived threats to those identities that affect cisgender attitudes toward transgender rights. Our subsequent experiments explored this idea, as detailed in chapters 4 through 6, while also taking into account the considerable literature that finds that men and women have very different attitudes about LGBT rights broadly and transgender rights specifically, as we noted in chapter 1.

We now turn to the second major issue related to transgender people that has made headlines and inspired public opinion surveys over the past few years: the right of transgender people to serve openly in the U.S. military.

Integrity, Equality, and Transgender Military Service

Most Americans don't think much about the people serving in our armed forces; because it is an all-volunteer force, it is not a salient topic for most people who are not interested in choosing to serve. In contrast, the issue of access rights to public bathrooms tends to be much more salient (and threatening) to all members of the public because it is more proximate and something experienced regularly. In July 2017, however, President Trump raised national focus on the issue with his series of tweets announcing that he would be reversing the Obama administration policy of allowing transgender people to serve openly in the military.

Debates related to LGBT rights and military service have made headlines for decades. The Carter administration adopted the first formal ban, claiming "homosexuality is incompatible with military service." In 1993, during the Clinton administration, Congress approved legislation codifying the ban into law, dubbed Don't Ask, Don't Tell (DADT)—gay and lesbian people were allowed to serve but only if they were closeted. Recruiters and supervisors were not supposed to ask about an individual's sexual orientation and gay men and lesbians were not supposed to tell anyone. Opposition to open inclusion in the armed forces stemmed from the role that military service played in bolstering the masculinity of those choosing to serve. The argument was that the inclusion of openly gay men (and lesbians) would threaten the understanding of the military as a place where "real men" serve. "Thus, individuals' discomfort with gays and lesbians is not simply a homophobic reaction; it reflects the fear that the organization will change in ways that do not permit it to bolster masculine identity and sense of superiority" (Mucciaroni 2008: 186).

The policy of discharging individuals found to be sincerely gay (as opposed to those making false admissions of homosexuality to avoid military service) led to the discharge of thousands of service members. Then-presidential candidate Bill Clinton raised the issue during the 1992 campaign and faced stiff opposition from the military and service members. Polls taken at the time were strongly divided. A CBS News/*New York Times* poll in February 1993 found 42% of the public in support of gay, lesbian, and bisexual people in the military and 47% opposed. Initial support for DADT was strong but by the end of the 1990s, that support began to fade. By 1997, most Americans no longer supported DADT and in 2007, polls found overwhelming majorities in favor of allowing gay men and lesbians to serve openly in the U.S. military.

President Barack Obama repealed DADT in 2011 but resisted calls at the time from LGBT advocacy organizations to also allow transgender people to serve openly. In 2014, then-Secretary of Defense Chuck Hagel said the military should "continually review its prohibition of transgender people" in the armed forces. He said, "Every qualified American who wants to serve our country should have an opportunity if they fit the qualifications and can do it." This stance was in conflict with Defense Department guidelines, written decades earlier, which described transgender people as sexual deviants. In July 2015, then-Secretary of Defense Ash Carter announced a plan to allow transgender people to serve openly, acknowledging that many transgender people were already serving in the military. He said, "We have transgender soldiers, sailors, airmen and Marines—real, patriotic Americans—who I know are being hurt by an outdated, confusing, inconsistent approach that's contrary to our value of service and individual merit" (Bromwich 2017).

Secretary Carter commissioned the Rand Corporation to compile a report about how allowing transgender service members would affect readiness and costs in the U.S. military. The report found that "the number of U.S. transgender service members who are likely to seek transition-related care is so small that a change in policy will likely have a marginal impact on health care costs and the readiness of the force" (Schaefer et al. 2016: 69). The report also suggested a net benefit to the military because of the increased inclusion and diversity the policy change would provide. The study estimated that 2,450 active-duty members were transgender and roughly 54 people would seek medical care to transition each year. That care would increase medical costs between $2.9 and $4.2 million per year, an estimated 0.13% increase.[6]

In an attempt to neutralize arguments from opponents, Carter also emphasized the part of the study that predicted higher rates of substance abuse and suicide if transgender service members did not have their needed procedures covered by the Pentagon. Transgender people would be permitted to join so long as they could demonstrate they had been stable in their new gender for at least 18 months. The policy was meant to come into effect on July 1, 2017. The inclusion of transgender people in military service was hailed by many media outlets as a victory for human rights, one that cemented Obama's historic LGBT rights legacy (Margolin 2016).

That victory proved to be short-lived. On July 26, 2017, President Trump sent out a series of three tweets reversing the 2016 decision by the Obama administration to allow transgender people to serve openly (see Figure 3.2). Trump tweeted that he consulted with military experts before making the decision and cited "tremendous medical costs and disruption that transgender in the military would entail." As noted earlier, these statements are in direct contrast to the findings in the 2016 Department of Defense study. Trump's initial efforts to implement the ban were blocked by the courts as unconstitutional. In March 2018, Trump followed up with a new attempt to implement the change, this time exempting those currently serving but only allowing additional transgender people to enlist if they agree to serve as the sex they were assigned at birth; again, the policy was blocked by the courts as unconstitutional and did not go into effect. Many political and military leaders criticized the proposed policy change. In separate statements in April 2018, the leaders of the U.S. Navy, Army, Air Force, Marine Corps, and Coast Guard testified to Congress that transgender service members do not harm military cohesion or discipline (*New York Times* 2018). Many elite Republicans also voiced disagreement with the Trump policy, including Republican Senators Dan Sullivan (R-AK), Lisa Murkowski (R-AK), and Joni Ernst (R-IA) (Enten 2017).

The Trump administration responded to these losses in the courts by trying to create a hostile work environment for transgender troops and rejecting their applications to enlist (Ferdman 2018). This meant the issue was generally kept out of the public eye and was never the topic of a ballot initiative campaign or public vote. Lawyers debated the issue and social media posts offered responses and analyses but there were no advertisements aimed at shifting general public opinion. While legal challenges delayed implementation of Trump's decision, those legal battles ended in Trump's favor with a Supreme Court decision in January 2019.

Trump's tweets and the very public battle over transgender troops pushed the issue onto the public agenda and as an item in various public opinion polls, but public opinion data on transgender troops is more limited than survey data on bathroom access rights. Before the issue hit the front pages, Taylor et al. (2018) included support for transgender troops in several of their national surveys, in October 2015 and in June 2016. In the first survey,

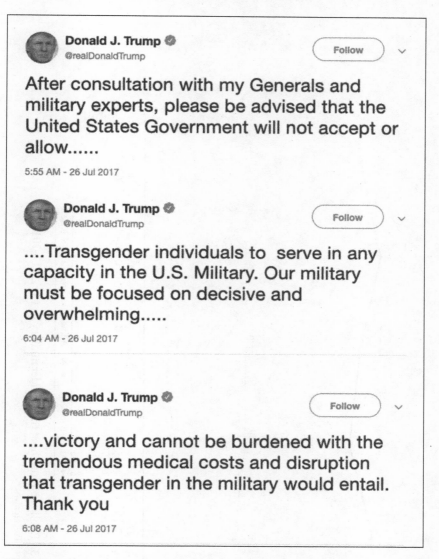

Figure 3.2. Trump tweets banning transgender troops, July 26, 2017.

respondents could choose to answer *don't know* while the latter forces a choice between support and opposition. In October 2015, over a third (35.5% of respondents) chose *don't know* while just 22% were supportive. In the forced-choice survey of June 2016, 68% of respondents were supportive. Taylor et al. note: "it seems that many Americans have yet to solidify their

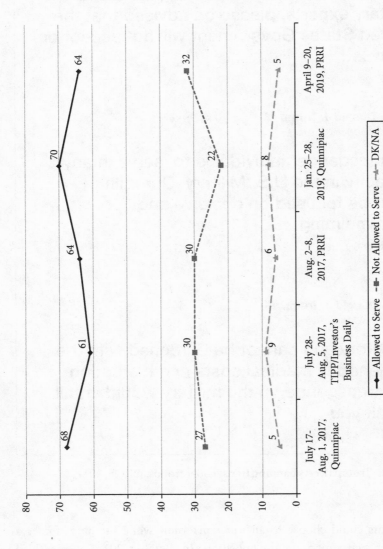

Figure 3.3. Public opinion about transgender military service, 2017–2019.

Source: Roper iPoll archive.

attitudes on many different topics related to gender identity and transgender people" (2018: 72).

As of June 2019, Roper's iPoll database lists five national surveys with questions on transgender service in the military: three in 2017 and two more in 2019. In 2017, support for transgender military service ranges from 61% to 68%, with 27% to 30% of respondents opposed, as shown in Figure 3.3. The issue was only in the news due to Trump's tweets; as the news cycle moved on, so too did public opinion pollsters. The news cycle returned to the issue in January 2019 when the U.S. Supreme Court ruled in Trump's favor. At that time, support had increased to 70% in favor with 22% opposed; however, an April 2019 poll found support back down to 2017 levels, with 64% in favor and 32% opposed. Also notable is the dramatically lower proportion of respondents declining to share an opinion about the issue compared to the results from the 2015 survey by Taylor et al. The overall lack of broader public debate meant that there were fewer settled attitudes, allowing more room for persuasive communication and the possibility that we could experimentally shift those attitudes.

Polls also show a clear and persistent partisan split on the issue, as shown in Figure 3.4. In 2017, 32% to 37% of Republicans supported transgender

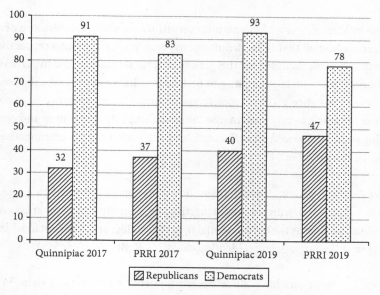

Figure 3.4. Support for transgender military service, by political party, 2017–2019.

Source: Roper iPoll archive.

troops while 57% to 60% were opposed. Among Democrats, the range was 83% to 91% in favor and 7% to 15% opposed. In the January 2019 poll, the split is slightly larger, with 40% of Republicans in favor and 50% opposed, and 93% of Democrats in favor and only 3% opposed. A fourth poll conducted by PRRI in April 2019 suggests a shift in attitudes, with more Republicans in favor (47%) and fewer Democrats in support (78%).

The public does have gendered attitudes about the military. It is traditionally seen as a place for men, and historically, it has struggled to include women and members of the LGBT community. Since its inception, the U.S. military has promised that it would "make men out of" the young men who joined it and service has been portrayed by recruiters as a way to prove one's masculinity (Knaff 2018; Huebner 2018). Media and society represent military men as idealized versions of American masculinity (Myers 2018). Although both men and women serve in the armed forces, the military is dominated by men, with women making up about 16% of the active duty force (Department of Defense 2018).

More than a decade ago, U.S. Air Force Psychiatrist George Brown linked the hypermasculine perception of military service to the unusually large number of transgender women he was seeing in his medical center.

The military places a high premium on virility, stoicism, machismo, assertiveness, and all that is, by definition, hypermasculine. It seems that active duty is a natural choice for the gender-dysphonic male in the hypermasculine phase who is attempting to make a last ditch effort to take the path of least resistance vis-à-vis society and family. He sees a chance to maximize his ambivalently present masculine self while de-integrating and purging his feminine self, all in the service of adaptation and accommodation. (G. R. Brown 2006: 541)

While some patients choose hypermasculine pursuits limited to contact sports, race car driving, or mountain climbing, an unknown number choose military service as the quintessential hypermasculine environment in which to purge their cross-gender identifications. (G. R. Brown 2006: 543)

Brown's perceptions have since been supported by empirical data. While men are more likely to serve in the U.S. military than women, the opposite is true for transgender people: 21.4% of the transgender population has served in the military, including 32.0% of those assigned male at birth and 5.5% of those assigned female at birth (Gates and Herman 2014).

Widespread conceptions of military service as a masculine pursuit naturally mean that the public will tend to think more about men than women when asked survey items about military service. This conception of the military as a place for men (including transgender men) helps balance out our overall set of experiments on transgender rights, allowing for comparisons between how attitudes about transgender rights that tend to bring transgender women to mind (e.g., bathroom access rights) compare to attitudes about transgender rights that tend to bring transgender men to mind.

The perception of military service as a masculine pursuit also means that messages supporting the inclusion of LGBT troops are likely to be seen as dissonant by recipients of those messages. This should be particularly true if the inclusive message comes from a military leader, as we do in the experiment described in the next section. Our previous research finds that dissonant messages are particularly powerful for changing minds about gay and lesbian rights (Harrison and Michelson 2017a). Here, we explore the power of a dissonant message to open minds to persuasion about transgender military service, combined with manipulations of the framing of those messages.

The 2018 Values Framing Experiment

We designed an online survey experiment that framed the issue of transgender military service as either about equality or integrity, a message delivered either by a military leader or a transgender rights leader. The experiment exposed participants to one of four versions of a mock newspaper article about the issue, including either statements from Admiral Mike Mullen, former Chairman of the Joint Chiefs of Staff or Mara Keisling, founder and executive director of the National Center for Transgender Equality. In addition to experimentally manipulating the elite messenger in the mock articles, the content varied to focus either on the value of integrity or on the value of equality.

Participants were asked to read a short statement that provided a definition for their randomly assigned value (integrity or equality). They were then asked to rate the degree to which they thought the value was important. On the next screen, they were asked to read a manipulated news story purporting to be from *USA Today* that quoted either Mullen or Keisling as advocating for transgender service members and claimed that Congress was currently debating the issue. The text for the story featuring Mullen and an integrity frame was titled "Ex Joint Chiefs Chairman Supports Transgender Troops" and included a photo of Mullen in uniform. The text read:

> Admiral Mike Mullen, former Chairman of the Joint Chiefs of Staff, is calling on Congress not to ban openly transgender service members from the military.
>
> Mullen, who was the highest-ranking military officer in the country from 2007 to 2011, released a statement yesterday as Congress began debate on a new effort to ban transgender troops.
>
> "No matter how I look at the issue, I cannot escape being troubled by the fact that Congress is considering a policy which forces young men and women to lie about who they are in order to defend their fellow citizens," Mullen said.
>
> "Thousands of transgender Americans are currently serving in uniform and there is no reason to single out these brave men and women," he continued. "It comes down to integrity—theirs as individuals and ours as an institution."
>
> In late March, the Pentagon requested that transgender troops no longer be able to serve in the United States military. The policy recommendation is currently being debated in Congress, with a vote expected later this month.

The article featuring Keisling and with the equality frame was titled "Transgender Equality Activist Supports Transgender Troops" and included her photo. The text read:

> Mara Keisling, founder and executive director of the National Center for Transgender Equality, is calling on Congress not to ban openly transgender service members from the military.
>
> Keisling, a national leader in the fight for transgender equality, released a statement yesterday as Congress began debate on a new effort to ban transgender troops.
>
> "Efforts to ban transgender servicemembers from serving in our nation's military are unconstitutional and violate the equal opportunity rights of transgender Americans," Keisling said.
>
> Keisling continued, "On this day and every day, I continue to stand with transgender people of all backgrounds—from service members and

students, to workers and parents—in celebration of their lives and with unwavering commitment for the fight for full equality."

In late March, the Pentagon requested that transgender troops no longer
be able to serve in the United States military. The policy recommendation is
currently being debated in Congress, with a vote expected later this month.

In the other two conditions, the mock news articles were altered to leave the
statements the same but to attribute them to the other elite messenger, with the
integrity framing linked to Keisling and the equality framing linked to Mullen.

After reading the mock article, participants were asked a series of questions
about their support for transgender rights, including allowing transgender
people to serve openly in the military. As a measure of behavior, they were
also given the opportunity to add their name to a petition to be sent to
Congress in support of transgender troops. The survey ended with a set of
demographic questions and a debriefing screen. (See Script Appendix for additional survey details.) We designed the experiment to test three hypotheses
about the power of dissonant framings:

H_1: All else equal, messages from Mullen will be more persuasive than
messages from Keisling.

H_2: A message from Mullen priming the value of equality will be more persuasive than a message from Mullen priming the value of integrity.

H_3: A message from Keisling priming the value of integrity will be more persuasive than a message from Keisling priming the value of equality.

Consistent with the Theory of Dissonant Identity Priming (Harrison and
Michelson 2017a), we expected messages from Mullen to be more persuasive than messages from Keisling. Keisling, as a transgender rights activist,
is a stereotypical messenger on this topic; Mullen, as a military leader, is a
dissonant messenger (while also a trusted source given his history of military service and leadership). Comparing messages from each elite messenger, we expected that messages from Mullen framing the issue as one of
equality would be more effective because it is more counter-stereotypical
(dissonant) for a military leader to choose that frame; similarly, we expected messages from Keisling using the integrity frame to be more effective
because it is more dissonant for an equal rights advocacy group leader to
choose that frame.

Results

Participants were recruited to the online survey experiment on MTurk, with workers paid $0.50 for a completed survey. Overall, we collected data from 816 participants; data were collected May 11–12, 2018. Those participants were randomly assigned to the following conditions: (1) Integrity/Mullen, n = 209; (2) Integrity/Keisling, n = 201; (3) Equality/Mullen, n = 201; (4) Equality/Keisling, n = 205. Overall, support for transgender military service was quite high, with 75% of respondents approving. A much smaller proportion of respondents, 27.1%, chose to sign the petition.

First, testing H_1, we combined participants in the equality and integrity conditions to examine whether messages from Admiral Mullen were more persuasive. An initial crosstab suggests that Mullen was not a more persuasive messenger: 76.8% of respondents assigned to a news story about Mullen said that they supported transgender troops, compared to 72.4% of participants assigned to a news story about Keisling; the difference is not statistically significant. Participants assigned to the Mullen stories were slightly more likely to sign the petition compared to participants assigned to read the Keisling stories: 31.7% compared to 28.8%; again, the difference is not statistically significant. Instead, attitudes are driven by ideology and partisanship (conservatives and Republicans are less supportive). Older participants are less supportive but younger participants are no more likely to sign a petition. Respondents with transgender friends are also more supportive and Anglo (White non-Latinx) respondents are more likely to sign the petition (see Appendix Table A3.1 for full results).

We turn next to H_2 and H_3, where we are more attentive to the framing content of the messages and the underlying values that are cued. There is some variation by condition on attitudinal and behavioral measures of support for transgender troops. An initial crosstab finds no difference between the two messages including statements from Mullen: in the stereotypical message condition (integrity), 75.1% of participants say they support transgender troops, compared to 78.6% of participants in the dissonant message condition (equality); the difference is not statistically significant. There is also no difference between the two messages including statements from Keisling: in the stereotypical condition (equality), 73.7% of participants say they support transgender troops, compared to 71.1% of participants in the dissonant condition (integrity); the difference is not statistically significant (see Table 3.3).

Table 3.3. Support for Transgender Military Service, by Condition, 2018 Values Framing Experiment

	Mullen/Integrity (N = 209)	Mullen/Equality (N = 201)	Difference (SE)
Percentage approving of transgender troops	75.1 (3.0)	78.6 (2.9)	3.5 (4.2)
Percentage signing petition	27.8 (3.1)	35.8 (3.1)	8.1* (4.6)
	Keisling/Integrity (N = 201)	Keisling/Equality (N = 205)	Difference (SE)
Percentage approving of transgender troops	71.1 (3.2)	73.7 (3.0)	2.5 (4.4)
Percentage signing petition	30.3 (3.3)	27.3 (3.1)	−3.0 (4.5)

Note: N = 816. Data collected May 11–12, 2018. * = statistically significant at $p \leq .05$, one-tailed. SE = standard errors.

Stronger support for our hypotheses is found when examining who signed the petition. Among those assigned to the Mullen conditions, 35.8% of respondents reading the news article with an equality frame signed their names to the petition compared to only 27.8% of respondents reading the article with an integrity frame; the difference of 8.1 percentage points is statistically significant. In contrast, among those assigned to the Keisling conditions, 30.3% in the integrity frame signed, compared to 27.3% in the equality frame; the difference is not statistically significant. We further tested these differences with multivariate regression models. For the two conditions with messages from Mullen, those in the equality condition are more likely to sign. Participants who read a story featuring Keisling, in contrast, were no more likely to sign based on the framed value, but admiring equality is a significant predictor. Participants were also more likely to sign if they claimed to have a transgender friend. Conservatives are less likely to sign in the Keisling conditions, and Anglo (White non-Latinx) people are more likely to sign in the Mullen conditions. Finally, participants are more likely to sign if they place a higher value on equality, but this only reaches statistical significance in the Keisling conditions (see Appendix Table A3.2 for full results).

While not all of our hypotheses are supported, we do find that a dissonant message from a military leader (a credible source) increases support for transgender troops compared to a stereotypical message from the same messenger or to supportive messages from a national transgender rights leader. Consistent with our earlier research on persuasive messages about LGBT rights (Harrison and Michelson 2017a), an elite cue can make the difference. That said, it is not *just* an elite message that matters but also the content of that message. A dissonant message priming the value of equality is more powerful than a message from the same elite messenger that primes the value of integrity, even when controlling for respondent attitudes about those values. In sum, the most powerful message for influencing attitudes and behavior on transgender troops was a dissonant message from a dissonant (and yet trusted) source.

Discussion and Conclusion

Looking back across our two studies aimed at shifting attitudes using appeals to core values, we recognized that these framing approaches were not effective in moving respondents to be more supportive of transgender rights. In the first experiment we found that raising fears about the safety of women and girls in public restrooms was an effective way to reduce support for bathroom access rights. Our interest, of course, is in increasing support for transgender rights, which suggested that we needed to take the opposite approach: to reassure people about their fears instead of threatening them. This insight helped us develop Identity Reassurance Theory—the idea that respondents needed to be reassured about their own identities to have the self-esteem needed to support the rights of those seen as threats to their own ingroups or to their own identities. That theory, outlined in chapter 2, guided the design of many of our experiments conducted in 2017 and 2018 and which we describe and analyze in the following three chapters.

The second values experiment was more successful but still not particularly satisfying. Using elite cues and value frames about equality and integrity showed some promise as means of motivating increased support for transgender rights but not consistently and the experiment did not suggest a broader framework for moving forward, especially given that our most effective mock newspaper article—using Admiral Mullen and an equality frame—was manipulated and deceptive. We were putting words into his mouth that weren't really there, which is both intellectually unsatisfying and not particularly helpful for giving advice to real-world activists and allies on how to win the fight for transgender rights. In other words, we did not want to pursue a research agenda that would only work in a laboratory or experimental situation, where participants could be debriefed; we wanted to find a strategy for messaging about transgender rights that could be implemented by those seeking to influence the mass public.

Those caveats notwithstanding, these two values framing experiments provided useful takeaways. As awareness of transgender rights increases, so too will discussions of whether and how public outreach and policies might need to be revised to better include them as full members of society. Moving beyond the current headlines about gender-neutral bathrooms and transgender troops may mean revisiting other elements of sex and gender in our culture, including our need for sex-marked identity documents or for sex segregation in competitive sports (H. F. Davis 2017). Attention to how these policies might spark backlash among certain subgroups of the population might help advocates and policymakers to frame their proposals to mitigate perceived threats and resistance.

Although bathroom access rights and transgender troops are perhaps the transgender rights issues most familiar to the U.S. public, other issues of transgender equality are also the subject of public debate and policymaking. Occasionally, stories about transgender athletes, often critically noting the unfair advantage of "biological boys" competing against girls, appear in the news and attract the public's attention. For example, in early 2017, the case of Mack Beggs, a transgender boy in Texas, leapt onto the front page when he won the state girls' wrestling championship. Beggs had asked to compete as a boy but Texas officials refused and forced him to compete as the sex he was assigned at birth and listed on his birth certificate (Domonoske 2017). In June 2018, a similar story arose when two 16-year-old transgender women, Andraya Yearwood and Terry Miller, came under fire after winning first and second place at track events at Connecticut's State Open Finals (Thorbecke 2018). Several parents of girls who had lost races to Yearwood and Miller started petitions urging the state to change the rules and force the transgender girls to compete as boys. In June 2019, still seeking relief after the petition effort failed and as Miller continued to win championships, the parents filed a federal Title IX discrimination complaint, claiming the state's policy on transgender athletes discriminates against girls (Pell 2019).

Public opinion polling on transgender participation in sports is scarce. Taylor et al. (2018) share findings from their 2015 and 2016 national surveys on transgender athletes in college sports but only related to students "who have had a sex change." Despite this fairly narrow definition of transgender, support in their polls is quite low in their October 2015 survey, with 30.1% in support of transgender athletes playing as their current gender, 34% opposed, and 35.9% undecided. In their June 2016 survey, which forced respondents to choose between support or opposition without a middle ground option, opposition dropped to 39.7% with the remaining 60.1% in favor. A Marist Poll in March 2017 asked respondents about *professional* sports teams signing a transgender player. Support is quite high, at 58%, while 29% were opposed and 13% were unsure. In our January 2019 gender attitudes survey (discussed in chapter 2) we found strong majorities of the public (67% to 68%) supportive of transgender athletes in professional sports. A PRRI poll in January 2018—the one public poll about transgender high school sports participation—split their sample to ask separate questions about transgender boys and girls: 61% of respondents supported transgender boys competing in high school athletic events with other male students while only 50% of respondents supported transgender girls competing with other female students. Additional survey data are needed to better understand attitudes about teenage transgender athletes and whether attitudes are stable or shifting over time and experiments are needed to explore how those attitudes might be changed.

Another takeaway from the two experiments described in this chapter was the need to vary our dependent variables to explore how people think and feel about transgender men compared to transgender women. As noted in chapter 2, our national gender attitudes survey found significant differences in levels of comfort with transgender men and transgender women in different contexts. The issue of public bathrooms and locker rooms generally focuses on the rights of transgender women because both advocates and opponents have often used rhetoric about transgender women in their persuasive messaging: advocates have focused on transgender women because they are particularly vulnerable; opponents have vilified transgender women as threats to public health and safety. On the other hand, the issue of allowing transgender people to serve openly in the military is more likely to bring to mind transgender men, reflecting the traditional conception of the military as a place for men to prove their masculinity and the fact that men make up 84% of the active duty force. Advocates for transgender rights policies need to be attentive not only to differences in how men and women think about transgender people but also to how those attitudes differ when the focus is on male and female subgroups of the transgender community.

4

Gender Roles, Masculinity, and Support for Transgender Rights

Masculinity, or the way that men display their gender, can be both toxic and fragile. Many boys are taught to reject "girl things" like dolls and the color pink and to assert their masculinity in their choice of clothing, hobbies, and demeanor. As Tey Meadows details in *Trans Kids* (2018), expressions of masculinity by young girls are much more likely to be dismissed as acceptable tomboy behavior. Expressions of femininity by young boys, on the other hand, are less likely to escape criticism: even small infractions are likely to be met with disapproval and social sanction.

The same applies to adult men. Advertisements for everything from body spray to assault rifles encourage men to assert or reclaim their masculinity. Vokey et al. (2013) found that hypermasculinity appeared in 56% of advertisements in U.S. men's magazines. "Advertisements depicting men as tough and violent (particularly towards women) is disturbing, because gender portrayals in advertisement images do more than sell products. They also perpetuate stereotypes and present behavioural norms for men and women" (Vokey et al. 2013, 562). In one fairly notorious recent example, the Bushmaster Man Card advertising campaign claimed that buying an assault rifle "declares and confirms that you are a Man's Man." In an October 2018 op-ed for the *New York Times*, columnist Nick Kristof (2018) noted the appeal to masculinity made by gun manufacturers:

> The last few decades have in many ways demoted working class white men—their jobs have become insecure, they may no longer be the family's chief breadwinner, women and people of color have gained ground—but firing an AR-15 or packing a concealed weapon offers beleaguered men a chance to reassert their masculinity; to such men, guns provide a sense of purpose, fulfilling a traditional manly role of protecting their families and their communities. Bushmaster, the gun company, has marketed one assault rifle with a photo of it and a headline: "CONSIDER YOUR MAN CARD REISSUED."

Transforming Prejudice. Melissa R. Michelson and Brian F. Harrison, Oxford University Press (2020) © Oxford University Press.
DOI: 10.1093/oso/9780190068882.001.0001

While these appeals to masculinity are widespread, very recently there has been some evidence that the advertising world is shifting. Fashion and body care brands, in particular, are embracing a wider range of expressions of masculinity, including men wearing aprons and make-up. Not all consumers welcome the shift, emphasizing the ongoing commitment to traditional understandings of gender roles. In January 2019, Gillette released a new television commercial clearly calling on men to reject toxic masculinity and its negative consequences; the ad quickly made its way onto YouTube's list of the top 20 most disliked videos of all time (Elephant 2019).

The same commitment to traditional (even toxic) understandings of gender is also at play when Americans consider their attitudes about transgender people and rights. Policing how other people express their gender is part of how men, in particular, shore up their own self-esteem about their gender and their masculinity. Weinstein et al. (2012) find empirical evidence that at least some very homophobic individuals hold same-sex attractions that are repressed due to shame, fear, and/or being raised by homophobic and oppressive parents. Individuals for whom gender and gender identity are particularly important aspects of their identities are more likely to enforce gender stereotypes on themselves and others and to feel threatened by and disapprove of transgender people.

In this chapter, we explore the role of gender identity, threats to masculinity, and support for transgender rights. First, we explore gender differences in attitudes toward public policies including transgender rights and the subgroup differences in these attitudes by support for traditional gender roles. We then turn to an exploration of the concept of toxic masculinity and how it relates to our Identity Reassurance Theory. In two randomized experiments, one conducted in a lab and one with a national online sample, we then explore the power of threats and boosts to masculinity to shift attitudes toward transgender people and rights. We find consistent evidence that men's attitudes are linked to the strength and importance of their gender identities.

Gender and Public Policy Attitudes

In 2019, the Democrat-controlled House of Representatives passed a bill called the Equality Act that would protect LGBT Americans from discrimination in housing, employment, public accommodations, and other places. The bill, originally introduced in 2015, addresses the fact that under federal and most states' laws, LGBT people are not explicitly protected from discrimination in many aspects of public life (Lopez 2019). Someone can be fired from a job, evicted from a home, or kicked out of a business just because an employer, landlord, or business owner doesn't approve of the person's sexual orientation or gender identity. It was also introduced in 2017 but died in committee. In the midst of the House debate, Gallup conducted its annual Values and Beliefs poll (May 3–7, 2017), asking about public opinion toward LGBT rights. One of the questions on the survey was "Do you think new civil rights laws are needed to reduce discrimination against lesbian, gay, bisexual, or transgender people, or not?" (Figure 4.1).

Unsurprisingly, conservatives, Republicans, and those who regularly attend church were the three groups most likely to respond that new civil rights laws were not needed; conversely, liberals and Democrats were the two groups most likely to see a need for such laws. Perhaps more surprising, though, is how sharply divided men and women were in their responses. Women strongly supported new LGBT civil rights laws by a margin of 61% to 35%; men opposed such laws by a margin of 40% to 58%. In other words, in this survey, there is a 21-percentage-point gap in support between men and women about whether LGBT people deserved federal civil rights laws to protect them from discrimination in public life.

The same survey asked about transgender access to public restrooms: "Do you think these policies [governing public restrooms] should require transgender individuals to use the restroom that corresponds with their birth gender or should these policies allow transgender individuals to use the restroom that corresponds with their gender identity?" As shown in Figure 4.2, there is a similar pattern: Republicans, self-identified conservatives, and regular churchgoers overwhelmingly responded that transgender people should use the bathroom that corresponds to their sex assigned at birth; self-identified liberals, Democrats, and those who attend church less often responded that they support transgender people choosing the bathroom that matches their gender identity. Again, however, there is a large gap between the opinions of men and women: 52% of women think transgender people should be able to use the bathroom of their gender identity compared to just 38% of men.

More recent surveys show that these deep divides by gender on transgender rights persist, even as support for transgender rights has increased overall. In an April 2019 PRRI survey, 67% of women favored allowing transgender people to serve openly in the military compared to 59% of men. On

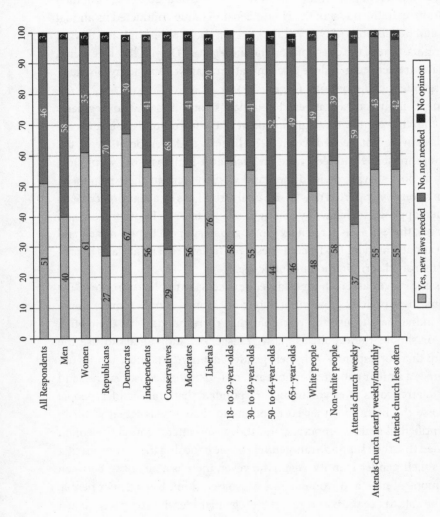

Figure 4.1. Support for laws protecting LGBT people from discrimination, by subgroup, 2017.

Note: Question wording: *Do you think new civil rights laws are needed to reduce discrimination against lesbian, gay, bisexual, or transgender people or not?* Data collected May 3–7, 2017. *Source:* https://news.gallup.com/poll/210887/americans-split-new-lgbt-protections-restroom-policies.aspx.

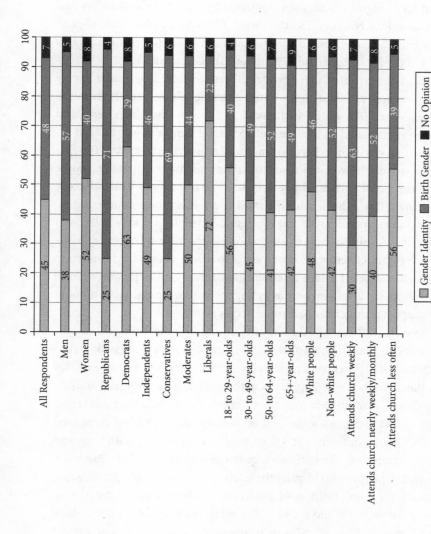

Figure 4.2. Attitudes about transgender bathroom policies, by subgroup, 2017.

Note: Data collected May 3–7, 2017. Question wording: *In terms of policies governing public restrooms, do you think these policies should [ROTATED] require transgender individuals to use the restroom that corresponds with their birth gender (or should these policies) allow transgender individuals to use the restroom that corresponds with their gender identity? Source:* https://news.gallup.com/poll/210887/americans-split-new-lgbt-protections-restroom-policies.aspx.

bathroom access policies, 51% of men said transgender people should use the bathroom corresponding to their assigned sex at birth compared to just 40% of women (R. P. Jones et al. 2019). While still falling below majority support for transgender rights, this marks an increase in support for transgender bathroom access rights among men compared to the 2017 Gallup survey and the 2016 American National Election Study (ANES). In 2016, 56% of men said transgender people should use the public restroom corresponding to their sex assigned at birth, as did 57% in the 2017 Gallup survey.

To confirm our expectations of gender differences based on similar survey questions, we analyzed data about transgender people and rights from the 2016 ANES. The 2016 ANES included 1,181 face-to-face interviews and 3,090 surveys conducted on the Internet, for a total sample size of 4,271. It included three survey items related to transgender people and rights. The first asked respondents how much discrimination against transgender people there is in the United States, either *none at all, a little, a moderate amount, a lot,* or *a great deal.* The second question is a feeling thermometer rating question, asking respondents to rate transgender people on a scale of 0 (cold) to 100 (warm). A third question asked about support for transgender bathroom access rights. Given previous survey responses, we expected women to perceive higher levels of discrimination against transgender people, to have warmer feelings toward them on the feeling thermometer scale, and to more strongly support transgender bathroom access rights.

The data support these expectations. Beginning with the feeling thermometer question, there are notable differences by gender, with men giving an average response of 51.9 degrees and women giving an average response of 58.9 degrees; the difference of 7 degrees is both substantively large and statistically significant. Women were also more likely to report believing that transgender people experience a great deal of discrimination (34.5%) compared to men (26.5%); the difference of 8 percentage points is again both large and statistically significant. The bathroom question asked: "Should transgender people—that is, people who identify themselves as the sex or gender different from the one they were born as—have to use the bathrooms of the gender they were born as, or should they be allowed to use the bathrooms of their identified gender?" Overall, 52% of respondents said transgender people should use the bathroom corresponding to their birth gender while 48% supported transgender bathroom access rights. Women were more likely to support the right of transgender people to use the bathroom of their gender identity (52.1%) while men were more likely to say that transgender people should have to use the bathroom of the gender they were identified as at birth (55.7%).

We further hypothesized that gender gaps would be less powerful predictors of attitudes about transgender people when controlling for attitudes about traditional gender roles. We explored this point using two ANES items, one about equal pay and one about women taking care of the home while the man of the family works. The first asked, "Do you favor, oppose, or neither favor nor oppose requiring employers to pay women and men the same amount for the same work?" The second item asked, "Do you think it is better, worse, or makes no difference for the family as a whole if the man works outside the home and the woman takes care of the home and family?" Possible responses to both items were 7-point Likert scales ranging from *favor a great deal* to *oppose a great deal*.

As shown in Table 4.1, attitudes toward gender roles are statistically significant predictors of attitudes toward transgender people. Respondents who favor equal pay for men and women have warmer feelings toward transgender people, see more discrimination against transgender people, and are more supportive of transgender bathroom access rights. Respondents who think it is better if a man works and a woman takes care of the home have cooler feelings toward transgender people, see less discrimination, and are less supportive of transgender bathroom rights. It is not just the gender of an individual that predicts attitudes toward transgender people and rights but how gender identities and gender norms are understood.

In our 2019 national gender identity attitudes survey, we found consistent evidence that gender identity predicts attitudes toward transgender people. As noted in chapter 2, our survey asked respondents their level of comfort with people of various sexual orientations and gender identities in various situations, including separate questions about transgender men and transgender women. Participants were asked about their level of comfort with transgender people in their families, as friends, at work, as a person they play sports with, as parents, as their doctor, as their representative in Congress, as the star of their favorite sports team, and as president of the United States. These questions were only asked of respondents who previously noted that they were familiar with the term *transgender*. We modeled responses to these items on a variety of control and contact variables, including gender, sexual orientation, race, age, education, whether the respondent has any family members or close friends who are gay or lesbian, and whether the respondent has any family members or close friends who are transgender or nonbinary.

Table 4.1. Attitudes Toward Transgender People and Support for Gender Equality, 2016 American National Election Study

	Feeling Thermometer		Perceived Discrimination		Bathroom Access Rights	
	Model 1 (SE)	Model 2 (SE)	Model 3 (SE)	Model 4 (SE)	Model 5 (SE)	Model 6 (SE)
Female	5.36* (.88)	4.65* (.91)	−.17* (.04)	−.12* (.04)	.25* (.07)	.18 (.10)
Equal pay	9.62* (1.37)	6.38* (1.45)	−.62* (.06)	−.51* (.06)	.64* (.11)	.22 (.15)
Man work	−13.64* (.91)	−6.73* (.99)	.28* (.04)	.07 (.04)	−.96* (.07)	−.47* (.10)
Age	—	−0.11* (.03)	—	.002 (.001)	—	−.004 (.003)
Income	—	0.26* (.06)	—	−.008* (.003)	—	.03* (.01)
Ideology	—	−6.13* (.41)	—	.16* (.02)	—	−.54* (.04)
Partisanship	—	−1.08* (.29)	—	.08* (.01)	—	−.18* (.03)
Constant	49.21* (1.37)	78.79* (2.73)	2.79* (.06)	1.75* (.12)	−.42* (.11)	1.60* (.33)

Note: N = 4,271. Models 1 through 4 are ordinary least squares regressions; models 5 and 6 are logistic regressions. Data are weighted to be nationally representative. Ideology is coded from 1 = *extremely liberal* to 7 = *extremely conservative*; partisanship is coded from 1 = *strong Democrat* to 7 = *strong Republican*. * = statistically significant at $p \leq .05$, two-tailed. SE = standard errors.

As shown in Table 4.2, gender, sexual orientation, and interpersonal contact are the most consistent predictors of attitudes toward transgender men and women in these various roles. Consistently, cisgender men are less supportive of transgender men and women compared to women (including cisgender women and transgender women; our respondents did not include any transgender men). Respondents who identify as heterosexual are consistently less supportive of transgender men and women compared to respondents who identify with another sexual orientation. Anglo (White non-Latinx) respondents are occasionally less supportive of transgender men and women compared to people of color but race is usually not a statistically significant predictor. Age is a more consistent predictor, with older respondents less supportive of transgender men and women compared to younger respondents. Similarly, respondents with higher levels of education

Table 4.2. Summary of Predictors of Attitudes Toward Transgender People, 2019 Gender Attitudes Survey

	Gender	Sexual Orientation	Race	Age	Education	Gay or Lesbian Friends or Family	Transgender or Nonbinary Friends or Family
Transgender man . . .							
. . . as part of your family	N+	N*	–	N+	–	P*	P*
. . . as one of your friends	N*	N*	–	–	–	P*	P*
. . . as one of the people you play sports with	N*	N*	–	N*	P*	P*	P*
. . . as one of your work colleagues	N*	N*	–	–	P+	P*	P*
. . . becoming parents	N*	N*	P*	N*	P+	P*	P*
. . . as your doctor	N*	N*	–	–	P+	P*	P*
. . . as the star of your favorite sports team	N*	N*	–	–	P+	P*	P*
. . . as your representative in Congress	N*	N*	–	N*	P*	P*	P*
. . . as president	N*	N*	P+	N*	P*	P*	P*
Transgender woman . . .							
. . . as part of your family	N*	N*	–	N*	–	P*	P*
. . . as one of your friends	N*	N*	–	N*	–	P*	P*
. . . as one of the people you play sports with	N*	N*	–	N+	P+	P*	P*
. . . as one of your work colleagues	N*	N*	–	N+	–	P*	P*
. . . becoming parents	N*	N*	P+	N*	–	P*	P*
. . . as your doctor	N+	N*	–	N*	P*	P*	P*
. . . as the star of your favorite sports team	N*	N*	–	N+	–	P*	P*
. . . as your representative in Congress	N*	N*	–	N*	P*	P*	P*
. . . as president	N*	N*	–	N*	–	P*	P*

Note: N = 995. P* = positive, statistically significant, $p \le .05$; N* = negative, statistically significant, $p \le .05$; P+ = positive, statistically significant, $p \le .10$; N+ = negative, statistically significant, $p \le .10$; – = not statistically significant. Data collected February 8–March 5, 2019.

are generally more supportive of transgender men and women compared to respondents with lower levels of education. Finally, respondents with gay, lesbian, transgender, and/or nonbinary family members or close friends are consistently more supportive of transgender men and women compared to respondents without interpersonal contact.

We found a consistent, negative correlation between gender and support for transgender rights, with men much less supportive than women. A substantial body of work finds gender to be a strong and reliable predictor of a whole host of political attitudes (Erikson and Tedin 2015). Other studies have found that gender is one of the most powerful cognitive schemas available (Brewer and Lui 1989; Starr and Zurbriggen 2017). However, research by Monika McDermott suggests that the true predictor of these different attitudes might be masculine and feminine personalities. These personality traits are strong predictors of support for traditional gender roles which are, in turn, strong predictors of political attitudes, even more so than is gender identity, or as the author writes, "biological sex" (McDermott 2016). McDermott argues that traditional understandings of gender-based differences in political attitudes and behaviors are based on gender expectations and traits of masculinity and femininity. These expectations are often challenged by the notion of transgender identity: transgender people often, by definition, do not conform to a traditional conceptualization of gender identity as binary and immutable (Burdge 2007). It follows, then, that men are less supportive of this nontraditional conceptualization: "Men's greater negativity toward transgender people is consistent with the notion that they are more invested than women in adhering to gender norms, presumably as a means of affirming their own masculinity and heterosexuality" (Norton and Herek 2013: 750). This means that attention to gender expectations and to self-identities as masculine or feminine may be a route toward influencing attitudes.

What is the precise mechanism? The answer, we suspect, is complicated and multifaceted but our hypotheses are rooted in existing work on masculinity and the desire to maintain a consistent gender identity, primarily among men. Crafting successful strategies and tactics in persuasion attempts when targeting men (or women) in strategic communication will need to take these considerations into account. This chapter examines the role of individual-level gender identity and conceptualizations of masculinity and femininity in predicting support of or opposition to transgender people and rights. We begin with a broad discussion of sex and gender, gender expression, and gender roles before turning to our experimental designs and results.

Gender, Gender Ideologies, and Expectations

The terms *sex* and *gender* are not interchangeable. Sex generally is understood as based on one's chromosomes and anatomy (including genitalia) and it is assigned at birth. Some individuals are assigned intersex (or *difference of sexual development*) at birth but most people are assigned male or female based on their appearance. Gender, in contrast, is socially constructed. It is how people identify—their internal knowledge of their own gender—which can differ from their assigned sex (National Center for Transgender Equality 2016a). In other words, sex is something labeled at birth based on anatomy; gender is something developed over time corresponding to one's knowledge and understanding of their own identity.

Considerable research finds men to be susceptible to perceived threats to masculinity, fearful of insufficient masculinity, and supportive of traditional gender norms. The *masculine overcompensation thesis* posits that when men are concerned about the social implications of losing their masculinity (e.g., being seen as gay or otherwise lacking masculine traits), they tend to overcompensate by exhibiting extreme masculine behaviors and attitudes to create the impression that they are, indeed, masculine in socially desirable ways (H. E. Adams, Wright, and Lohr 1996; Burke 1991; Burke and Stets 2009; Heise 2007). Masculine overcompensation has been cited as the cause of relatively benign behaviors such as buying sports cars at the onset of midlife crises as well as behaviors with broader negative implications including escalation of the Vietnam War by President Lyndon Johnson (Fasteau 1974; Kimmel 1996). Anti-gay hate crimes "are tied closely to rigid and hierarchical ideas about masculinity that depend on differentiating 'real' men from women as well as gay and bisexual men" (Wade 2016: para. 8).

Men heavily invested in performing masculinity at extreme levels—a phenomenon often referred to as *toxic masculinity* (Karner 1996)—are more likely to engage in domestic violence against their female partners (Macmillan and Gartner 1999), to sexually harass women (Maass et al. 2003), and even to commit mass shootings (Bridges and Tober 2017; Wade 2016). Contemporary conceptualizations of toxic masculinity rely on reaffirming superiority and dominance, leading certain men to abuse people and power because of what Enloe (2017: 16) calls "the sustainability of patriarchy." As many boys grow into men, "they learn that they are entitled to feel like a real man, and that they have the right to annihilate anyone who challenges that sense of entitlement" (Kimmel 2012, quoted in Wade 2016, para. 9). In contrast, men who identify as feminists are less transphobic than men who do not consider themselves feminists (Brassel and Anderson 2019). Toxic masculinity also underlies anti-transgender violence. The stereotype of transgender women, in particular, as predatory or as deceptive fuels and is used to justify violence against them by men who feel deceived or threatened.

We hypothesized that threats to traditional gender identity norms (masculinity and femininity) should also be significant predictors of attitudes about transgender people. The concept of transgender identity likely threatens those for whom the concept of a traditional, immutable gender is essential to their own identity. Conversely, bolstering and even strengthening gender identities should have the reverse effect of improving attitudes toward transgender people or at least mitigating the negative effects of toxic masculinity. As posited by our Identity Reassurance Theory, bolstering one's sense of one's gender identity should reduce reactance and make people more willing to receive and process supportive information about transgender rights. We conducted two experiments to investigate these two key concepts, identity threat and identity bolstering, and how they affect attitudes toward transgender people and rights.

Identity Threat

There are a variety of studies that examine the relationship between masculinity threat and subsequent attitudes and behavior. For example, Wilkinson (2004) finds that men's anti-gay attitudes are linked to fear of appearing feminine; Glick et al. (2007) find that threatening respondents' masculinity made them more negative toward effeminate gay men but not toward masculine gay men. Perhaps most relevant to our work, Willer et al. (2013) conducted an experiment to investigate how threats to masculinity and femininity affect attitudes and behavior, finding differential effects for men and women. Men who are told that they are feminine are subsequently more supportive of war, more homophobic, more interested in purchasing an SUV, and more supportive of dominance hierarchies and male superiority compared to men who are told that they are masculine. These reactions are particularly strong among men with higher levels of testosterone as measured by saliva tests.

Identity loss theory, originating from economic decision making, suggests that because many people view gender as having only two discrete social categories, violating these expectations "evokes anxiety and discomfort in oneself and in others. Gender identity, then, changes the 'payoffs' from different actions" (Akerlof and Kranton 2000: 716–717). In other words, when a conventional binary conceptualization of gender expression is threatened, attitudes and behaviors toward that which threatens the identity (such as transgender people and rights) should change as well. Existing research shows that identity threat translates to more negative attitudes toward gay and lesbian people. Willer et al. (2013) found increased homophobia among men whose masculinity was threatened. In part, their finding stems from the same threat to gender traditionalism that LGBT identity and rights represent. We hypothesized that the findings would be replicated when asking participants about transgender bathroom access rights because the issue can trigger a visceral threat to masculinity.

As Cavanaugh (2010: 4) notes: "Nowhere are the signifiers of gender more painfully acute and subject to surveillance than in sex-segregated washrooms. The perceived loss of a binary gender axis, the grid upon which normative heterosexuality depends for cogency and intelligibility, incites anxiety about gender incoherence." The policy issue of transgender bathroom access is a threat to the underlying ontological structure of the strict binary gender expression (Roughgarden 2013). For some people, the idea that they might encounter a transgender person while using a public bathroom or locker room is perceived as a real (and intensely personal) potential threat (Schilt and Westbrook 2015; Westbrook and Schilt 2014).

Based on existing work, we hypothesized that our experimental design to threaten gender performance would affect men and women differently. Specifically, we hypothesized that gender differences in support for transgender people and rights would be exacerbated by threats to men's masculinity given the perceived inherent threat to male gender identity often posed by transgender rights but did not anticipate a similar response from women.

We further hypothesized that effects should vary by strength of gender identity. People vary in the degree to which they support and find personally relevant core dimensions of gender-differentiated normative standards (that men should be dominant and independent and that women should be helpful and concerned about others) (Wood et al. 1997). Strength of gender identity and connection to it can vary across one's lifespan in response to an array of factors (Ely 1995; Martin and Ruble 2010; Sinclair, Hardin, and Lowery 2006; Tobin et al. 2010; White and Gardner 2009). We hypothesized that men with strong gender identities will be more sensitive to manipulated threats to their masculinity compared to men with gender identities that are less central to their identity.

The Gender Identity Threat Experiment

Our first experiment related to masculinity explores the power of identity threat in shifting attitudes about transgender bathroom access (for full results, see Harrison and Michelson 2019). We focus on the powerful effects of priming, which has been shown effective at manipulating gender self-concepts among both men and women (McCall and Dasgupta 2007; Haines and Kray 2005; Rudman and Phelan 2010). Priming can increase an identity's salience and, subsequently, related concern for identity-based interests, especially when a strongly held identity is threatened (Klar 2013). Priming gender identity and threats to gender norms can test the power of gender construction in shaping attitudes and behavior, particularly toward issues like transgender rights that draw so heavily on very personal concepts of gender.

We conducted a 2016 laboratory experiment among undergraduate students at a large Midwestern university that experimentally manipulated threats to participants' masculinity or femininity to test their effects on attitudes and behaviors toward transgender people and key rights for that community. Again, we expected that threatening a male respondent's masculinity would increase their opposition to transgender rights, and that this effect would be stronger among men who self-report that gender is essential to their identity. At the same time, we expected that threatening a female respondent's femininity would neither increase nor decrease their opposition to transgender rights. Specifically, we hypothesized that:

H1: Men will be less supportive of transgender rights compared to women.
H2: Threatening a male respondent's masculinity will increase his opposition to transgender rights.
H3: Threatening a female respondent's femininity will not affect her support for transgender rights.
H4: Men who self-report that their gender is essential to their identity will be more likely to increase their opposition to transgender rights when their masculinity is threatened, compared to men who self-report that their gender is not essential to their identity.

The laboratory experiment included 182 participants (89 men and 93 women) of a variety of races and ethnicities (49% White non-Latinx, 7% Black, 5% Latinx, 18% Asian American, 2% other, 19% mixed). Most reported their political ideology as progressive (64%) while 27% said they were moderates and 9% said they were conservatives. Only 15% reported that they personally knew someone who was transgender or gender nonconforming. Male and female participants were randomly separated into six groups, with 29 to 31 people randomly assigned to one of six conditions. Replicating Willer et al. (2013), two-thirds of our participants were assigned to take the Bem Sex Role Inventory (BSRI) and one-third were assigned to complete the Big 5 personality test (L. R. Goldberg 1993; Tupes and Christal 1961). Of those assigned to the BSRI, half (one-third of all participants) were randomly assigned to the gender threat condition and half (one-third of all participants) were assigned to the nonthreat condition. The BSRI measures how strongly a respondent identifies psychologically with traditional gender roles including masculinity and femininity.

Upon completing the BSRI, respondents received a false BSRI score that was either threatening or nonthreatening to their masculinity or femininity. Although participants were administered the real BSRI, the scores they were shown were false. An example of a false feminine score is shown in Figure 4.3. Each score was accompanied by an explanation reading: "Based on your responses, your score is within the [FEMININE/MASCULINE] range of responses." Men randomly assigned to the threatening condition were told that their score was in the feminine range, while men randomly assigned to the nonthreatening condition were told that their score was in the masculine range. Similarly, women in the threatening condition were told that they had a masculine score, while women in the nonthreatening condition were told that they had a feminine score (see Script Appendix for full details).

Assignment to the Big 5 treatment acts as a placebo: participants in these groups also answered a series of survey items about themselves: a traditional set of items meant to measure their personalities. Participants in this placebo condition were all then shown the same false report of moderate or above-average personality attributes.

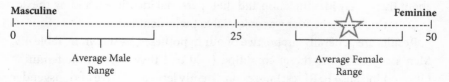

Figure 4.3. False report of feminine score on BSRI, 2016 laboratory experiment.

YOUR RESULTS:

1. Extraversion (your level of sociability and enthusiasm): 38% (moderate)
2. Agreeableness (your level of friendliness and kindness): 29% (moderate)
3. Conscientiousness (your level of organization and work ethic): 42% (moderate–above average)
4. Emotional stability (your level of calmness and tranquility): 40% (moderate)
5. Intellect (your level of creativity and curiosity): 50% (moderate–above average)

We assumed that receiving a (false) report of moderate to above-average personality scores on relatively benign traits would neither prime nor threaten gender identity.

All participants were then asked two related questions about transgender bathroom access rights, an issue prominent in the news at the time: (1) support for transgender access to public bathrooms and locker rooms that match their gender identity and (2) how respondents would vote on a hypothetical ballot initiative on transgender access to public bathrooms and locker rooms that match their gender identity. Participants were debriefed at the conclusion of the experiment.

Results

Overall, 95% of women in the sample supported transgender access to public bathrooms and locker rooms compared to 84% of men. Similarly, 88% of women said they would definitely or probably vote to protect transgender access on a hypothetical ballot initiative compared to 74% of men. Both of these differences are statistically significant. Respondents were then asked about their party identification and their personal identity, including the degree to which their gender was essential to their identity.[1]

Results are generally supportive of our hypotheses, as shown in Table 4.3. Men assigned to the threat condition (told that they were in the feminine range on the false BSRI test) were consistently less supportive of transgender rights compared to those assigned to the nonthreat condition (told that they were in the masculine range) or to the baseline Big 5 condition. There were

Table 4.3. Support for Transgender Rights, by Gender and Experimental Condition, Gender Identity Threat Experiment

	Condition		
	Nonthreatening	Threatening	Placebo (Big 5)
MEN			
Bathroom access (% yes access)	89.7% (26/29)	70%[a,b] (21/30)	93.3% (28/30)
Ballot bathrooms (% yes access)	82.8% (24/29)	60.0%[a,b] (18/30)	80.0% (24/30)
WOMEN			
Bathroom access (% yes access)	96.8% (30/31)	90.3% (28/31)	96.8% (30/31)
Ballot bathrooms (% yes access)	100% (31/31)	83.9%[a] (26/31)	80.7% (25/31)

Note: N = 182. Data collected May 2–16, 2016. Numbers in parentheses are the number reporting yes/ cell size. [a]indicates a statistically significant difference between the threatening and nonthreatening conditions within each gender; [b]indicates a statistically significant difference between the threatening and Big 5 placebo conditions.

also statistically significant differences on the hypothetical ballot measure about access to public bathrooms and locker rooms. In contrast, women assigned to the threat condition were generally no more or less supportive of transgender bathroom access rights compared to women assigned to the nonthreat and baseline conditions, with one exception: Women assigned to the threat condition were less likely to say that they would vote to support transgender access rights on a hypothetical ballot measure compared to women in the nonthreat condition, and this difference is statistically significant.

Before moving on to test for differential effects by strength of gender identity, we examined whether men and women who self-report that gender is essential to their identity are less supportive of transgender rights (see Table 4.4). Overall, 72% of female respondents said that gender was essential to their identity as did 48% of male respondents. Among men who reported that gender is essential to their identity, 74% supported transgender access rights to public bathrooms and locker rooms that match their gender identity compared to 94% of men with nonessential gender identities. Similarly, 60% of men who reported that their gender is essential to their identity would vote to protect transgender access rights on a hypothetical ballot initiative

Table 4.4. Support for Transgender Rights, by Gender and Strength of Gender Identity, Gender Identity Threat Experiment

	Men		Women	
	Not Essential	Essential	Not Essential	Essential
Bathroom access (% yes access)	93.5% (43/46)	74.4%[a] (32/43)	96.2% (25/26)	94% (63/67)
Ballot bathrooms (% yes protect access)	87.0% (40/46)	60.5%[a] (26/43)	92.3% (24/26)	86.6% (58/67)

Note: N = 182. Data collected May 2–16, 2016. Numbers in parentheses are the number reporting yes/ cell size. [a] indicates a statistically significant difference between subgroups (essential vs. nonessential) within each gender.

compared to 87% of men with nonessential gender identities. Both of these differences are statistically significant. Among women, in contrast, there were no statistically significant differences in support for transgender rights across levels of gender identity strength.

While strength of gender identity proved an important predictor of support for transgender bathroom access rights, the data do not support our theory about the interaction between gender identity strength and threats to one's gender identity. Instead, our multivariate analyses confirmed that men were less supportive than women and also found that conservative political ideology was a fairly consistent predictor of opposition to transgender rights. Respondents who were Anglo (White non-Latinx) also tended to be less supportive compared to other respondents. Reviewing the results, we hypothesized that if threatening male undergraduate students' masculinity reduced support for bathroom access rights, then increasing support for those rights might require taking the opposite approach: to reassure men about their masculinity instead of threatening it. This insight led to our Identity Reassurance Theory as described in chapter 2.

Identity Bolstering

Ehrlich and Gramzow (2015: 1019) note, "It is well established that self-affirmation reduces a host of self-serving and group-serving biases." They further find, however, that group-level affirmations can sometimes exacerbate group biases. Building on those findings, Villicana et al. (2018) find that group affirmation can be more effective than individual self-affirmation for reducing racism but only when there is a high level of psychological proximity between the aspect of self being affirmed and the outgroup being evaluated; the effect of group affirmation is limited to those who highly identify with the social identity that is affirmed. Other research on affirmation is more directly relevant to our research project. Martínez et al. (2015) note that anti-gay prejudice helps men affirm their masculinity by distancing themselves from men who violate gender norms. We hypothesized that affirming masculinity in another way—and specifically not through anti-gay prejudice—might lead to more positive, supportive attitudes among men. Perhaps most central to our study, Brough et al. (2016) find that men's willingness to engage in green behaviors (a behavior seen as feminine) can be decreased by threatening their masculinity and can be increased by affirming their masculinity. Similarly, Gal and Wilkie (2010) find that men are more likely to engage in activity perceived as stereotypically feminine if their masculinity has been affirmed.

The Gender Identity Bolstering Experiment

Our second experiment exploring the power of gender identity takes a somewhat similar approach to the 2016 laboratory experiment but here, we were experimentally *bolstering* gender identity (participant masculinity or femininity) rather than *threatening* it. For this experiment, we hypothesized:

H1: Men will be less supportive of the right of transgender people to serve openly in the military compared to women.
H2: Men who are told that they are very masculine will be more supportive of the right of transgender people to serve openly in the military compared to men who are not told that they are very masculine.
H3: Women who are told that they are very feminine will be more supportive of the right of transgender people to serve openly in the military compared to women who are not told that they are very feminine.

The online survey experiment was conducted in August 2018 via Lucid's academic platform. Respondents were first asked several demographic questions including their gender identity. They were then told that they were about to answer questions as part of a national survey asking a large number of adults about their political interests and attitudes. Both men and women then responded to 22 statements about gender identity, all on a 7-point Likert scale ranging from *strongly disagree* to *strongly agree*. Each statement was drawn from the Male Role Norms Inventory Short Form (Levant, Hall, and Rankin 2013). Men responded to statements like "Men should be the leader in any group"; "It is important for a man to take risks, even if he might get hurt"; and "Men should watch football games instead of soap operas." Women responded to statements like "Women should have soft voices"; "Women should not be competitive"; and "Women should not brag about their achievements" (see Script Appendix for full details).

After responding to these items, respondents were randomly assigned to receive either a score or a prompt to continue on with the survey. Respondents who received a score were (falsely) led to believe their score was a result of a tabulation of their responses to the gender role statements; however, everyone received the same score exaggerating their femininity or masculinity (for women and men, respectively). As seen in Figure 4.4, female respondents received a score of 44 and male respondents received a score of 6 along with text highlighting how feminine or masculine the results were, along with a scale (shown in Figure 4.4).

To mask the intent of the experiment, respondents were then told they were moving on to a new set of questions and that similar to the previous section of the survey they were items that were being administered nationally to large numbers of adults to investigate and measure differences in political interest and attitudes. As a manipulation check, respondents were asked two questions about the degree to which they were feeling happy or good, on 7-point Likert scales ranging from *extremely unhappy* or *extremely bad* to *extremely happy* or *extremely good*. Experiments conducted by Rivera and Dasgupta (2017) find that men randomly assigned to a condition where they completed a Male Role Norms Scale (MRNS) inventory and were (falsely) told that they were very masculine were more likely to express positive feelings on these two scales compared to men in the control condition. Men in the treatment group in our experiment were also more likely to express positive feelings on these two scales, although the differences are small.

Participants were then asked a series of questions about their attitudes toward transgender people and rights. Instead of answering questions about

Women received the message:

> YOUR SCORE: 44. Based on your responses, your score is within the VERY FEMININE range of responses.
>
> Your score is at the high end of the scale, suggesting that you are <u>very feminine compared to most adult women.</u>
>
> Extensive research shows that feminine women tend to be different in important ways that affect future professional success and personal relationship quality.

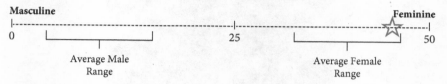

Men received the message:

> YOUR SCORE: 6. Based on your responses, your score is within the VERY MASCULINE range of responses.
>
> Your score is at the high end of the scale, suggesting that you are <u>very masculine compared to most adult men.</u>
>
> Extensive research shows that masculine men tend to be different in important ways that affect future professional success and personal relationship quality.

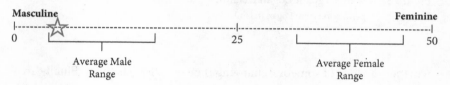

Figure 4.4. Gender identity bolstering scales.

access to bathrooms and locker rooms, we asked respondents their attitudes about transgender people openly serving in the military, an issue prominent in the news in 2017 and 2018 (see chapter 3). Embedded in the first question about military service was a photo of U.S. Air Force Staff Sergeant Logan Ireland, a masculine-presenting transgender airman wearing a camouflage tactical vest and pants and holding a semiautomatic weapon (Figure 4.5). Respondents were asked whether they agree or disagree with a policy allowing transgender people to serve in the military.

They were also asked their voting intention on a hypothetical ballot initiative about transgender people serving in the military and whether they agreed or disagreed with seven statements about transgender people, including whether they would mind living next door to a transgender person, whether transgender people violate the traditions of American culture, and

Figure 4.5. Staff Sergeant Logan Ireland.
Published with permission from Logan Ireland.

whether the idea of someone changing their sex disgusts them. Finally, they were asked whether they would be willing to sign an online petition urging lawmakers to allow transgender people to serve in the military. The survey ended with several more demographic questions as well as a debrief about the misleading nature of the masculinity/femininity score.

Results

Overall, we collected 990 responses, 47% men ($n = 469$) and 53% ($n = 521$) women. Respondents ranged in age from 18 to 94, with a mean age of 45.5; most respondents (72%) were Anglo (White non-Latinx); 8% identified as Black, 7% as Latinx, 5% as Asian, and the remainder as mixed or another race. About one in four (22.5%) reported that they personally knew someone who is transgender. One in three (29%) described their ideology as conservative or very conservative while 33% described their ideology as liberal or very liberal and the remaining 38% described themselves as moderates. We randomly assigned half the men ($n = 233$) and half of the women ($n = 236$) to the control condition and the other half of the men ($n = 236$) and women ($n = 261$) to the treatment condition.

As expected, we found stronger effects among male participants. In response to exposure to the photo of Sergeant Ireland and the question about transgender people serving openly in the military, participants could respond using a Likert scale from 1 = *strongly disagree* to 7 = *strongly agree*. The mean response for all participants was 4.97; male respondents were slightly less supportive and thus were below the mean (4.77), whereas female respondents were slightly more supportive and thus above the mean (5.16).

Participants in the treatment condition were more supportive of military service but the difference is not statistically significant. In a multivariate regression (not shown) controlling for other factors, only political ideology is a statistically significant predictor of responses, with more liberal respondents more likely to support transgender troops. Looking separately at male and female participants, the gap between treatment and control persists and the difference for male respondents is larger but in neither case is the effect statistically significant (Table 4.5). This pattern of weak differences persists in multivariate regressions (not shown) controlling for other factors (age, education, race, ideology, and interpersonal contact with a transgender person). Among women, support for transgender troops is stronger among liberals and younger respondents. For men, liberal ideology and knowing a transgender person predict support for transgender troops.

We also asked respondents how they might vote on a state ballot initiative on the issue of transgender troops. Overall, 76.4% of respondents (73.3% of men and 79.1% of women) said they probably or definitely would vote yes while 23.5% (26.7% of men and 20.9% of women) said they would probably or definitely vote no. Participants assigned to the treatment group were much more likely to say they would vote yes, particularly among men, for whom the difference is statistically significant (Table 4.6).

In addition to our focus on transgender military troops, we asked participants to respond to a series of statements meant to measure their levels of transphobia and support for transgender rights. Participants were asked whether they agreed or disagreed with the following statements:

1. I would not mind if my neighbor was transgender.
2. Transgender people violate the traditions of American culture.
3. Businesses should be able to refuse services to transgender people.

Table 4.5. Mean Support for Transgender Military Service, by
Treatment Condition, Gender Identity Bolstering Experiment

	Control	Treatment	Difference (SE)
All respondents ($N = 990$)	4.88	5.06	.18[+] (.12)
Women ($N = 521$)	5.11	5.21	.10 (.16)
Men ($N = 469$)	4.64	4.90	.27[+] (.19)

Note: Data collected August 3, 2018. [+] = statistically significant at $p \leq .10$, one-tailed. SE = standard errors.

Table 4.6. Would Vote for Transgender Military Service,
by Treatment Condition, Gender Identity Bolstering Experiment

	Control	Treatment	Difference (SE)
All respondents ($N = 990$)	3.05	3.13	.08 (.06)
Women ($N = 521$)	3.19	3.19	.001 (.08)
Men ($N = 469$)	2.88	3.06	.17* (.10)

Note: Data collected August 3, 2018. Dependent variable (*ballot*) is coded 1 = definitely would vote no, 2 = probably would vote no, 3 = probably would vote yes, 4 = definitely would vote yes. * = statistically significant at $p \leq .05$, one-tailed. SE = standard errors.

4. The idea of someone changing their sex disgusts me.
5. Transgender people are sick and need help from a mental health professional.
6. Transgender people deserve health insurance that covers all transgender-related issues.
7. Congress should pass laws to protect transgender people from discrimination in housing, restaurants, and other public places.

We recoded these items so that higher scores indicated support for transgender people and rights. Assignment to the treatment condition had no effect on responses to these items, whether examined separately for men and women or for all respondents, as individual items, or as a combined index.[2] Instead, responses are consistently predicted by political ideology, with liberals more likely to give supportive answers. Age and personal contact with a transgender person are also, in some models, predictive of support.

We next examined our measure of political behavior: willingness to sign an electronic petition to one's member of Congress. We hypothesized that individuals assigned to the treatment condition would be more likely to sign the petition compared to individuals assigned to the control condition. Overall, 37.8% of participants in the treatment group signed, including 37.6% of women and 38.1% of men. This supportive behavior was less frequent among participants in the control group, among whom 34.3% signed (33.5% of women, 35.2% of men). The differences are not statistically significant. These findings persist in multivariate regressions controlling for other variables (not shown). Instead, willingness to sign is strongly predicted by ideology, for both men and women, and in addition women with higher reported levels of education are also more likely to sign.

In sum, men assigned to a treatment condition that reassured them of their masculinity were more likely to support allowing transgender people to serve openly in the military but were no more or less likely to be supportive of transgender people and rights more generally. Women assigned to a treatment condition that reassured them of their femininity did not differ in their attitudes compared to the control group, but women overall were more supportive of transgender troops compared to men.

Discussion and Conclusion

The nature of masculinity has changed over time and while there are several encouraging contemporary examples of changing conceptualizations of masculinity, toxic masculinity and its effects persist in many ways. In particular, opposition and resistance to LGBT rights is a way for some men to assert their masculinity and as such, there is sometimes a strong link between attitudes toward transgender rights, gender roles, and one's own gender identity. Gender and gender norms are strong predictors of attitudes toward transgender people and rights and our experimental manipulations about gender roles were able to both increase and decrease support for transgender rights, albeit only among men. When male respondents received threatening feed-back about their masculinity, they were less supportive of transgender rights. Male participants exposed to affirmations about their masculinity were more likely to support allowing transgender troops to serve openly in the U.S. military but were no more or less supportive of other transgender rights. Further experiments may find that different methods or messages affirming masculinity may be more effective on a broader array of issues. Raising the issue of gender in any way—priming gender, even if it is an affirming message—may have the unintended consequence of raising the salience of existing attitudes on these issues, which may account for the inconsistent results from our second experiment on this theme. Other methods of reaffirming self-esteem and existing identities and values may be more productive routes to opening minds to persuasion. We turn in the next two chapters to an exploration of these ideas, including appeals to positive emotions, moral elevation, and ac-knowledgment of the initial discomfort that people may feel when thinking about transgender people.

5

Emotions and Moral Elevation

In the early afternoon of a January day in New York City, Wesley Autry was waiting with his two young daughters, ages four and six, to catch a subway train. Just as a train was approaching, Cameron Hollopeter, a young man standing nearby, suffered a seizure and fell onto the tracks. Without hesitation, Wesley jumped down and threw himself on top of Cameron's body in the space between the tracks, holding him down as the train passed over them. Five cars rolled over them, leaving grease on Wesley's knit hat, before the train came to a stop. Hearing screams, Wesley called out, "We're okay down here, but I've got two daughters up there. Let them know their father's okay." He heard cries of wonder and applause. Wesley didn't think much of what had happened; he visited Cameron at the hospital later that day and then headed to his job as a construction worker.

The people of New York, and the world, thought otherwise. Wesley became known as the Subway Hero, the Subway Samaritan, and the Hero of Harlem. He was flooded with gifts and cash and the mayor of New York awarded him the Bronze Medallion, New York City's highest award for exceptional citizenship and outstanding achievement.

What you're probably feeling right now as you read Wesley's story of selfless bravery is called moral elevation, an feeling that is elicited when people witness acts of moral beauty like charity, gratitude, loyalty, or generosity (Algoe and Haidt 2009; Haidt 2003a, 2003b; Keltner and Haidt 2003). The idea is that when exposed to or encouraged to think about examples of moral elevation, people report feeling inspired, uplifted, more open to others, and more motivated to engage in positive behavior that is to the benefit of others (Algoe and Haidt 2009; Schnall, Roper, and Fessler 2010). Considerable scholarship shows that moral elevation increases the feeling of warmth, admiration, and affection for the person(s) performing the exemplary behaviors, spurring a desire to emulate that moral exemplar to become a better person (Haidt 2003a). This leads to prosocial behaviors such as charitable donations, volunteering, helping the experimenter, and organizational citizenship, even

Transforming Prejudice. Melissa R. Michelson and Brian F. Harrison, Oxford University Press (2020) © Oxford University Press.
DOI: 10.1093/oso/9780190068882.001.0001

if those behaviors are not directly related to the moral exemplar (see Van de Vyver and Abrams 2017).

In other words, watching video reports about people like the Hero of Harlem inspires others to become better people themselves. Emotional reactions to videos that evoke moral elevation are particularly well suited to our work because reactions to transgender people are also often emotional, rather than rational. If negative emotions depress support for transgender people and rights, then positive emotions should mitigate those negative reactions, or perhaps even generate support. Signaling moral elevation is also a way to bolster one's self esteem, the key to avoiding reactance and opening minds to attitudinal change as modeled by our Identity Reassurance Theory.

This chapter is dedicated to testing the applications of these kinds of interventions in terms of transgender rights. We test whether moral elevation and positive emotions can nudge people to be more supportive of transgender people. We posit that the desire to be a better person and to act virtuously will boost self-esteem and reduce reactance, allowing those experiencing the positive emotion to be nudged into being less prejudiced or more supportive of equal rights for members of a marginalized group such as transgender people. We explore the power of emotions to encourage recipients of our messages to draw on their better angels and rise to the call to support equality and justice. Specifically, we present the results of two experiments attempting to shift affect and emotion away from those with a negative valence toward those with a more positive one, generating greater support (or at least a more neutral stance) for public policies supporting transgender people.

Emotion in Social Psychology

One of the most common obstacles to transgender people and rights is also one of the most complicated: emotional reactions to transgender identity. Because political discussion and debate often evoke strong emotions, they provide elites with the opportunity to use emotional language to appeal to the public (Holbrook and O'Shaughnessy 1984; Vakratsas and Ambler 1999). Social psychologists have offered divergent views on how emotion itself is structured (Marcus 2003; Scherer 2000). On the one hand, contemporary studies of attitudes suggest that emotion can be conceived as falling along a single bipolar dimension ranging from negative to positive (valence), with intensity increasing as one moves away from the center toward the poles. This view emphasizes an evaluative component of social judgment (Eagly and Chaiken 1993; Fiske and Taylor 1991; McGuire 1985; Schwarz and Bohner 2001) and is a reasonable approximation for how many people divide the world into "likes and dislikes" (Brader 2006).

However, others contend that such a focus on valence and summative judgments is likely to discount the role of specific emotions: if we only view emotions from the perspective of negative valence, reactions to politics like fear, disgust, and disappointment would fall under the same category. However, common sense dictates that these emotions are not only very different from each other but also likely to lead to different attitudes and behaviors in the political domain. The same is, of course, true for positive emotions: as Brader (2006: 52) notes, "emotions such as enthusiasm, sympathy, and serenity" are all positive but reflect much more than a simple "like" heuristic. In other words, we should consider the impact of individual, discreet emotions to best understand their effects and how they could be mitigated.

Plutchik (1980) outlines his psychoevolutionary theory of emotion, considered to be one of the most influential classifications of general emotional responses, by focusing on eight primary emotions: anger, fear, sadness, disgust, surprise, anticipation, trust, and joy. Relying on an evolutionary fight-or-flight perspective and the desire to reproduce, he argues that these emotions trigger behaviors that increase the likelihood of survival. Plutchik explicitly asserts that his concepts of emotion are applicable to all evolutionary levels, including humans, and despite emotions being displayed in different ways in different species, there are commonalities and patterns that can be identified. Overall, the theory was developed to explain psychological defense mechanisms, with eight defense mechanisms proposed to be manifestations of the eight core emotions, summarized by his wheel of emotions (see Figure 5.1).

The wheel visually illustrates the core concepts of Plutchik's theory: There are four pairs of bipolar emotions: joy versus sadness, anger versus fear, trust versus disgust, and surprise versus anticipation. Emotions are related in a bipolar fashion, with each able to be expressed at different intensities and in different combinations to form different emotions. Finding the right antidote to any particular emotion can help to either diminish or at least soften its effect. Along these lines, we theorize that eliciting positive emotions and diminishing negative ones might reduce reactance and open minds to persuasion on transgender rights.

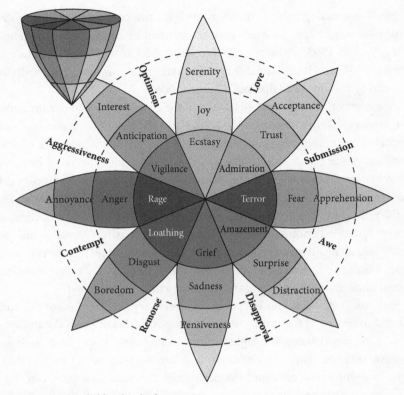

Figure 5.1. Plutchik's wheel of emotions.
Note: Reprinted with permission from *American Scientist*. Figure 6 from Plutchik (2001: 359).

Emotion and Transgender Identity

The first step in determining how to counteract emotion in terms of responses to transgender people and rights is understanding which emotions are most likely to be evoked and what effects those emotions can have. From there, we can test different strategies and tactics to offset the effects and (hopefully) move the needle in the other direction, toward acceptance of transgender people and support for public policies needed by transgender people. This chapter uses the experimental evoking of emotions to test several related ideas. After an exploration of disgust and fear, the emotions most likely to be felt when people think about transgender people, we move to a description of a set of experiments evoking emotions of participants and thus increasing openness to transgender rights. The first experiment described in this chapter evokes emotions to test the effects of heightened fear versus heightened happiness, using exposure to photos of spiders and puppies. Next we explore the power of moral elevation, the concept introduced earlier, which has been used in multiple experiments to increase prosocial behavior and attitudes toward members of outgroups. We use randomized exposure to short videos including one about the Hero of Harlem to explore the effect of a heightened sense of moral elevation on attitudes toward transgender rights.

Disgust

Disgust can be a potent element in political and moral attitude formation, specifically as it relates to LGBT people (Herek 1984; Inbar et al. 2009; Inbar et al. 2012; Inbar and Pizarro 2014). As an abstract concept, disgust signals that things are toxic or harmful, playing an evolutionary role in maintaining purity, safety, and cleanliness (Cosmides and Tooby 2000). Individuals who experience disgust are biologically driven to avoid contamination, which in the political realm manifests as prejudice against members of the group evoking the threat, including people who are members of the LGBT community, obese, mentally ill, homeless, immigrants, people with physical disabilities, or members of ethnic and racial outgroups (Clifford and Jerit 2018; Herek and McLemore 2013). Political actors have long appreciated the power of disgust as a rhetorical tool to shape political attitudes, particularly toward LGBT rights (Hatemi and McDermott 2012; Kam and Estes 2016; Nussbaum 2010; Smith 2007; Gadarian and Van Der Vort 2017). However, political elites may not always accurately anticipate how disgust will shape attitudes (Clifford et al. 2015; Kam and Estes 2016). While stigma against gay men, lesbians, and transgender people is often driven in part by disgust toward them (Miller et al. 2017; Herek and McLemore 2013), disgust as a rhetorical tool can backfire and have a boomerang effect, leading to increased indignation against those trying to use disgust to drive those prejudiced attitudes toward LGBT people (Gadarian and Van Der Vort 2017).

Disgust continues to be used by opponents of LGBT rights as a tool for heightening negative emotions toward LGBT people because language and rhetoric are critical elements in shaping social perceptions of minority groups (Schneider and Ingram 1993; Smith 2007; Albertson and Gadarian 2015). Research shows that disgust has the potential to increase negative affect toward gay and lesbian rights both explicitly and implicitly (Terrizzi et al.

2010; Inbar et al. 2012; Cunningham et al. 2013). Disgust can also predict opposition to transgender rights (Miller et al. 2017). Disgust has even been shown to be strong enough to drive political attitudes regardless of partisan affiliation and cues (Clifford and Wendell 2015).

Fear

Fear is a related emotion also used to generate negative attitudes and reduce support for members of marginalized groups. Brader (2005) finds that messages featuring content and imagery associated with threat decrease the salience of prior beliefs and encourage recipients of the fear appeals to reconsider their attitudes. Scholars find that prejudice against gay men and lesbians is based more on disgust than on fear but those studying attitudes toward transgender people find that transphobia (fear of transgender people) does indeed play a role. For example, Nagoshi et al. (2008) find that transphobia is based on fear of expressed deviations from conventional gender identities, which may be interpreted as a threat to their own social identities and status (see chapter 4). Worthen (2013) posits that cisgender men are threatened by transgender women (and gender nonconforming men) because they are relinquishing their male privilege. More specifically, transgender women are a threat for some cisgender men; they tend to view them as men who have been feminized which means "then all men can be feminized which would ultimately result in the breakdown of the conventional social norms in which men are dominant and women are subordinate" (Glotfelder 2012: 71).

Sara Ahmed (2004) writes extensively about the role of fear in cultural politics. Fear allows for the conservation of power and for existing social norms to be preserved. When previously invisible others gain visibility, those attached to the social norms of the present tend to fear change and the loss of control which leads them to establish *the other* as dangers to their very life and existence. Payne and Smith (2014) extend this understanding of the fear of the other to the introduction of transgender children to elementary schools which leads to what they label "the big freak out." These children represent a threat to societal notions of gender norms and the binary gender system; thus, the presence of transgender children in schools causes fear and anxiety.

Fear not only decreases support for transgender people and their rights but is even used as a defense in criminal court, as when a man who has violently attacked or murdered a transgender woman claims a *trans panic defense* for his actions. The trans panic defense is when a defendant argues that "the post-intimate discovery that his transgender female victim had male genitalia was so upsetting that it provoked him into a heat of passion" (Lee and Kwan 2014: 80). The trans panic defense is based on discomfort with gender identity and/or nonconformity, anger at the victim's alleged deception, and fear by the male defendant that if others find out he was sexually intimate with a transgender woman they will think he is gay: in other words, that his attraction to someone he later learns has male genitalia is a sign of latent homosexuality. "First and foremost, the defendant's violence may be motivated by his fear of being seen as gay. . . . The heterosexual man who believes in traditional gender roles may also see the fact of his having had sex with a transgender female as a threat to his masculine identity that has to be quashed" (Lee and Kwan 2014: 109). Legal scholars do not support trans panic defenses but they continue to be used to influence juries.

Disgust, fear, and other negative emotions clearly play a prominent role in how people respond to transgender people, whether they are elementary school children or intimate partners. As discussed in chapter 3, fear is also at play in discussions of bathroom access rights in that opponents of those rights often frame the debate as about fear of assault of girls and women in women's restrooms. In the experiments described in this chapter, we sought to find positive emotions that might act as antidotes to the negative emotions that are sometimes felt by opponents of transgender people and rights. Our hypothesis is that many of those negative emotions can be mitigated or ameliorated by evoking strongly valanced, positive emotions prior to asking questions about transgender people and rights. The overall goal is to evoke positively valanced emotions like happiness and moral elevation, thus bolstering the self-esteem of participants and making them more open to persuasion. In this chapter, we describe two experiments testing the effects of evoking those positive emotions. The first experiment randomly assigned participants to view photos meant to elicit either the positive emotion of happiness or the negative emotion of fear. The second experiment randomly assigned treatment condition participants to view videos meant to evoke moral elevation compared to videos meant to provide amusement or serve as a control. In both experiments, we expected participants in the treatment conditions to be more supportive of transgender people and rights.

The Puppies and Spiders Experiment

We conducted a survey experiment to investigate the impacts of manipulating emotional elicitation prior to answering questions about transgender people and rights. Respondents answered some initial demographic questions before being asked to evaluate a series of photographs designed to elicit fear or happiness. We aimed to evoke fear using a set of 10 photos of very large spiders and happiness using a set of 10 photos of puppies. The instructions indicated that we were studying the effects of different emotions on attitudes and thoughts. Respondents in the fear condition (spiders) were told, "In this particular study, we're interested in FEAR and things that people find scary or frightening." They then clicked through 10 photographs of very large spiders and were asked to rate them on a scale from 1 = *not very scary* to 5 = *extremely scary*. Respondents in the happiness condition (puppies) were also told they were taking part in a study studying the effects of emotions on attitudes and thoughts but were told in the instructions that we were interested in the effects of happiness or joy and things that people find cute or endearing. They then clicked through a series of 10 photographs of puppies and were asked to rate the photos on a scale from 1 = *not very cute* to 5 = *extremely cute*.

As a manipulation check, we asked respondents immediately after treatment to answer two feeling questions, one asking how good or bad they were feeling (a 7-point Likert scale ranging from *extremely bad* to *extremely good*) and another asking how happy or unhappy they were feeling (a 7-point Likert scale ranging from *extremely unhappy* to *extremely happy*). Respondents then answered a series of questions about transgender people, rights, and policies, including how they would vote on a hypothetical ballot initiative about transgender access to bathrooms that correspond with their gender identity; whether businesses should be able to refuse services to transgender people; if the idea of someone changing their sex disgusts them; whether transgender people deserve health insurance that covers all transgender-related issues; and whether the respondent would be willing to sign a petition urging lawmakers to support transgender people by passing laws that protect their rights (see Script Appendix for full survey details).

We expected participants assigned to view photos of puppies to feel happier and thus express stronger support for transgender rights: ·

H_1: Participants assigned to the puppies condition will report feeling better and happier than participants assigned to the spiders condition.

H_2: Participants who report more positive emotions will report stronger support for transgender rights compared to participants who report more negative emotions.

H_3: Participants who report feeling more positive emotions will be more likely to sign a petition in support of transgender rights compared to participants who report more negative emotions.

Results

Data were collected on the Lucid academic platform[1] on August 3, 2018. Overall, we collected 987 valid responses, of whom 51.5% were female and 48% were male (including two transgender men); another two respondents identified as nonbinary. Most respondents (70%) identified as Anglo (White non-Latinx), with another 11% identifying as Black, 8% as Latinx, 5% as Asian American, and the remainder as mixed race. Political ideology was spread out fairly evenly, including 32% identifying as liberal or very liberal, 38% as moderate, and 30% as conservative or very conservative. Respondents ranged in age from 18 to 87, with a mean age of 45. Almost half (49%) identified as Democrats or leaning toward the Democratic Party, 38% as Republicans or leaning toward the Republican Party, and the remaining 13% as political independents. One in five (22%) said they personally knew someone who was transgender or gender nonconforming.

Our analysis looked for differences between respondents assigned to the positive emotion (puppies) and negative emotion (spiders) conditions, including their reported feelings immediately after viewing the photos and their responses to the questions about transgender people and rights.

The experiment successfully manipulated respondent emotions, confirming our first hypothesis. Participants assigned to the spiders condition were significantly less likely to say that they felt good or happy and the differences are statistically significant (Table 5.1). In fact, one participant was so disturbed by the spider photos that he wrote to one of the authors at the email address listed on the final debrief screen of the survey to complain how scared they had made him feel.

Support for transgender people and rights varied significantly by dependent variable. While an overwhelming majority of respondents said they would not mind having a transgender neighbor and supported antidiscrimination laws to protect transgender people, majorities also said that

Table 5.1. Manipulation Check, Puppies and Spiders Experiment

	Puppies (SE)	Spiders (SE)	Difference (SE)
Feeling good (1–7 scale)	5.53 (.06)	4.72 (.07)	.81* (.10)
Happiness (1–7 scale)	5.38 (.06)	4.74 (.07)	.65* (.10)

Note: N = 987 (N = 486 in control/spiders, N = 501 in treatment/ puppies). Data collected August 3, 2018. * = statistically significant at $p \leq .01$, two-tailed. SE = standard errors.

the idea of someone changing their sex disgusted them and that transgender people were mentally ill. Only a third were willing to sign the petition to protect transgender rights. While there are some small differences in support for transgender people and rights between participants randomly assigned to the puppies and spiders conditions, none of these differences are statistically significant (Table 5.2). In contrast with results from experiments explored in other chapters, there is no measurable difference in how participants respond to items related to transgender rights compared to items related to transphobia; there are simply no measurable differences when comparing participants in the puppies and spiders groups.

We combined responses to the eight attitudinal items into a simple additive index, using the full range of potential answers. This generated an index with scores ranging from 0 for participants who did not give a supportive answer to any question to 8 for participants who gave supportive answers to all 8 items. As with the analysis of individual items, there is no difference between index scores for respondents in the spiders condition and the puppies condition. There is also no difference between participants in the two conditions on willingness to sign the petition (Table 5.2).

Adding in the role of emotion, however, provides support for our hypotheses. In a multiple regression examining the role of both assignment to treatment and control and reported emotions, individuals who were assigned to the puppies condition and who report feeling better and happier have slightly higher scores on the attitudinal index (Table 5.3). This effect persists when controlling for age, race, gender, political ideology, and reported personal contact with transgender people—the effect is substantively small but

Table 5.2. Support for Transgender People and Rights, Puppies and Spiders Experiment

	% Supportive All (A)	% Supportive Spiders (B)	% Supportive Puppies (C)	Difference (C–B)
1. Would vote yes on hypothetical ballot measure in support of transgender bathroom access rights	53.0	54.7	51.3	−3.4% pts.
2. I would not mind if my neighbor was transgender	84.5	85.4	83.6	1.8% pts.
3. Transgender people violate the traditions of American culture	70.8	70.4	71.3	0.9% pts.
4. Businesses should be able to refuse services to transgender people	77.8	76.3	79.2	2.9% pts.
5. The idea of someone changing their sex disgusts me	65.3	64.4	66.3	1.9% pts.
6. Transgender people are sick and need help from a mental health professional	70.6	68.5	72.7	4.2% pts.[+]
7. Transgender people deserve health insurance that covers all transgender-related issues	62.4	63.0	61.9	−1.1% pts.
8. Congress should pass laws to protect transgender people from discrimination in housing, restaurants, and other public places	77.0	76.1	77.8	1.7% pts.
Index of attitudinal items	5.61 (SE = .08)	5.58 (SE = .11)	5.64 (SE = .11)	.06 (SE = .15)
Signed petition to Congress supporting anti-discrimination law to support transgender people	34.4	35.2	33.5	−1.7% pts.

Note: $N = 987$ ($N = 486$ in control/spiders, $N = 501$ in treatment/puppies). Data collected August 3, 2018. Responses to items 3 through 6 are reverse-coded; percentage supportive for these items are those disagreeing. [+] = statistically significant at $p \leq .10$, one-tailed. SE = standard errors.

Table 5.3. Emotion and Support for Transgender Rights, Puppies and Spiders Experiment

	Attitudinal Index (SE)	Sign Petition (SE)
Puppies condition	−.664* (.324)	−.053 (.071)
Feelings	−.004 (.007)	.0005 (.002)
Puppy feelings (interaction term)	.023* (.010)	.002 (.002)
Age	−.007+ (.004)	−.002* (.001)
Anglo	−.007 (.156)	.001 (.03)
Female	.381* (.137)	.001 (.030)
Ideology	−.967* (.061)	−.114* (.013)
Know transgender	.347* (.166)	.096* (.036)
Constant	7.68* (.287)	.664* (.063)

Note: $N = 982$. Data collected August 3, 2018. * = statistically significant at $p \leq .05$, + = $p \leq .10$, one-tailed. SE = standard errors.

statistically significant, supporting our second hypothesis. Individuals with more liberal political ideologies, women, and those reporting interpersonal contact are more supportive of transgender rights. In contrast, there is no measurable effect on willingness to sign the petition; individuals who are younger, are more liberal, or report personal contact are more likely to have signed the petition but there are no measurable differences by treatment condition or by reported emotions.

Takeaways from the puppies and spiders experiment are both encouraging and disheartening. That viewing photos of cute puppies can put recipients of messages in a good mood and thus slightly increase their support for transgender people and rights is evidence that evoking positive emotions is a productive avenue for shifting attitudes. On the other hand, it is not feasible to send everyone daily puppy photos (or maybe videos) so that they will treat other people in their lives equally. Advocacy campaigns might heed these results, however, and think of creative ways to place targets of communication in a positive headspace when trying to persuade them to be more supportive of transgender people and rights.

The Moral Elevation Experiment

Our second emotion manipulation experiment focused on moral elevation, the emotion triggered by watching a virtuous act such as saving a stranger from being run over by a train. Often, moral elevation encourages others to similarly act in virtuous or compassionate ways, to be their better selves. Crucially for our purposes, moral elevation differs from happiness in that it has a proven track record of motivating emulation, including prosocial and affiliative behavior. Moral elevation is distinctive in how it causes people to feel and to act: "elevation is a response to acts of moral beauty in which we feel as though we have become (for a moment) less selfish, and we want to act accordingly" (Algoe and Haidt 2009: 106).

The term *moral elevation* was coined by Jonathan Haidt, drawing inspiration from Thomas Jefferson. As he explains in detail in his 2006 book *The Happiness Hypothesis*, Jefferson wrote in a 1771 letter that reading great novels could trigger beneficial emotions and that reading about the fidelity and generosity of a hero, for example, elicits a desire in the reader for a "covenant to copy the fair example" (Haidt 2006: 195). Jefferson calls this feeling (what Haidt terms *moral elevation*) the opposite of disgust—it is "the sense of rising on a vertical dimension, away from disgust" (Haidt 2006: 195).

Given that disgust, as noted earlier, can elicit negative attitudes toward transgender people and rights, we hypothesized that eliciting the opposite feeling—moral elevation—should elicit more positive attitudes. Other scholars have shown that watching videos that induce feelings of moral elevation cause viewers to be less prejudiced against gay men while watching videos that are merely amusing (inducing happiness) or that do not elicit any particular emotion (control videos) do not (Lai, Haidt, and Nosek 2014). If moral elevation can reduce prejudice against gay men, then perhaps it can also reduce prejudice against transgender people.

Transgender advocacy groups including the Movement Advancement Project have evoked moral elevation in some of their public campaigns such as in a television advertisement released in July 2016.[2] The video opens to show a transgender woman and her friends sitting down at a restaurant. She excuses herself to use the restroom but is intercepted by a male waiter who directs her to use the men's restroom. The door of the men's restroom opens to show two menacing men as the voiceover notes the danger that the transgender woman faces if she were to choose that option. Another woman passing by notices what is happening and comes over to intervene on the transgender woman's behalf, as does another woman exiting the women's restroom. The two cisgender women then accompany the transgender woman into the women's restroom, defying the waiter. The video isn't only about moral elevation: it includes a definition of what transgender means and frames the issue as about safety, equality, and privacy. But the moral elevation component is clear—the video is not only making an argument about the right of transgender people to use the restroom of their gender identity but also providing a model of how a supportive bystander might behave in a similar situation.

We modeled our moral elevation experiment closely on that of Lai et al. (2014), using the same video clips used in their experiment (which they have generously shared online).[3] The control video is a clip about how flutes are made. The two amusement-inducing videos include clips from a standup routine by Jerry Seinfeld and a flash mob dancing to the song "Do Re Mi" from *The Sound of Music*. The moral elevation videos include a clip from *The Oprah Winfrey Show* where a musician talks about a mentor who turned him away from street gangs, a story about girls on a softball team carrying an injured player from the other team around the bases, and the story of the Hero of Harlem saving a stranger from being run over by a New York City subway train (as detailed in the opening of this chapter).

Using the same six videos, we hypothesized that individuals randomly assigned to watch one of the moral elevation videos would be more supportive of transgender rights compared to individuals randomly assigned to watch one of the amusement videos or the control video. Lai et al. note (2014: 782): "If moral elevation is the functional opposite of social disgust, then it may be effective at reducing sexual prejudice in a way that goes beyond simply being a positive emotion." As they further note, positive emotions should also theoretically reduce prejudice, including by promoting perceived similarity between groups (although they are not aware of any published evidence to support that theory) but they do not find evidence to support this hypothesis. Individuals randomly assigned to watch one of the amusement videos were no less likely to express implicit or explicit sexual prejudice than were individuals randomly assigned to watch the control video. Consistent with their findings, we hypothesized:

H_1: Participants assigned to the moral elevation condition will be more supportive of transgender rights compared to participants assigned to the control condition.

H_2: Participants assigned to the moral elevation condition will be more supportive of transgender rights compared to participants assigned to the amusement condition.

H_3: Participants assigned to the amusement condition will be no more supportive of transgender rights compared to participants assigned to the control condition.

Results

Data were collected on the Lucid academic platform[4] from May 29 through June 16, 2019. Respondents who failed the manipulation check, indicating that they had not viewed the assigned video, were eliminated. This left us with 1,013 usable responses, of whom 47% identified as male (including two transgender men) and 53% identified as female; one respondent identified as genderqueer/genderfluid. Most respondents (72%) were Anglo (White non-Latinx), and they ranged in age from 18 to 84 with a mean age of just over 46. Nearly half (48%) were Democrats or leaning toward the Democratic Party, another 16% were independents, and 36% were Republicans or leaning toward the Republican Party. Just over one-fifth (22%) said that they personally knew someone who was transgender or gender nonconforming.

Roughly half of our 1,013 respondents ($n = 503$) were assigned to watch one of the three moral elevation videos and the other half to either the control video ($n = 149$) or an amusement video ($n = 361$). To test our hypotheses, we examined four different measures of support for transgender rights, including two measures of attitudes and two measures of behavior: (1) responses to an index of transphobia generated from answers to 4 questions, (2) responses to an index of support for transgender rights generated from answers to 10 questions, (3) responses to an item asking how the respondent would vote on a hypothetical ballot measure about "whether transgender people should be able to use the bathroom of their choice," and (4) responses to an invitation to sign a petition (requiring the respondent to give their full name and ZIP code) "urging lawmakers to support transgender people by passing laws that guarantee them the same rights as other Americans" (see Script Appendix for full survey details).

The transphobia scale, our first measure of support, was generated using four questions coded from 1 = *most transphobic* to 4 = *least transphobic*, allowing for scores ranging from 4 to 16. Higher values are more supportive while lower values indicate less support and stronger feelings of transphobia. About one-third ($n = 371$) of respondents gave the most supportive response to each item, for an index score of 16. Consistent with our hypotheses, respondents randomly assigned to watch a moral elevation video scored higher on the scale compared to respondents randomly assigned to watch either the control video or an amusement video, indicating higher levels of comfort with transgender people, supporting our first two hypotheses (Table 5.4). These differences persist in a multivariate model including other predictors of transphobia, including gender, ideology, partisanship, and whether the respondent personally knows someone who is transgender or gender nonconforming (see Appendix Table A5.1). There is no measurable difference in transphobia between respondents assigned to watch the control video or an amusement video, supporting our third hypothesis.

The index of support for transgender rights, our second measure of support, included a battery of 10 questions, again with each item scored from 1 = *least supportive* to 4 = *most supportive*. Scores here range from a low of 10 to a high of 40 and are more spread out, with only 13% ($n = 134$) giving the highest level of support. Here there is less support for our hypotheses; the differences in support for transgender rights are small and not statistically significant (Table 5.5).

The third and fourth measures of support examine political behavior: support for a ballot measure for transgender bathroom access rights and willingness to sign a petition to lawmakers in favor of equal rights for transgender

Table 5.4. Transphobia, by Condition, Moral Elevation Experiment

	Mean Transphobia Score (SE)	Difference From Control (SE)	Difference From Amusement (SE)
Control ($N = 149$)	12.40 (.28)	—	—
Amusement ($N = 361$)	12.58 (.19)	.17 (.34)	—
Moral elevation ($N = 503$)	13.01 (.15)	.61* (.32)	.44* (.24)

Note: N = 987. Data collected May 29–June 16, 2019. * = statistically significant at $p \leq .05$, one-tailed. SE = standard errors.

Table 5.5. Support for Transgender Rights, by Condition, Moral Elevation Experiment

	Mean Support for Transgender Rights (SE)	Difference From Control (SE)	Difference From Amusement (SE)
Control (N = 149)	30.13 (.62)	—	—
Amusement (N = 361)	30.77 (.40)	.64 (.75)	—
Moral elevation (N = 503)	31.09 (.34)	.96[+] (.71)	.32 (.53)

Note: N = 987. Data collected May 29–June 16, 2019. [+] = statistically significant at $p \leq .10$, one-tailed. SE = standard errors.

Table 5.6. Behavioral Measures of Support for Transgender Rights, by Condition, Moral Elevation Experiment

	Vote Yes on Ballot Measure	Difference From Control (SE)	Difference From Amusement (SE)
Control (N = 149)	55.0%	—	—
Amusement (N = 361)	53.5%	1.6% pts. (4.9)	—
Moral elevation (N = 503)	62.6%	7.6% pts.* (4.5)	9.2% pts.* (3.4)
	Sign Petition to Lawmakers	**Difference From Control (SE)**	**Difference From Amusement (SE)**
Control (N = 149)	35.6%	—	—
Amusement (N = 361)	36.3%	0.7% pts. (4.7)	—
Moral elevation (N = 503)	38.4%	2.8% pts. (4.5)	2.1% pts. (3.3)

Note: N = 987. Data collected May 29–June 16, 2019. * = statistically significant at $p \leq .05$, one-tailed. SE = standard errors.

people. Overall, 58% (n = 590) of our 1,013 respondents said they would vote in favor of the ballot measure and 37% (n = 377) were willing to sign the petition with their name and ZIP code.

As shown in Table 5.6, results for the ballot measure are consistent with our hypotheses: respondents assigned to watch a moral elevation video were more likely to say they would vote in favor of transgender bathroom access rights compared to respondents assigned to watch either the control video or an amusement video; these differences are both substantively large and statistically significant. There is no difference in support between those assigned to watch the control and amusement videos. In contrast, the differences in willingness to sign the petition are negligible. The differences in support for the ballot measure persist in a multivariate analysis that takes into consideration other predictors of support for transgender rights, including gender, political ideology, partisanship, and whether the respondent personally knows someone who is transgender or gender nonconforming (not shown).

Discussion and Conclusion

Our Theory of Identity Reassurance and previous scholarship on the power of negative and positive emotions suggest that evoking positive emotions should move recipients of persuasive messages to be more open to messages about transgender people and rights. This was expected to be particularly true for messages evoking moral elevation given previous published experiments on how it can generate prosocial behavior and reduce anti-gay attitudes. Consistent with those expectations, we found that evoking happiness through viewing photos of cute puppies or watching a video modeling virtuous and selfless behavior motivated our experiment participants to report more supportive attitudes about transgender people. At the same time, the experiments generated mixed results for the power of those positive emotions to motivate changes in behavior, measured by willingness to sign online petitions or by intention to vote in favor of a ballot measure supporting transgender rights. Overall, results from these two experiments provide evidence that appeals to emotion are a productive line of research for advocates and allies seeking to reduce transphobia. Further experiments are needed to better understand how these results might be used in interpersonal conversations or in advocacy campaigns by transgender rights groups.

For decades, the role of emotion was dismissed by political scientists who instead tended to favor a rational actor model that imagined individuals making fact-based, unemotional evaluations of political ideas and candidates (Downs 1957). The past few decades have seen a renewed appreciation for the far messier and accurate reality that politics is and always has been about emotion. "To ignore the important role of emotion means to ignore what might in fact be the most critical component to our understanding of how people process political information and make sense of the political world" (Redlawsk 2006: 10). Fear drives policies meant to marginalize and to erase transgender people while pride brings LGBT people and their allies into the public streets to celebrate the diversity of sexual orientation and gender identity with glitter and rainbows. Disgust underlies the trans panic defense used to escape punishment for violent attacks and murders against transgender women but moral elevation may lead bystanders to intervene when a transgender woman is denied access to a public restroom.

In the next chapter, we review our final set of experiments, exploring the power of acknowledgment of discomfort and the sharing of journey stories. Then, in chapter 7, we pull together the findings from all of the experiments in this book to offer actionable strategies for those hoping to harness the power of the Theory of Identity Reassurance to change minds about transgender people and rights.

6

Feeling a Little Uncomfortable, and That's Okay

During the 2016 fight in North Carolina to repeal HB2, the bill that required transgender people to use the public restroom that corresponded to their sex as assigned at birth (see chapter 3), Freedom for All Americans released a television advertisement meant to persuade voters that the bill had been a mistake.[1] The advertisement featured Zeke Christopoulos, a transgender man, and his professional coworkers Patricia Hickling Beckman and Chester A. Spier.

The ad opens with a shot of the three coworkers wearing business clothing and with Zeke's voiceover: "All of us take pride in our work and we're proud to call North Carolina home." The camera then zooms in on Patricia facing Zeke and saying, "I remember when I learned that Zeke was transgender and had transitioned from female to male and I . . . I was a little uncomfortable at first." Zeke, nodding and smiling, replies, "and I get that." The advertisement goes on to discuss the negative impact of HB2 on the state's economy and how it hurts transgender people like Zeke. The ad closes with the voiceover: "HB2 just goes against what North Carolinians are and what kind of state we want to live in" while the words "No Discrimination in North Carolina" flash on the screen. The message is clear: it might make you a little bit uncomfortable but you can still do the right thing and be the kind of person who does not discriminate. The advertisement encourages viewers to push past their individual discomfort and to draw on their commitments to equality.

We argue that discomfort is a central feature of attitudes toward transgender people and rights. Noble (2005) explores the experience of discomfort among immigrants, borrowing from Giddens (1990) the idea of "ontological security." Noble defines ontological security as "the confidence or trust we have in the world around us, both in terms of the things and the people with which we share our lives, and hence which provide stability and a continuity to our identity" (2005: 113, citing Giddens 1990). Noble argues that the disruption of ontological security creates profound discomfort, heightened by

Transforming Prejudice. Melissa R. Michelson and Brian F. Harrison, Oxford University Press (2020) © Oxford University Press.
DOI: 10.1093/oso/9780190068882.001.0001

"the prevailing Western mood of existential insecurity: a world in which we are no longer sure who we can trust, whether our identities and communities are meaningful any more" (2005: 119, citing Furedi 1997: 171). This discomfort in turn produces "the active, affective regulation of the inappropriate existence of others" (Noble 2005: 115).

Rather than shaming respondents for their beliefs or feelings, advocates are instead attempting to acknowledge these attitudes without judgment, similar to the HB2 advertisement described in the opening of this chapter.[2] Advocates suggest that this approach will lessen audience discomfort, encourage re-engagement with one's core values, and allow people to be more open to information about transgender people and rights.[3] Gender is a centrally important concept for many people and societies and therefore, for some people the mere existence of transgender identity creates uncertainty about the presumed stability of gender. As a result, discomfort is an especially prevalent emotional response for many people toward transgender people. As Poteat, German, and Kerrigan note:

Because transgender individuals challenge societal norms for gender expression, negative attitudes toward them can serve as a psychological defense against discomfort with gender non-conformity and allow the expression of the core belief in gender conformity. (2013: 28)

This idea is also supported by the findings of Miller et al. (2017: 1, 11) that attitudes toward transgender rights "often reflect social norms and morality about bodies . . . both how gender is presented via the body and how the body is altered." They also find that disgust—a particularly guttural form of discomfort—is a predominant influence on attitudes toward transgender people and policy issues (for more on the role of disgust and other emotional reactions to LGBT people, see chapter 5).

Advocates for members of the disability community have long used the acknowledgment of discomfort in a similar way. Experimental research proves acknowledgment can be a successful strategy for alleviating interpersonal discomfort and improving support for a minority or stigmatized group. In this chapter, we explore the use of acknowledgment to test whether it is an effective method of inducing respondents to be more open to persuasive communication about transgender rights. We begin with an online survey experiment. Those results show that, contrary to expectations, acknowledgment increases respondent discomfort and has no effect on transgender-related policy support. While we find limited support for the efficacy of acknowledgment as a persuasive strategy, we do find clear evidence that people continue to respond differently (and more negatively) to transgender women than to transgender men. We follow up on that online experiment with a face-to-face survey experiment that, rather than simply acknowledging discomfort, also focuses on the second aspect of the process: the idea that an individual can change their mind and become more supportive. Just as Patricia does in the HB2 advertisement, a person can be "a little uncomfortable at first" but still can embark on a journey toward acceptance.

Existing research shows that many people feel strong discomfort or disgust toward transgender people, affecting both policy support and openness to contact and potentially limiting opportunities for opinion change (Casey 2016). Elected officials may also feel this discomfort, depressing their willingness to pursue protections for transgender individuals. Taylor and Lewis note that legislators, particularly Republicans, are known to be "sometimes repulsed" by transgender people and are often "not comfortable with transgender persons unless they pass well" (2015: 122). Mitigating these negative visceral reactions to transgender people is therefore often seen as a necessary first step toward reducing bias and increasing support for transgender rights. In chapter 5, we explored the power of evoking moral elevation, the emotional opposite of disgust, as a strategy for reducing prejudice. In this chapter, taking our cue from real-world advocacy organization strategies, we test the power of acknowledgment.

Acknowledgment

Given that many people may feel discomfort (or even disgust) toward transgender people and the negative consequences of that feeling for treatment of transgender people (both interpersonally and politically), our focus is on the most effective way to reduce such discomfort. Indeed, reducing discomfort and bias against members of stigmatized groups can increase willingness to engage in social relationships, support for particular policies that benefit those groups, and other prosocial behaviors (Conover 1988; Jones and Rachlin 2006; Lauber, Nordt, Falcato, and Rössler 2004; Loewenstein and Small 2007).

One method of reducing discomfort or stigma is to directly acknowledge it. Acknowledgments tend to ease interactions because they address (and do not ignore) underlying tension and discomfort in an interaction (Singletary and Hebl 2009). Research has found acknowledgment to be an effective way of reducing bias against visibly disabled people (Hebl and Kleck 2002; Hebl and Skorinko 2005) and to date, this strategy has most often been studied in the context of employment discrimination against physically disabled people. For example, F. Davis (1961) found that when individuals made explicit statements about their own physical disabilities, others were less likely to view them with disdain, pity, or contempt (also see Hebl and Kleck 2002). People who openly acknowledge their physical disability are also evaluated more positively by interviewers and coworkers than those who do not (Hastorf, Wildfogel, and Cassman 1979; Hebl and Skorinko 2005; Mills, Belgrave, and Boyer 1984). As Lyons et al. (2018: 3) argue, "This may be due, in part, to the fact that acknowledging one's visible disability helps others overcome their initial negative reactions and attributions of the target individual as fragile, inefficacious, or pitiful and helps to shape others' perceptions, activate positive stereotypes, reduce negative stereotypes, avoid discrimination, and gain acceptance."

More recent experiments have replicated this effect in interpersonal interactions with other groups such as gay and lesbian individuals (Singletary and Hebl 2009) and ethnic and racial minorities (Barron, Hebl, and King 2011). Research on transgender patients and medical providers has found that acknowledgment can reduce discomfort and ease interactions and "may transform underlying heteronormativity and gender-normativity in the physician–patient relationship" (Harbin, Beagan, and Goldberg 2012: 159). Building on this scholarship, we hypothesized that acknowledgment would similarly reduce discomfort and bias toward transgender people. By acknowledging the elephant in the room, discomfort should be reduced and bias in turn lessened.

To be clear, we are not suggesting that being transgender is a disability, visible or otherwise. However, to the extent that the existence of transgender identity challenges a fundamental concept (gender) that structures many aspects of American life and history (Jackman 1994), many people may feel a fundamental or strong (negative) sense of discomfort. This in turn leads to "the active, affective regulation of the inappropriate existence of others" (Noble 2005 115). In other words, when ontological security is threatened, people express that discomfort by attempting to regulate and limit the supposed threat and the people who may represent it—in this case, transgender people. Substantial existing scholarship from various disciplines suggests that acknowledgment of the discomfort and uncertainty felt by many people about interacting with transgender people may help decrease their feelings of unease and increase support for transgender rights. While we echo many scholars and activists in noting that stigmatized individuals should not bear the sole responsibility for reducing discrimination against them, we also support any relatively low-cost or scalable approaches that can reduce discrimination and improve the lives of members of stigmatized groups. If effective, acknowledgment could be a useful strategy easily implemented in television ads and other educational or persuasive efforts to improve life for transgender people.

The Karl and Kathy Experiment

This experiment[4] was designed to examine two main questions. The first question is simply whether acknowledgment is an effective strategy for reducing bias toward transgender people. Second, we test whether the object of acknowledgment has any unique impact on reducing discomfort or improving attitudes toward transgender people. Scholarly research on acknowledgment has referred to acknowledgment in different ways. Here, we present three variations of acknowledgment: acknowledging that people may not know much about transgender people (*unfamiliarity* condition), that being transgender carries stigma and unfair treatment (*stigma* condition), or that a cisgender person may feel uncomfortable about transgender people or identity (*discomfort* condition). As a control condition, some respondents were assigned to view a message encouraging recycling, using the same photos and text of similar length. We use photos in all of the experimental conditions following Flores et al. (2017), who found that text-only appeals on transgender rights were ineffectual while appeals including photos, regardless of the person in the photo, increased the effectiveness of persuasive appeals on transgender rights.

As a related concern, as noted in chapter 2, attitudes toward transgender women are significantly more negative than attitudes toward transgender men. Therefore, we examine whether the strategy of acknowledgment is more or less effective based on the gender of the person featured in the experimental condition.

Experimental Design

Prior to the experiment, we conducted a separate online survey to test the likelihood that participants would find it plausible that the people in the photographs we intended to use (the authors) were transgender. Participants were recruited via Amazon's Mechanical Turk; respondents were paid $0.50 to complete the survey, consistent with fair wages and best practices on the site.[5] Participants were asked to evaluate a series of 20 photographs of cisgender and transgender individuals, including some well-known transgender people such as Caitlyn Jenner and Laverne Cox as well as more anonymous members of the public, including the authors. We asked participants to indicate for each photograph whether they believed the depicted individual was male, female, or transgender.

A total of 330 participants completed the survey, including 170 who identified their own gender as female (51.5%), 158 as male (48%), and 2 as gender nonconforming. Most participants identified their race as Anglo (White non-Latinx) (80%) and as both straight and cisgender (89%).

Our survey respondents correctly identified 9 out of 10 cisgender photos as depicting cisgender individuals but only correctly identified 3 out of 10 transgender photos as depicting transgender individuals (typically, the two celebrities and a transgender woman who worked in the Obama White House, Raffi Freedman-Gurspan) (see Table 6.1). Brian was (incorrectly) identified as transgender by 24% of non-LGBT respondents and Melissa was (incorrectly) identified as transgender by 13% of non-LGBT respondents. We took this as evidence that they would be plausibly accepted as transgender messengers in the study, allowing for effective experimental manipulation of their gender identities.

For the main experiment, participants were randomly assigned to read a short paragraph about either recycling (control) or transgender rights (treatments), accompanied by a visual image of one of the authors, identified as Karl or Kathy. Treatment conditions acknowledged the general lack of knowledge about or unfamiliarity with transgender people, including the statement "It can be hard to understand what it means to be transgender, especially if you've never met a transgender person before." This mirrors contemporary persuasive efforts by LGBT groups such as the television advertisement released by the transgender advocacy group Movement Advancement Project in July 2016 described in chapter 5.[6] Additional treatment conditions

Table 6.1. Correct Gender Identifications, Photos for Acknowledgment Experiment

	Number of Correct Photo Identifications		
	Full Sample (N = 330)	Cisgender respondents (N = 328)	Non-LGBT respondents (N = 294)
Correct identifications of Brian as cisgender	74.9%	75.4%	75.9%
Correct identifications of Melissa as cisgender	80.7%	80.9%	82.7%
Correct answers, all 10 cisgender photos	91%	91%	91%
Correct answers, all 10 transgender photos	32%	32%	31%

N = 330. Data collected February 6, 2017.

added a phrase about either the stigmatized aspect of transgender identity ("In many places, the law allows people to treat transgender people like me unfairly . . . ") or how thinking about what it means to be transgender could be uncomfortable ("Some people feel uncomfortable thinking about what it means to be transgender . . . "). Because the unfamiliarity language was being used at the time by LGBT advocates, we keep this language in subsequent conditions and build further on the acknowledgment strategy by additionally acknowledging stigma or discomfort. We refer to these as the *unfamiliarity, stigma,* and *discomfort* conditions, respectively (see Script Appendix for full survey details).

In addition, we examine whether the efficacy of these messages differed if the condition included an image of a man versus a woman, with the expectation that the respondent would then think about transgender men or transgender women when choosing their responses to our dependent variable items. Note that even in the control conditions, respondents were also exposed to one of the same photos, allowing for consistent comparisons for assignment to conditions priming respondents to think about men or women (see Figure 6.1). We expect that priming individuals to think about transgender women, relative to transgender men, will limit the effectiveness of acknowledgment as a strategy given existing hostilities toward transgender women above and beyond those toward transgender men.

After exposure to the treatment or placebo text, participants were asked a series of questions about how they were feeling, their support for transgender rights, and a set of demographic questions.

Control/Male (Karl)

"Hi, my name is Karl. It can be hard to understand what it means to recycle, especially if you've never recycled before. Recycling means taking things that would otherwise be thrown away and using them for something new.

In many places, it's legal to have only public trashcans but no public recycling bins, including in public restrooms, which means many people throw away items like bottles, cans, and paper towels that could easily be recycled.

It's important to pass laws that make it easier to recycle to give the environment the protection it deserves."

Treatment/Female (Kathy)

"Hi, my name is Kathy, and I am transgender. It can be hard to understand what it means to be transgender, especially if you've never met a transgender person before.

Being transgender means that I know myself to be a different gender than what people thought I was when I was born. When I was growing up, people thought I was a man, but I knew that I was a woman.

In many places, the law allows people to treat transgender people like me unfairly, including when they are trying to find a job or even when trying to use a public restroom. I can even be fired just for being who I am.

It's important to pass laws that give transgender people like me the equal protection we deserve."

Figure 6.1. Examples of control and treatment conditions, acknowledgement experiment.

Hypotheses

H_1: Individuals exposed to a supportive message about transgender rights will be more likely to say they support those rights compared to individuals exposed to a message about recycling.

H_{1A}: Individuals exposed to a supportive message about transgender rights that notes that transgender may be an unfamiliar concept will be more likely to say that they support those rights compared to individuals exposed to a message about recycling.

H_{1B}: Individuals exposed to a supportive message about transgender rights that notes that being transgender carries stigma and unfair treatment will be more likely to say that they support those rights compared to individuals exposed to a message about recycling.

H_{1C}: Individuals exposed to a supportive message about transgender rights that notes that some people are uncomfortable with the idea of what it means to be transgender will be more likely to say that they support those rights compared to individuals exposed to a message about recycling.

H_2: Individuals exposed to a message about transgender rights from a male-presenting messenger will be more likely to say they support those rights compared to individuals exposed to the same message from a female-presenting messenger.

Results

Data were collected in an online survey using Amazon's Mechanical Turk on September 26, 2017. Respondents were compensated $0.50 for completing the survey, consistent with fair wages and best practices on the site.[7] Overall, we collected 975 usable responses, including a roughly even split of male (52%) and female (48%) respondents. Respondents were mostly Anglo (White non-Latinx) (76%) and 89% identified as both straight and cisgender; most identified as Democrats (53%) while another 34% identified as Republicans and the remaining 13% as politically independent. They ranged in age from 19 to 74, with a mean age of 37. More than one-third (35%) said that they personally know someone who is transgender.

Immediately after viewing the treatment or control text and photo, respondents were asked a series of questions about how they were feeling, including the degree to which they were feeling uncomfortable and the degree to which they were feeling sympathetic. Responses were measured on a 5-point Likert scale ranging from 1 = *not at all* to 5 = *extremely*. We expected that participants randomly assigned to the treatment conditions would feel (1) less comfortable than participants randomly assigned to the control conditions since they had just been faced with the uncomfortable issue of transgender people and rights and (2) more sympathetic since they had just been exposed to information about a group of people being discriminated against.

These expectations are supported by the data. After viewing the treatment or control text, respondents were asked, "When you think of what you just read, how much do you feel each of these emotions" and rated themselves on various emotions using 5-point Likert scales coded from 1 = *not at all* to 5 = *extremely*. In the control group, 78% of respondents reported feeling *not at all uncomfortable* compared to only 61% of respondents in the treatment groups. The mean level of reported discomfort was 1.40 (SE = .06) in the control group and 1.78 (SE = .04) in the treatment group, a statistically significant difference of .38 points (SE = .09, $p < .01$). In the control group, only 24% reported feeling *very sympathetic* or *extremely sympathetic* compared to 43% of respondents in the treatment groups. The mean level of reported sympathy was 2.51 (SE = .09) in the control group and 2.97 (SE = .05) in the treatment groups, a statistically significant difference of .45 points (SE = .11, $p < .01$).

Moving on to our formal hypotheses, we examined differences in responses to a series of questions about transgender rights:

1. How would you feel if a transgender person moved next door?
2. Do you favor or oppose laws protecting transgender people against job discrimination?
3. Do you think business owners in your state should be able to refuse to provide products or services to transgender people, if doing so violates their religious beliefs?
4. Do you think health insurance policies should cover medical treatments for transgender people, such as mental healthcare, surgery, or hormone replacement therapy?

5. Which of the following comes closer to your view, even if neither is exactly right? *Laws should require transgender people to use facilities like public bathrooms based on the sex they were assumed to be at birth*, OR *Laws should allow transgender people to use facilities like public bathrooms based on their current gender identity.*

Responses to the first four questions were measured with 5-point Likert scales, coded from 1 = *very unhappy* to 5 = *very happy* for the first question and coded from 1 = *strongly oppose/disagree* to 5 = *strongly favor/agree* for questions 2–4. Question 5 had binary responses, reflecting the two competing options regarding transgender bathroom access policy.

Responses did not differ significantly on any the five dependent variables when comparing participants assigned to the treatment and control conditions (not shown). This finding persists in multivariate models controlling for various other predictors of attitudes toward transgender rights, including age, gender, race, income, education, partisanship, political ideology, sexual orientation, and whether the participant reports personally knowing a transgender person (see Appendix Table A6.1).

Overall, the acknowledgment conditions succeed in increasing reported discomfort and sympathy among respondents but do not affect transphobia or support for transgender rights. Instead, the only consistent predictor of attitudes was political ideology, with conservatives less supportive compared to liberals. Predictors of transphobia and support for transgender equality, including comfort with a transgender neighbor and support for a law protecting transgender people from job discrimination, were also predicted by gender, sexual orientation, and contact: women, LGB (lesbian, gay, and bisexual) people, and people who said they personally knew a transgender person were more supportive compared to men, heterosexuals, and people who did not report personal contact. On the issues of transgender public policy, people with personal contact were also more supportive of transgender health care coverage and women were more supportive of bathroom access rights. These findings persist when separately examining respondents assigned to the different acknowledgment conditions (not shown).

Finally, we turn to our second hypothesis, that due to the intersection of transphobia and sexism male messengers will be more effective than female messengers. As in our initial analysis of H_1, we combine all acknowledgment treatments.

For most of our dependent variables and conditions, neither messenger is effective: participants randomly assigned to a treatment condition message delivered by Karl or by Kathy are no more supportive of transgender people or rights than participants randomly assigned to a control message from Karl or Kathy, with one notable exception: Karl is a more persuasive messenger on the issue of transgender bathroom access rights (Tables 6.2 and 6.3). This finding persists in multivariate models that include control variables such as political ideology (see Appendix Table A6.2). Among men, support is stronger in the treatment condition compared to the control condition *only* when the messenger is male (Table 6.2). When we combine the treatment and control conditions, the gender of the messenger does not predict support among men but women are more supportive when the messenger is male compared to when the messenger is female (Table 6.3). Overall, these findings suggest that messaging that primes recipients to think about transgender men rather than transgender women might be more effective at generating support for transgender bathroom rights.

Overall, these tests provide little evidence that acknowledgment is a persuasive strategy in the contexts of transgender rights. Our analyses show that acknowledgment—both in general and when specifically acknowledging unfamiliarity, stigma, and discomfort—only increased participants' discomfort (albeit also their feelings of sympathy) and had no effect on support for transgender rights. Instead, political ideology was the most consistent predictor of support for transgender people and rights. At the same time, there is some evidence that the gender of the messenger does matter, at least on the very gendered issue of transgender bathroom access. As noted in chapter 2, the mass public has very different attitudes about transgender men and transgender women. This is likely to interact with policy debates on transgender issues depending on whether the policy calls to mind transgender women (as with debates about bathroom access) or transgender men (as with debates about transgender military service). Our results suggest that deliberately priming recipients of a message about transgender bathroom access rights to think about transgender men rather than transgender women might be a powerful method of increasing support. This is not the usual messaging used by advocacy organizations. We encourage further research to test whether it is persistently more effective.

Table 6.2. Support for Transgender Bathroom Access Rights, by Condition, Acknowledgment Experiment

	Kathy			Karl		
	Control	Treatment	Difference	Control	Treatment	Difference
All respondents	65.0 (4.8)	63.4 (2.5)	1.6 (5.4)	62.1 (5.0)	66.3 (2.4)	4.2 (5.5)
Women	72.0 (6.4)	66.8 (3.5)	5.1 (7.5)	76.1 (6.4)	74.4 (3.3)	1.6 (7.2)
Men	59.1 (7.1)	59.7 (3.6)	0.5 (7.9)	49.0 (7.2)	59.1 (3.5)	10.1[+] (7.9)

Note: N = 975. Data collected September 26, 2017. [+] = $p \leq .10$, one-tailed. Standard errors in parentheses.

Table 6.3. Support for Transgender Bathroom Access Rights, by Gender of Messenger, Acknowledgment Experiment

All Respondents			Men			Women		
Kathy	Karl	Difference	Kathy	Karl	Difference	Kathy	Karl	Difference
63.7 (2.2)	65.5 (2.2)	1.8 (3.1)	59.6 (3.2)	57.1 (3.1)	2.4 (4.5)	67.9 (3.1)	74.8 (2.9)	6.8* (4.2)

Note: N = 975. Data collected September 26, 2017. * = $p \leq .05$, one-tailed. Standard errors in parentheses.

Our takeaway from this experiment was that simple acknowledgment of discomfort, even with detailed information about stigma, was insufficient to bolster self-esteem in a way that would open recipients of persuasive messages to persuasion. Instead, that acknowledgment needed to be accompanied by additional information about how to move past discomfort and toward acceptance: what practitioners refer to as a journey story. Recall the HB2 advertisement that opened this chapter, where Patricia notes that she was a little uncomfortable *at first*. She has moved past that discomfort to support her transgender coworker. Our next experiment tested the power of sharing a personal story of attitudinal change.

The Journey Story Experiment

Our journey story experiment uses the true story of a mom and her transgender daughter. In the treatment condition, participants read a brief definition of what it means to be transgender with a short vignette about the mom's journey story, including a photo of the mom with her daughter (Figure 6.2). Participants in the control condition saw the transgender rights symbol and read the same brief definition (Figure 6.3) but did not see the photo and story of the mom and daughter. Reflecting the demographics of the experimental location (San Jose, California), the experiment was conducted in both English and Spanish (see Script Appendix for Spanish-language materials). The top of each survey exposed participants to the relevant graphic and text.

The survey then asked participants their level of comfort around transgender people, whether they think transgender people are born that way, and their support for various transgender policies. We hypothesized that participants randomly assigned to the treatment condition would be more likely to say they are comfortable around transgender people, more likely to say transgender people are born that way, and more supportive of transgender rights and transgender-supportive policies.

Hypotheses

H_1: Exposure to the story about the journey of the transgender girl and her mom will increase comfort with transgender people compared to exposure to the control text.

H_2: Exposure to the story about the journey of the transgender girl and her mom will increase the likelihood of individuals saying that transgender people are born that way, compared to exposure to the control text.

H_3: Exposure to the story about the journey of the transgender girl and her mom will increase support for transgender rights, compared to exposure to the control text.

California Halloween 2018 Survey

Being transgender means that you know yourself to be a different gender than what people thought you were when you were born. For example, a person who was thought to be male and raised as a boy but who knows herself to be a woman might call herself transgender.

Kimberly Shappley used to think people who said they were transgender were confused or mentally ill. Then she realized, and gradually accepted, that her child was transgender. Identified as a boy at birth, Kai was most definitely a girl. "She knows who she is," Kimberly says.

Even if you have not supported transgender people in the past, it's okay to change your mind and support transgender rights.

Figure 6.2. Treatment condition text and image, journey story experiment.
Photo printed with permission from Kimberly Shappley.

California Halloween 2018 Survey

Being transgender means that you know yourself to be a different gender than what people thought you were when you were born.

For example, a person who was thought to be male and raised as a boy but who knows herself to be a woman might call herself transgender.

Figure 6.3. Control condition text, journey story experiment.
Note: In the experiment, the transgender symbol was in a heart and on a striped background.
© Can Stock Photo / grebeshkovmaxim.

As hypothesized, participants in the treatment condition were more likely to say they are comfortable around transgender people, more likely to say transgender people are born that way, and more supportive of transgender rights.

Results

Surveys were collected on October 31, 2018, from 3:30 p.m. until 9 p.m. Surveys were collected in front of a private home on Willow Glen Avenue in San Jose, California, a street known in the neighborhood for its lavish Halloween displays and heavy foot traffic. Reflecting the expected demographics of trick-or-treating families, surveys were printed in English on one side and Spanish on the other; adults passing by the house were asked to complete a survey in exchange for receiving a $2 Dunkin' gift card. Solicitations of passersby to complete the survey were made in both English and Spanish. Overall, 233 surveys were collected, including 200 in English (102 control surveys and 98 treatment surveys) and 33 in Spanish (21 control surveys and 12 treatment surveys). Data were double entered by two undergraduate research assistants to minimize error in transferring the data from the paper surveys into a spreadsheet. After eliminating eight low-quality surveys, we were left with 226 usable responses.

Consistent with H_1, assignment to the treatment condition made individuals more likely to say that they are comfortable around transgender people. In the control group, 77% of respondents said they feel comfortable when around someone who is transgender; in the treatment group, this proportion increases to 84.3%. Looking at the original coding, where the dependent variable is a 4-item Likert scale coded from 1 = *uncomfortable* to 4 = *comfortable*, there is a statistically significant difference in comfort between the treatment group (mean = 3.796) and the control group (mean = 3.664) of 0.132 (SE = .08, p = .05).

Assignment to the treatment condition also made individuals somewhat more likely to say that transgender people are born that way as opposed to it being a choice or the result of how individuals are raised, consistent with H_2. Here, the difference is smaller: in the control group, 66.4% of individuals think transgender people are born that way compared to 71.2% of individuals in the treatment group; the difference is not statistically significant.

To test H_3, we examined six separate survey items about transgender rights. For each item, respondents were asked on a 4-item Likert scale whether they agreed or disagreed with the following items:

1. Legal protections that apply to gay and lesbian people should also apply to transgender people.
2. Transgender people are sick and need help from a mental health professional.
3. Congress should pass laws to protect transgender people from job discrimination.
4. Congress should pass laws to protect transgender people from discrimination in public accommodations like restaurants and movie theaters.
5. Transgender people should have to use the public restroom that corresponds to their gender as assigned at birth.

6. Business owners should be able to refuse services to transgender people if it conflicts with their religious beliefs.

Because of how these items were phrased, an individual wanting to give the most supportive answers would disagree with items 2 and 6. On the other hand, individuals not bothering to read the items might simply agree with each, checking the leftmost box on the paper survey. We discarded the eight surveys where every leftmost box was checked, with the assumption that those individuals were not giving honest answers.

Support for transgender rights varied between the six items from a low of 43.3% for bathroom access rights (Q5) to a high of 81.7% for protection against job discrimination (Q3). For five of the six items, respondents in the treatment condition are more supportive of transgender rights compared to respondents in the control condition. Despite the small size of the experiment, these differences are at times quite large, reaching double digits and statistical significance for items about whether transgender people are sick and whether they should be protected from discrimination (Table 6.4).

We combined the six items into an additive index, first reverse-coding as needed so that each item ranged from 1 = *disagree* to 4 = *agree*. This

Table 6.4. Support for Transgender Rights, Journey Story Experiment

	Control Group	Treatment Group	Difference (SE)
Q1. Legal protections as for gays and lesbians.	78.3	77.9	−0.4 (.05)
Q2. Transgender not sick (reverse-coded)	69.2	81.7	12.5* (.06)
Q3. Protect against job discrimination	76.7	87.5	10.8* (.05)
Q4. Protect against public accommodation discrimination	75.6	83.8	8.2 (.05)
Q5. Bathroom access	40.0	47.1	7.1 (.07)
Q6. Business owners can't refuse for religious reasons (reverse-coded)	74.2	80.0	5.8 (.06)
Index	20.41	21.20	0.79* (.42)

Note: $N = 226$. Data collected October 31, 2018. * = statistically significant at $p \leq .05$, one-tailed. SE = standard errors.

created an index ranging from 12 (least supportive) to 24 (most supportive).[8] Comparing treatment to control, there is a statistically significant difference in support for transgender rights policies between the treatment group (mean = 21.198) and the control group (mean = 20.412) of 0.786 (SE = .42, p = .03). In sum, we find compelling evidence supporting H_3, that assignment to the treatment condition increased support for transgender rights.

Discussion and Conclusion

Simply acknowledging discomfort about transgender people is not an effective strategy for mitigating discomfort or prejudice. On the contrary, noting that discomfort is a common or understandable response only serves to increase reported discomfort. We conclude that participants in the first experiment described in this chapter saw the text in the treatment conditions as giving them permission to report how they truly felt and that it would be seen as normal or appropriate. Instead of being influenced by the experimental messages, attitudes were strongly predicted by political ideology.

On the other hand, sharing a mother's journey story to acceptance increased reported comfort with and acceptance of transgender people and rights. Participants in the Journey Story experiment were given permission to change their minds, even if they are "a little uncomfortable at first," the same message delivered by Zeke's coworker in the Freedom for All Americans advertisement shared in the beginning of this chapter. When people are provided a concrete example of someone changing their mind and actively confronting their discomfort, they are given permission to change their own mind and be more supportive of transgender rights.

There appears to be a fine line between acknowledging discomfort and normalizing discomfort. In the Journey Story experiment, respondents were exposed to a story about a specific mother who overcame her previous opposition to the identity she came to learn her daughter holds. In the earlier acknowledgment experiments, no such specificity for the thought evolution was given; instead, respondents were made to feel uncomfortable and even sympathetic but were not given a clear path to take toward more positive emotions and attitudes. Future work in acknowledgment will need to find the right balance between providing cover and granting permission to remain opposed to transgender rights because others are and providing a model scenario where someone tells a personal story about how they confronted their own discomfort. In other words, context and specificity (e.g., a journey story) appear to be the strongest communication strategy to encourage people to look past their own discomfort and opposition to transgender people and rights. Our findings support the widespread use of journey story narratives by advocacy campaigns, including videos used by the Movement Advancement Project and the Human Rights Campaign. Future experiments should explore the power of a personal journey story shared via interpersonal communications such as by transgender rights allies with their friends and neighbors.

In the next chapter, concluding the book, we review and discuss the findings from all of the experiments described in this book and the opportunities and challenges that lie ahead for those hoping to further transform public opinion about transgender people and rights.

7

Transforming Prejudice From the Inside Out

> When we speak, we are afraid our words will not be heard or welcomed. But when we are silent, we are still afraid. So it is better to speak.
>
> —Audre Lorde, "A Litany for Survival" (1978)

We started chapter 1 with lyrics to the song "A Little History Repeating" because when we began our inquiry into transgender attitudes and transgender history, some of what we read felt familiar. "These people are sick!" "We need to protect our kids!" In many ways, the angst, misunderstanding, fear, and rhetoric used against transgender people in contemporary American life echo what was used against gay men and lesbians throughout the 20th century and in many places, still today. As much as there is similarity between the fight for visibility and rights for transgender people and those in the past for other sexual minorities—as much as history is repeating—we quickly came to realize how much was different as well. Guided by lessons learned from the past as well as reflections on key differences in attitudes and behavior toward transgender people, we conducted the work described in this book to help accelerate the pace with which transgender people are recognized as full and equal members of our society.

In the experiments described in this book, we sought a better understanding of the causes of widespread discomfort and opposition to transgender people and rights and, ultimately, the best ways to convince others to be more respectful and supportive given the very real constraints of contemporary public opinion. Our most successful efforts gave people the space to evolve their opinions and to be their best selves while acknowledging that they might be engaging in attitudinal journeys or still feel some discomfort. We appealed to their better angels, to their sense of moral elevation, and to their commitments to honesty and justice. At the same time, we gave them

Transforming Prejudice. Melissa R. Michelson and Brian F. Harrison, Oxford University Press (2020) © Oxford University Press.
DOI: 10.1093/oso/9780190068882.001.0001

space to acknowledge lingering discomfort or past negative attitudes. We held their hands and gently nudged them toward more supportive attitudes without shaming them or criticizing their past or persistent prejudice.

In multiple instances, these strategies worked: our Theory of Identity Reassurance, supported by the multiple experiments in this book, points to a variety of fairly simple but powerful tools. The key is reassuring recipients of persuasive messages about their own identities and their own self-esteem so that their gut reactions to members of these marginalized communities are softened and their reactance is minimized. It's about making them feel better about themselves so that they can be more open to accepting others.

Our experiments were conducted in a variety of settings, including online surveys, in a university lab, and face-to-face on public sidewalks. Across different platforms, we found that reassuring recipients of persuasive messages that supporting transgender rights is not a threat to their gender identity but is a way for them to feel good about themselves can lead to meaningful change. Broockman and Kalla (2016) demonstrated that face-to-face conversations using the strategy of perspective taking (asking people to think about a time they themselves were discriminated against) could change attitudes about transgender rights. Similarly, we are nudging recipients of messages to take a different perspective, to look at the issue as being about themselves, about their self-esteem and pride in their identity, as a route to reducing reactance and opening minds to change.

In chapter 1, we described how the past, present, and future of transgender rights differ from those of rights for gay men and lesbians. We reviewed the science of persuasion and the barriers to persuasion on transgender rights, including the small size of the population and the limited and negative portrayal of most transgender characters on screen. We reviewed other predictors of attitudes toward transgender people including emotions and values and provided a road map to the various experiments presented in chapters 2-6.

In chapter 2, we described the known predictors of attitudes toward transgender people and how those attitudes vary based on context. To revisit the findings from our national survey, we found stronger support from women, more prejudice against transgender men compared to against transgender women, and stronger resistance to transgender people in positions of power or intimacy such as raising children or serving as elected officials. We also shared results from the Jack Reed experiment, testing the power of the Theory of Dissonant Identity Priming from our previous work and illustrating the need for a new method to change minds about transgender rights. We then introduced our new Theory of Identity Reassurance.

Chapter 3 examined the power of core values including equality, freedom, and integrity. In one experiment, we found that raising fears about the safety of women and girls in public restrooms was an effective way to reduce support for bathroom access rights—a strategy widely used by opponents of transgender public access rights—but it was not effective to use those same values to increase support. Another experiment, using elite cues and value frames about equality and integrity, showed inconsistent results and was intellectually unsatisfying. At the same time, those experimental data provided helpful feedback about the need to be attentive to the strength of masculine identities among male targets of persuasive messages and the need to disaggregate our research to explore the different ways public attitudes vary when the focus is on male and female subgroups of the transgender community.

In chapter 4, we explored the strategy of experimentally manipulating the salience of gender expression of recipients by either threatening their masculinity or femininity or bolstering it. In both of the experiments described in that chapter, our hypothesis was confirmed, adding further support to our Theory of Identity Reassurance: findings were particularly strong and consistent among male respondents, who were both less likely to support transgender rights when their masculinity was threatened and more likely to support transgender rights when their masculinity was reassured.

Chapter 5 detailed another way in which we tested our theory, using media designed to make people feel good, either just by making them happy or by evoking feelings of moral elevation. In one experiment, we either evoked fear by asking respondents to view photos of large spiders or evoked happiness by asking respondents to view photos of puppies. When participants reported feeling happier, they were more likely to support transgender rights. The second experiment in chapter 5, which used short videos to manipulate participant mood, was even more powerful and closely linked both to our theory and to the advocacy strategies of transgender rights organizations. Those viewing videos known to generate feelings of moral elevation were more likely to support transgender rights both compared to those watching a placebo video and compared to those watching videos merely meant to evoke feelings of amusement. When thinking about how good humans can be to each other and perhaps inspired by the stories of personal selflessness in these videos, our respondents were also led to be their best selves.

In chapter 6, mirroring strategies used by advocacy organizations, we explored the power of acknowledging the discomfort or prejudice that people feel when thinking about transgender people and rights. In one experiment, we found that different sorts of acknowledgment messages were insufficient on their own for moving people to be more supportive. Instead, these messages may have given respondents permission to express their existing discomfort. We also found that messengers presenting themselves as transgender men may be more effective than messengers presenting themselves as transgender women at nudging the public to support transgender bathroom rights. In our second experiment described in this chapter, we used as our treatment story the personal journey of the mother of a transgender girl; here, our message to respondents was that they too could change their attitudes even if, like the mother in the story, they have not always been supporters of transgender rights. This experiment was much more successful, again providing support for our Theory of Identity Reassurance.

The Transforming Prejudice Toolbox

In many ways, tackling the challenges ahead for transgender people and policy is similar to the history of gay and lesbian rights like marriage equality. As we have outlined throughout this book, however, to say that history is repeating is a bit of a misnomer: while similar in some ways, the past, present, and future of transgender advocacy differs quite a bit in some important ways as well.

One major difference is the lack of availability of arguably the most powerful tool in the gay rights advocacy toolbox: the power of interpersonal contact. When Harvey Milk called on gay men and lesbians to come out to their families and friends, he knew that many Americans knew and loved closeted gay and lesbian people. Calling on them to share their sexual orientations with their loved ones would allow them to use the power of those personal relationships to open minds to change. Multiple scholarly studies demonstrate clearly that this strategy worked (Rimmerman 2015; Ayoub 2016; Garretson 2018; Harrison and Michelson 2017a). For transgender people, however, this strategy is made more challenging due to their small numbers and the reality of possible harassment and assault. Only 0.6% of the U.S. population is estimated to be transgender and the decision to come out as transgender to others carries with it the very real threat of violence (Flores et al.

2016; Hoffarth and Hodson 2018). Three times as many American adults now tell pollsters that they know a gay or lesbian person compared to how many report that they personally know a transgender person (GLAAD 2015). The low levels of transgender contact reported today are similar to the levels of gay and lesbian contact Americans reported in the early 1990s; however, levels of transgender contact have not increased as much over time due to the much smaller size of the community. Nick Adams, GLAAD's Director of Transgender Representation, recently quipped: "more Americans think they've seen a ghost than think they've met a trans person" (Pride on Screen 2019).

The most recent GLAAD reports are that transgender representation in film in media is increasingly frequent and positive. The 2019 *Where We Are on TV* report documents a record high number of 26 regular and recurring transgender characters across the three tracked platforms (broadcast, cable, and streaming), including 17 transgender women, 5 transgender men, and 4 nonbinary characters (Where We Are on TV 2019). In contrast, the same report finds 407 lesbian, gay, and bisexual regular and recurring characters. While the numbers represent a record high on both counts, the absolute level of transgender character visibility is still quite low. This means that most people have never seen a transgender character. Adams notes: "Media representations for transgender people right now are still in a very pre-Ellen, pre-Will and Grace stage. We haven't had that one thing that breaks out, that really hits mainstream America in this way that wakes them up and makes them realize that we're just people" (Pride on Screen 2019). Instead, most Americans have seen transgender characters depicted as sex workers or violent killers, such as CeCe, the homicidal villain (and transgender girl) on 2015's *Pretty Little Liars*. While most Americans don't think they know a transgender person, "their heads are filled with this broken mental template about who trans people are, and it's been partially created by the last several decades of Hollywood telling really twisted, distorted, stereotypical cliché-ridden narratives about who trans people are" (Adams, Pride on Screen 2019).

Given the numbers and the reality of frequent violence against transgender people, there simply aren't enough closeted transgender people who can safely come out to their friends and family and transform attitudes in the same way that many in the gay and lesbian community did. While Hollywood's record is (slowly) improving, the rate of positive depictions of transgender characters on film and television is not reaching enough American viewers (particularly as programming becomes increasingly diverse and person-alized) for parasocial contact to remake the broken stereotypes held by Americans. While these are powerful, proven methods, interpersonal and mediated contact with transgender people is limited in how far it can take us toward acceptance and inclusion. The fight for transgender people and their rights requires allies—everyday Americans, like you—to use the persuasive methods described in this book to work for change.

Transforming prejudice against transgender people will be challenging for many reasons. But as Barack Obama told a conference of student leaders back in July 2006, far before his election to the presidency: "Making your mark on the world is hard. If it were easy, everybody would do it."[1] Allies have family members and friends that consider them trusted sources and this is a tool they can use to generate attitude change. Speaking about transgender rights to people you know is powerful because they are people you know, not strangers. They are more likely to listen to you given that they seek your ap-proval. That said, significant challenges remain.

First, there remains a serious amount of misinformation about and vis-ceral discomfort toward transgender people. As has been the case with gay men and lesbian women throughout history, many Americans are uncom-fortable with transgender people and rights. Negative depictions in film and media are partly responsible for these feelings. Recognizing the cause, how-ever, does not make overcoming that discomfort any easier, and as noted in chapter 6, simply recognizing the discomfort can legitimize it rather than diminish it. Conversations about transgender rights need to push beyond that discomfort, to shift people to focus on broader values of equality and freedom, and to cue a desire to be a good person, to exhibit moral virtue.

Second, transgender identity challenges deeply held beliefs about gender and the gender binary. Even as transgender visibility is increasing and more people come to learn that they have a transgender family member, friend or coworker, most of the aisles of toy and department stores are segregated into pink and blue, gender reveal parties are increasingly frequent and elaborate, and the national political conversation about the women who are running for (and winning) political office reminds Americans that politics is about politicians of two different genders. As we went to press, the country was focused on the victories of the U.S. women's national soccer team and on how team co-captain Megan Rapinoe, the "purple-haired lesbian goddess," was flattening France like a crêpe (Theisen 2019). Social media focused not just on the team's dominance at the 2019 World Cup but on the chasm in pay and prestige that separates the national men's and women's teams, a chasm based on a binary understanding of gender as the appropriate way to group competitive athletes. This attachment to and constant reinforcement of the gender binary can make acceptance of transgender and gender nonconforming people seem personally threatening. That gender is mutable, contrary to what many people have been taught since early childhood, can trigger an emotional and even existential response. It shakes the foundations of one's identity and that can be merely curious or deeply disturbing.

Third and relatedly, transgender identity has the potential to threaten men's sense of masculinity. As we have noted repeatedly, women tend to be more supportive of transgender people, and men who report their gender as essential to their identity are less likely to support transgender rights. Not all men feel this way. Some men are supporters of transgender people and hold no prejudice against them; they are allies and advocates. But some men are deeply threatened by transgender people and especially by transgender women, whom they may see as engaging in deception either to access spaces meant to be safe for women and girls such as public restrooms or to trick them into engaging in homosexual behavior. This manifests not just in strongly negative attitudes but often into violence. Transforming the prejudices of these men will be exceedingly difficult.

These challenges are significant but significant opportunities exist as well. Multiple studies have noted the relative fluidity of attitudes about transgender rights, reflecting the lack of information and exposure of most Americans and also the opportunity to generate attitudinal change (Broockman and Kalla 2016; Taylor et al. 2018). There is also an unusually high level of willingness of Americans to change their minds about transgender people and admit to doing so, a contrast to the usual tendency of survey respondents to portray themselves as firm and consistent in their beliefs. In an April 2019 PRRI poll, large majorities of Americans said that their views about transgender rights had changed over the last five years (usually in a positive direction). As shown in Figure 7.1, there is movement toward more support for transgender rights among Republicans, Democrats, moderates, liberals, and independents. The survey also found positive attitude change among evangelicals, White mainline Protestants, non-White Protestants, Catholics, and those unaffiliated with a church. In fact, every single group surveyed moved in a positive direction except for one: self-identified conservatives. This is encouraging evidence that attitudes are still settling and further change is possible.

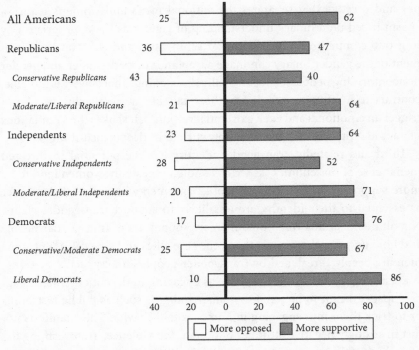

Figure 7.1. Self-reported change in support for transgender rights, by party and religious affiliation, PRRI April 2019 survey.

Note: Question wording: "Compared to your views five years ago, are your current views about rights for transgender people generally much more supportive, more supportive, more opposed, or much more opposed?" *Source*: Jones et al. (2019). Data collected April 9–20, 2019.

Why Change Is Needed: Issues Facing Transgender People

Transgender people have been fighting for equality for decades. Transgender women Marsha P. Johnson and Sylvia Rivera were leaders of the Stonewall Riots in 1969 that marked the symbolic launch of the modern gay rights movement. Yet, 50 years later, the ability of transgender people to live openly and without fear of discrimination or violence lags far behind that of gay men and lesbians.

Many issues are vitally important to the lives of transgender people, including employment and housing nondiscrimination, violence, the criminal justice system, health care, and access to other public spaces. At times, specific issues jump to the forefront, such as the 2016–2017 national conversation about transgender bathroom access rights and the 2017–2019 conversation about transgender troops serving openly in the U.S. military. But the issues that have garnered presidential attention and made headlines are not necessarily the priorities of the transgender community. Other challenges are more constant and more central to the day-to-day lives of transgender people, affecting their ability to live openly and without fear of being treated unfairly, verbally or physically attacked, or even killed. These issues are particularly pressing for transgender people of color. In 2015 the National Center for Transgender Equality (NCTE), along with scholars, methodologists, and other LGBT organizations, published the U.S. Transgender Survey Report (USTS), a study of 27,715 transgender people in the United States (James et al. 2016). USTS respondents reported alarmingly high levels of mistreatment, harassment, and violence; severe economic hardship and instability; and negative impacts on their physical and mental health. The executive summary of the USTS notes:

> Respondents reported high levels of mistreatment, harassment, and violence in every aspect of life. One in ten (10%) of those who were out to their immediate family reported that a family member was violent towards them because they were transgender, and 8% were kicked out of the house because they were transgender. (p. 4)

The alarmingly high rate at which transgender people are of violent assault, including murder, is vastly under-covered by the mainstream media. Rates of violence are especially high for transgender women and particularly against Black transgender women. Dozens of transgender people are murdered every year and thousands more are the victims of violent physical attacks (Human Rights Campaign Foundation 2018; James et al. 2016). In 2019, at least 25 transgender women were murdered, almost all of whom were Black. In 2018, 26 transgender women were murdered and most of those victims were also Black. These statistics likely underestimate the true extent of this violence due to under-reporting and misgendering of victims.

In the year prior to completing the USTS survey, 46% of respondents were verbally harassed and 9% were physically attacked because of being transgender. During that same time period, 10% of respondents were sexually assaulted and nearly half (47%) reported being sexually assaulted at some point in their lifetime. Among the respondents who had a job, 30% of respondents reported that in the past year they had been fired, denied a promotion, or experienced some other form of mistreatment in the workplace due to their gender identity or expression such as being verbally harassed or physically or sexually assaulted at work.

The 2015 USTS survey also noted persistent challenges facing gender nonconforming young children. The majority of respondents who were out or perceived as transgender while in elementary school (K–12) experienced some form of mistreatment, including being verbally harassed (54%), physically attacked (24%), and sexually assaulted (13%) because they were transgender. Further, 17% experienced such severe mistreatment that they left a school as a result.

Transgender prisoner rights are also a pressing concern, particularly given the threat to the safety of transgender people who are incarcerated. As noted earlier, nearly 9% of all transgender people reported in 2015 that they had been physically attacked in the previous year because of their gender identity; among incarcerated transgender people (including individuals held in jails, prisons, and juvenile detention centers), that figure jumps to nearly 30% (James et al., 2016). A case that made headlines in June 2018 noted the inconsistent policies in place in Philadelphia: while police are required to use a suspect's preferred name and pronouns, suspects are held in facilities that correspond to their government-issued identification unless they have had gender confirmation surgery. In the case in question, transgender activist ReeAnna Segin was placed in a men's prison, prompting concerns about her safety (Boren 2018).

The policies of the Philadelphia police department are not unique, according to the NCTE; they are endemic to many U.S. police departments (Young and McMahon 2019). In a sign of recognition of the problem, the Department of Justice released a video for law enforcement on July 20, 2016 on how police officers could engage with transgender people in ways that are respectful and professional. The opening vignette in the video depicts an interaction between an officer and a transgender woman pulled over for having a broken taillight. After confirming that her driver's license is her most recent form of identification, the officer asks if she would prefer to be addressed as ma'am or sir but otherwise the conversation is no different than what one would expect. The screen then cuts to Sergeant Brett Parson at the Department of Justice Community Relations Service (CRS), who comments:

Hey, I don't have to be in the room with you to know what probably just happened. Somebody just snickered, laughed, or made a joke. Trust me,

I know; I'm a cop too. As police officers, we use humor to deal with things that make us uncomfortable or afraid. We're human, and we know we mean no harm. It's our way of coping. But we have to admit it: to outsiders, it's perceived as unprofessional and disrespectful. Remember, you never get a second chance to make a first impression. If someone feels disrespected, they're less likely to trust us or cooperate. (CRS 2016a)

Parson goes on to give more information about relevant terminology such as the difference between sexual orientation and gender identity, the difference between transgender men and women (although all of the transgender people featured in the video are women), and to talk viewers through two more vignettes, one that dramatizes a police interview of a victim of assault and one about a report of a man in the women's restroom at a restaurant.

Another video released by CRS in November 2016 details a training conducted in Jackson, Mississippi to improve police officers' perceptions and behavior regarding the transgender community (CRS 2016b). CRS annual reports from 2017 and 2018 confirm that the videos are still being used and the office is facilitating *Law Enforcement and Transgender Community* trainings when requested by local law enforcement offices.

These videos are notable in how closely they hew to the argument we are making with Identity Reassurance Theory. Those watching are asked to remember that they are professionals whose primary concern is public safety. They are reassured that their initial discomfort and perhaps derisiveness is normal, even if the public might not understand. They are reminded that treating transgender people respectfully will help them to do their jobs. In the second vignette in the July 2016 CRS video, one police officer misgenders the transgender woman who has called to report being assaulted. His colleague pulls him aside and reminds him to be respectful. They return to the victim and he apologizes and asks if she would prefer to be addressed as ma'am or sir. It is a journey story, much like the journey story experiment we shared in chapter 6. Even if you are initially uncomfortable, you can change. You can be the morally virtuous law enforcement officer you aspire to be.

The widespread discrimination, abuse, and violence toward transgender individuals and rights underscore the urgent need for shifts in both public policy and public opinion. In addition to the frequent overall mistreatment identified in the USTS, there are intersectional patterns as well. USTS respondents of color reported deeper and broader patterns of discrimination than White respondents and as noted earlier transgender women of color are victims of homicide with alarming frequency. How do we push back against this discrimination, hate, and violence against transgender people? Or, to put it another way, "How do bodies that do not matter become bodies that matter?" (Boyd 2006: 136).

Expanding the Field

Our work here focused on transgender men and women merely scratches the surface of the many ways in which gender is currently understood. Some transgender people understand gender in a binary but mutable way, allowing for transitions between one gender and the other; other people reject this binary notion of transness completely (Tompkins 2014). People who identify as nonbinary, genderqueer, or genderfluid, to name just a few additional identities, are also part of the gender spectrum and are also stigmatized and discriminated against. Monro (2005: 14) argues for a pluralist model of gender that rejects the social construction that there are only male and female people and that "everything else must be temporary or abnormal." Some transgender people understand the process of transition as bringing their gender expression into alignment with their inner selves, as either male or female, but increasingly people identify as nonbinary or gender fluid, especially younger members of the transgender community (Monro 2019).

Expanding society's definition of gender will require further examination of ongoing debates over transgender rights issues. For example, as Wilchins, Riki Anne (1997) notes, arguing that transgender people should have the right to access existing male and female-only bathrooms of their preferred identity may unintentionally serve to cement the gender binary. True gender diversity includes people with fluid, multiple, and other gender identities. Scholars and advocates interested in equality for all must continue to expand the boundaries of their research agendas to include work on how to reduce prejudice against those who identify at any and all points along the gender continuum.

Scholarship is also fairly limited when it comes to how best to reduce prejudice against those at the intersection of different forms of marginalization, including race and ethnicity, socioeconomic class, and ability. The epidemic of violence against Black transgender women is increasingly on the public's radar but as Meier and Labuski (2013: 320) note: "transgender people face ubiquitous—and often more insidious—forms of structural violence every day," including access to housing bank loans, promotions, health care, college, adoption services, or the social safety net. On July 2, 2019, the executive director of the Center for Transgender Medicine and Surgery in New York, Joshua Safer, released a coauthored piece in the *Annals of Internal Medicine* describing new medical guidelines for treating transgender patients in primary care settings. The abstract notes: "Barriers to accessing appropriate and culturally competent care contribute to health disparities in transgender persons, such as increased rates of certain types of cancer, substance abuse, mental health conditions, infections, and chronic diseases" (Safer and Tangpricha 2019).

Hate crime statistics from the FBI, incomplete because they are based on self-reported data from local law enforcement agencies, nevertheless show that violence against transgender people has risen consistently over the past five years (Allen 2019). The source of this increased violence is unclear but what is clear is that the message from the top—the White House—is that transgender people do not deserve equality. On May 24, 2019, the Health and Human Services Office for Civil Rights proposed a new rule that would have allowed health care providers to decline to offer services that conflict with their religious beliefs, including caring for transgender patients. Earlier that same week, Trump's Department of Housing and Urban Development proposed a rule change to allow homeless shelters to turn people away based on their gender identity (Huetteman 2019). Trump's rhetoric, in addition to these and other actions like the ban on transgender troops, has contributed to a national environment more hostile to LGBT people. He has rolled back protections for transgender students in public schools, reversed a federal policy protecting transgender people from job discrimination, rolled back accommodation of transgender inmates in federal prisons, and refused to investigate claims of anti-transgender discrimination in public schools (Holden 2018).

In their 2018 book *The Remarkable Rise of Transgender Rights*, Jami Taylor and her coauthors document the remarkable victories of the transgender rights movement at both the local and national levels, including public policies and legal victories, all achieved despite the very small size and limited visibility of the transgender community. Yet, they also note the backlash and danger embodied by the Trump administration, including the remaking of the federal judiciary, which might limit further advances or even lead to reversals of previous legal victories. Unfortunately, these cautionary notes have proven true. Trump has taken executive actions and appointed judges hostile to transgender rights (and LGBT rights more generally). Positive change moving forward requires stronger public support and visibility of the need to protect transgender people and their rights. Shifting public attitudes, even just one conversation at a time, can lead to meaningful change at the national level. We hope that individuals and organizations interested in advocating for transgender equality will use the methods and messages explored in this book to continue to transform prejudice.

Although the gay rights movement launched at Stonewall in 1969 included transgender activists and leaders, battles over public opinion and policy have consistently focused on gay and lesbian rights, with bisexual people generally invisible and transgender people either deliberately excluded or forgotten. As Taylor et al. (2018) note, many of the legislative protections for gender identity have been quietly slipped into bills focused on gay and lesbian rights while in other instances, those protections for transgender people have been removed to win votes, as with the Employment Non-Discrimination Act (ENDA) of 2007. An earlier version of the bill died in committee, leading Massachusetts Democrat Barney Frank to introduce a new version that removed gender protections, focusing only on sexual orientation. That bill was endorsed by the Human Rights Campaign—the largest LGBT advocacy group in the country—and was evidence of debate among activists about whether it was better to move forward on gay and lesbian rights if that was all that was possible or if it was important to include transgender rights as well, even if that meant progress was delayed or uncertain. In the end, even the less inclusive ENDA bill of 2007 did not pass. The episode is an important reminder of the need for gay and lesbian allies to continue to fight for gender identity protections alongside sexual orientation protections. Unity is strength. Stronger together. United we stand. Pick your favorite slogan but the underlying theme is clear: gay and lesbian allies as well as allies from outside the LGBT community need to work together to continue to transform prejudice and advance transgender rights.

In May 2019, the House of Representatives passed the Equality Act, adding protections for LGBT people from discrimination in employment, housing, credit, public places and services, federally funded programs, and jury service. While unlikely to pass in the Republican-controlled Senate, this was an important victory in that it is the first time that an ENDA bill has made it to a floor vote in either chamber of Congress despite repeated efforts dating back to 1974. The marriage equality victory of 2015 did not eliminate for many Americans (those lacking state or local protections) the real threat of being married on Sunday and fired on Monday. Gay men and lesbians are still not recognized as full U.S. citizens (Engel 2016). The fight for public opinion and public policy change remains and victory is more certain if the LGBT community and their allies continue to stand united, to talk about equality with their friends and family, and to take issues of LGBT rights into consideration when making their political decisions, including how they cast their votes for elected office.

Transgender advocacy groups have produced and distributed videos that encourage viewers to treat transgender people with respect. The Movement Advancement Project video we described in chapter 6 is the most well known because it aired during the 2016 Super Bowl. The ad dramatizes two cisgender women standing up to support a transgender woman's right to use the women's restroom at a restaurant. A video released by the NCTE in July 2016 shares stories and statements from transgender people and their families and notes, "Support is critical. Don't worry about being perfect, it's still important to try" (NCTE 2016b). The video ends with suggestions for how to give that support, including just listening, letting transgender people be themselves, and pushing back when people make jokes or offensive comments at the expense of transgender people.

Those are all good ways to be supportive. Here are a few more based on our Identity Reassurance Theory and the results of our experiments:

1. Don't be afraid to start the conversation. Transforming prejudice sooner rather than later means making it a social priority and making it the topic of frequent discussion. It's okay to not know the perfect thing to say; what matters more is showing that the issue is important enough for you to want to talk about it.
2. Acknowledge potential discomfort but don't leave it there. Encourage others to push past that discomfort and be their best selves.
3. Share your own journey story or that of others to provide a model of how one can move from opposition to support.
4. Emphasize the feeling of moral elevation that comes from being on the right side of history and of doing the right thing even when it is difficult.

As is the case for many outgroups, changing attitudes and reducing bias is difficult but not impossible. The only way that change is impossible is if we don't try. A recent piece by Tessa Charlesworth and Mahzarin Banaji (2019) examined changing implicit and explicit attitudes toward multiple groups, including sexual minorities, between 2007 and 2016. During that time period, they found considerable decreases in prejudice against gay men and lesbians. These changes in prejudice were at a rate even faster than changes in prejudice toward members of other stigmatized groups (based on race, skin tone, age, disability, and body weight). The authors partially attribute these rapid changes to the issue's higher social priority and rate of discussion. In other words, because gay rights were a major topic of conversation between 2007 and 2016, including the battle for marriage equality, minds changed faster. As we noted in our 2017 book *Listen, We Need to Talk*, following the conventional wisdom of avoiding controversial topics (religion and politics) may please Miss Manners but it also will preserve existing biases.

This is where allies come in. We are both cisgender but we have been working for years on strategies and messages that can help move the public to be more supportive of transgender people and transgender rights because we want to live in a society where everyone is treated with equal dignity and respect. We want our transgender friends, coworkers, and neighbors to feel as safe and included in our communities as we do. We want the hate, the violence, and the murders to stop. The journey of 1,000 miles begins with one step. The transformation of prejudice begins with a single conversation.

In today's hyperpartisan and ideological political environment, persuading others to rethink their current position on any political issue is exceedingly difficult, let alone asking people to rethink their biases and prejudices. Opening minds to persuasion toward transgender people and rights requires a rhetorical flanking maneuver in one of two ways: (1) making an indirect appeal and evading direct attack on existing attitudes (since that will likely evoke reactance) or (2) generating reduced barriers and thus an increased willingness to receive and process persuasive messages. To generate change, transforming prejudice requires open and perhaps uncomfortable conversations. We urge allies of transgender and gender nonconforming people and other marginalized and stigmatized groups to channel their inner equality and justice superhero and do the right thing.

APPENDIX

Table A2.1. Attitudes Toward Transgender People and Support for Gender Equality, 2016 American National Election Study

	Discrimination Against Transgender People (SE)	Bathroom Access (SE)
Gender	−.22*	.26*
	(.07)	(.07)
Equal pay	.10*	−.22*
	(.03)	(.03)
Woman stay home	.20*	−1.00*
	(.07)	(.07)
Constant	1.81*	3.9*
	(.08)	(.07)

Note: $N = 3{,}430$. Data is weighted to be nationally representative. Discrimination is coded 1 = *a great deal* to 5 = *none at all*. Bathroom access is coded 1= *feel very strongly that transgender people should use the bathroom of the gender they were born with* to 6 = *feel very strongly that transgender people should be able to use the bathroom of their identified gender*. * = statistically significant at $p \le .01$. SE = standard errors.

Table A2.2. Comfort With LGBT People, by Situation, 2019 Gender Attitudes Survey

	% Very Comfortable	% Somewhat Comfortable	% Comfortable (Sum)
As part of your family			
Heterosexual people	89.3	7.0	96.2
Gay men	66.6	16.9	83.5
Lesbians	67.1	15.6	82.7
Bisexual men	63.0	17.2	80.2
Bisexual women	66.6	16.5	83.1
Transgender men	51.5	14.1	65.7
Transgender women	51.0	17.0	68.1
People with nonbinary gender	62.3	15.1	77.4
As one of your friends			
Heterosexual people	90.7	6.3	97.0
Gay men	70.6	18.1	88.7
Lesbians	71.5	16.3	87.8
Bisexual men	66.6	17.6	84.2
Bisexual women	70.5	15.9	86.4
Transgender men	52.4	17.3	69.6
Transgender women	53.5	16.9	70.4
People with nonbinary gender	63.0	14.4	77.4
As one of your work colleagues			
Heterosexual people	89.8	6.7	96.5
Gay men	72.3	18.2	90.5
Lesbians	71.4	17.1	88.5
Bisexual men	65.5	20.0	85.5
Bisexual women	70.6	18.0	88.7
Transgender men	53.1	17.6	70.7
Transgender women	53.3	19.0	72.3
People with nonbinary gender	65.1	12.7	77.7
As someone you play sports with			
Heterosexual people	88.6	7.7	96.3
Gay men	66.8	18.9	85.6
Lesbians	69.1	17.4	86.5
Bisexual men	64.5	17.5	82.0

Table A2.2. *Continued*

	% Very Comfortable	% Somewhat Comfortable	% Comfortable (Sum)
Bisexual women	67.8	17.3	85.1
Transgender men	49.7	17.7	67.4
Transgender women	49.8	17.5	67.3
People with nonbinary gender	63.4	14.4	77.7
Becoming parents			
Heterosexual people	88.8	6.4	95.3
Gay men	56.2	17.8	74.0
Lesbians	58.3	17.5	75.8
Bisexual men	55.2	19.2	74.3
Bisexual women	60.4	16.7	77.1
Transgender men	44.2	16.1	60.3
Transgender women	45.8	16.3	62.1
People with nonbinary gender	57.5	14.4	71.9
As your doctor			
Heterosexual people	88.0	7.5	95.5
Gay men	60.1	17.9	78.0
Lesbians	62.5	17.4	79.9
Bisexual men	56.1	20.7	76.8
Bisexual women	62.1	18.4	80.5
Transgender men	41.6	16.3	57.9
Transgender women	44.6	16.8	61.4
People with nonbinary gender	58.9	13.7	72.6
As your representative in Congress			
Heterosexual people	87.4	8.3	95.6
Gay men	62.6	20.0	82.7
Lesbians	64.2	17.2	81.4
Bisexual men	59.5	19.0	78.5
Bisexual women	63.3	17.6	80.9
Transgender men	46.2	16.5	62.6
Transgender women	47.0	17.3	64.3

Continued

Table A2.2. *Continued*

	% Very Comfortable	% Somewhat Comfortable	% Comfortable (Sum)
People with nonbinary gender	59.3	13.4	72.6
As the star of your favorite sports team			
Heterosexual people	87.9	8.4	96.3
Gay men	67.9	18.6	86.5
Lesbians	68.5	17.0	85.6
Bisexual men	65.5	18.7	84.2
Bisexual women	68.5	17.3	85.8
Transgender men	49.7	16.9	66.6
Transgender women	49.0	18.5	67.5
People with nonbinary gender	62.3	14.4	76.7
As president of the United States			
Heterosexual people	86.3	8.1	94.5
Gay men	56.7	19.0	75.7
Lesbians	59.1	17.2	76.3
Bisexual men	56.0	17.7	73.7
Bisexual women	59.2	16.9	76.1
Transgender men	42.0	16.1	58.1
Transgender women	42.5	15.3	57.8
People with nonbinary gender	56.9	15.4	72.3

Note: Comfort items were only asked of respondents who said they definitely knew what each term meant. This generates samples of $N = 1,353$ for questions about heterosexuals, 1,183 for gay men, 1,192 for lesbians, 1,175 for bisexuals, 995 for transgender people, and 292 for nonbinary gender people. Data collected February 8–March 5, 2019. See Script Appendix for full survey wording.

Table A3.1. Support for Transgender Troops, Mullen Versus Keisling Conditions, 2018 Values Framing Experiment

	Support for Transgender Troops (SE)	Signed Petition (SE)
Mullen condition	.052	.072
	(.20)	(.17)
Age	−.162*	−.063
	(.05)	(.05)
Age squared	.002*	.0005
	(.001)	(.001)
Gender	−.004	.253
	(.21)	(.18)
Income	.043	−.020
	(.04)	(.04)
Education	.041	−.086
	(.08)	(.06)
Ideology	−.769*	−.346*
	(.15)	(.12)
Party identification	−.198*	−.076
	(.07)	(.06)
Anglo (White non-Latinx)	−.101	.514*
	(.24)	(.22)
Transgender friends	.449[+]	.611[+]
	(.27)	(.20)
Admire integrity	.263*	−.083
	(.12)	(.13)
Admire equality	.259*	.477*
	(.10)	(.13)
Constant	2.541*	−1.124
	(1.29)	(1.24)

Note: $N = 805$. Data collected May 11–12, 2018. Logistic regression models. Gender is coded as 1 = *female*, 2 = *male*; income is coded from 1 = *less than $20,000/year* to 9 = *more than $90,000/year*; education is coded from 1 = *less than high school* to 8 = *graduate degree*; ideology is coded from 1 = *very liberal* to 5 = *very conservative*; party identification is coded from 1 = *strong Democrat* to 7 = *strong Republican*. Analysis excludes transgender and gender nonconforming respondents ($n = 7$). * = statistically significant at $p \leq .05$, [+] = $p < .10$ one-tailed. SE = standard errors.

Table A3.2. Petition Signers for Transgender Troops, Dissonant Versus Stereotypical Conditions, 2018 Values Framing Experiment

	Admiral Mike Mullen Conditions (SE)	Mara Keisling Conditions (SE)
Dissonant condition	.256*	−.111
	(.12)	(.13)
Age	−.035	−.097
	(.06)	(.07)
Age squared	.0003	.0009
	(.001)	(.001)
Gender	.191	.403
	(.24)	(.27)
Income	.004	−.030
	(.05)	(.05)
Education	−.060	−.184[+]
	(.09)	(.10)
Ideology	−.206	−.494*
	(.17)	(.18)
Party identification	−.118	−.039
	(.09)	(.09)
Anglo (White non-Latinx)	.761*	.209
	(.30)	(.32)
Transgender friends	.721*	.642*
	(.28)	(.31)
Admire integrity	−.023	−.208
	(.18)	(.20)
Admire equality	.291[+]	.739*
	(.18)	(.21)
Constant	−2.007	−.022
	(1.77)	(1.93)

Note: N = 405 (Mullen); N = 400 (Keisling). Data collected May 11–12, 2018. Logistic regression models. Gender is coded as 1 = *female*, 2 = *male*; income is coded from 1 = *less than $20,000/year* to 9 = *more than $90,000/year*; education is coded from 1 = *less than high school* to 8 = *graduate degree*; ideology is coded from 1 = *very liberal* to 5 = *very conservative*; party identification is coded from 1 = *strong Democrat* to 7 = *strong Republican*. Analysis excludes transgender and gender nonconforming respondents (n = 7). * = statistically significant at $p \leq .05$ + = $p < .10$, one-tailed. SE = standard errors.

Table A4.1. Transphobia and Transgender Rights Attitudes, by Treatment Condition, Gender Identity Bolstering Experiment

	Control	Treatment	Difference (SE)
All respondents (N = 990)			
Neighbor	3.30	3.33	.04 (.06)
Culture	3.05	3.13	.07 (.07)
Businesses refuse	3.30	3.32	.02 (.06)
Change sex	3.00	3.00	.01 (.07)
Need help	1.87	1.89	.02 (.07)
Health insurance	2.75	2.77	.02 (.07)
Pass laws	3.18	3.13	−.05 (.06)
Women (N = 521)			
Neighbor	3.47	3.47	.01 (.07)
Culture	3.18	3.22	.04 (.09)
Businesses refuse	3.47	3.43	.03 (.08)
Change sex	3.13	3.08	.05 (.10)
Need help	1.70	1.77	.07 (.08)
Health insurance	2.87	2.86	.01 (.09)
Pass laws	3.34	3.21	.13 (.08)
Men (N = 469)			
Neighbor	3.11	3.18	.07 (.09)
Culture	2.92	3.02	.11 (.10)
Businesses refuse	3.11	3.20	.09 (.10)
Change sex	2.86	2.90	.04 (.10)
Need help	2.06	2.02	.04 (.10)
Health insurance	2.62	2.67	.05 (.10)
Pass laws	3.00	3.04	.04 (.10)

Note: Data collected August 3, 2018. Items are coded from 1 = *least supportive* to 4 = *most supportive* of transgender people or rights. See Script Appendix for wording of dependent variables. None of the differences examined here are statistically significant. SE = standard errors.

Table A5.1. Effect of Viewing Moral Elevation Video on Transphobia and Transgender Rights, Moral Elevation Experiment

	Transphobia Index (SE)	Transgender Rights Index (SE)	Ballot Measure (SE)	Petition (SE)
Moral elevation video	.390*	.246	.212*	.071
	(.19)	(.39)	(.09)	(.14)
Female	.753**	1.47**	.110	.188
	(.19)	(.40)	(.09)	(.14)
Democratic partisanship	.184**	.731**	.120**	.146**
	(.05)	(.11)	(.02)	(.04)
Know transgender	.265	.841	.290**	.366*
	(.23)	(.48)	(.11)	(.16)
Liberal ideology	1.225**	2.649**	.508**	.245**
	(.11)	(.22)	(.05)	(.08)
Constant	7.338**	17.708**	.646**	−2.520**
	(.39)	(.80)	(.17)	(.29)

Note: $N = 1,013$. Data collected May 29–June 16, 2019. ** = statistically significant at $p \leq .01$, * = at $p \leq .05$, two-tailed. SE = standard errors.

Table A6.1. Support for Transgender People and Rights, Acknowledgment Experiment

	Neighbor (SE)	ENDA (SE)	Religious Exemption (SE)	Health Care (SE)	Bathroom Access (SE)
Treatment (acknowledgment)	.037 (.17)	.002 (.16)	.129 (.16)	−.116 (.15)	.262 (.21)
Female	.499* (.14)	.255+ (.14)	−.147 (.13)	.103 (.12)	.416* (.17)
Age	.005 (.006)	.004 (.006)	.002 (.01)	.003 (.01)	.009 (.01)
Education	−.029 (.05)	.062 (.05)	.015 (.05)	.057 (.04)	.067 (.06)
Income	.028* (.01)	.024+ (.01)	−.020+ (.01)	.004 (.01)	.020 (.02)
Partisanship	.063 (.05)	.046 (.05)	−.020 (.05)	.025 (.05)	−.003 (.07)
Ideology	−.465* (.07)	−.648* (.06)	.676* (.06)	−.625* (.06)	−.878* (.09)
Anglo (White non-Latinx)	.067 (.17)	.292 (.16)	−.040 (.15)	−.071 (.14)	.069 (.21)
Straight	−.729* (.25)	−.928* (.34)	−.134 (.25)	−.434+ (.24)	−.735+ (.42)
Know transgender	.558* (.15)	.369* (.15)	−.302 (.14)	.357* (.13)	.406* (.19)
Constant	—	—	—	—	3.745* (.79)

Note: N = 948. Data collected September 17, 2017. * = statistically significant at $p < .05$; + = $p < .10$, one-tailed. Ordered Logit model cut-point estimates not shown. Models for Neighbor, ENDA, Religious Exemption, and Health Care are Ordered Logit models, reflecting the ordered nature of the dependent variables (5-point Likert scales). Model for Bathroom Access is a Logit model, reflecting the dichotomous nature of the dependent variable. Partisanship is coded from 1 = *strong Republican* to 7 = *strong Democrat*. Ideology is coded from 1 = *extremely liberal* to 7 = *extremely conservative*. Income is an ordinal variable with 21 categories ranging from 1 = *less than $10,000* to 21 = *more than $150,000*. Education is coded from 1 = *some grade school* to 7 = *graduate degree*. SE = standard errors.

Table A6.2. Support for Transgender People and Rights, by Gender of Messenger, Acknowledgment Experiment

	Neighbor (SE)		ENDA (SE)		Religious Exemption (SE)		Health Care (SE)		Bathroom Access (SE)	
	Kathy	Karl	Kathy	Karl	Kathy	Karl	Kathy	Karl	Kathy	Karl
Treatment	−.061 (.23)	.195 (.24)	.244 (.22)	−.278 (.25)	.326 (.23)	−.026 (.23)	−.062 (.21)	−.121 (.22)	−.035 (.29)	.646* (.32)
Female	.575* (.20)	.384* (.20)	.165 (.19)	.342+ (.20)	−.076 (.18)	−.164 (.19)	.077 (.17)	.053 (.18)	.199 (.24)	.560* (.26)
Age	−.010 (.01)	.201* (.01)	−.003 (.01)	.013 (.01)	.013+ (.01)	−.011 (.01)	−.001 (.01)	.005 (.01)	.004 (.01)	.015 (.01)
Education	.029 (.07)	−.095 (.07)	.115+ (.07)	.010 (.07)	−.007 (.07)	.032 (.07)	.027 (.06)	.080 (.07)	.147+ (.09)	−.033 (.10)
Income	.032+ (.02)	.024 (.02)	.016 (.02)	.039* (.02)	−.006 (.02)	−.038* (.02)	.007 (.02)	−.005 (.02)	.003 (.02)	.037 (.03)
Partisanship	−.016 (.08)	.144+ (.08)	.002 (.07)	.076 (.07)	.071 (.07)	−.097 (.07)	−.120+ (.07)	.181* (.07)	−.070 (.09)	.067 (.09)
Ideology	−.544* (.10)	−.408* (.25)	−.729* (.09)	−.595* (.09)	.814* (.09)	.579* (.09)	−.730* (.20)	−.541* (.08)	−.910* (.13)	−.879* (.13)
Anglo (White non-Latinx)	.206 (.23)	−.044 (.25)	.346 (.22)	.176 (.24)	−.285 (.21)	.280 (.24)	−.343+ (.20)	.281 (.21)	.060 (.28)	.142 (.31)
Straight	−.194 (.39)	−1.133* (.34)	−.429 (.48)	−1.281* (.48)	−.660+ (.36)	.334 (.37)	.016 (.35)	−.910* (.33)	−.309 (.58)	−1.186+ (.64)
Know transgender	−.525* (.21)	−.592* (.22)	−.270 (.21)	−.461* (.22)	.314 (.21)	.321 (.20)	−.398* (.19)	−.327+ (.19)	−.385 (.27)	−.414 (.28)
Constant	—	—	—	—	—	—	—	—	4.140* (1.15)	3.442* (1.10)

Note: Kathy $N = 472$; Karl $N = 476$. Data collected September 17, 2017. * = statistically significant at $p < .05$; + = $p < .10$, one-tailed. Ordered Logit model cut-point estimates not shown. Models for Neighbor, ENDA, Religious Exemption, and Health Care are Ordered Logit models, reflecting the ordered nature of the dependent variables (5-point Likert scales). Model for Bathroom Access is a Logit model, reflecting the dichotomous nature of the dependent variable. Partisanship is coded from 1 = *strong Republican* to 7 = *strong Democrat*. Ideology is coded from 1 = *extremely liberal* to 7 = *extremely conservative*. Income is an ordinal variable with 21 categories ranging from 1 = *less than $10,000* to 21 = *more than $150,000*. Education is coded from 1 = *some grade school* to 7 = *graduate degree*. SE = standard errors.

Script Appendix

Note: All online survey experiments and the laboratory experiment began by obtaining informed consent. The two face-to-face surveys were granted exemption. Unless otherwise indicated, the questions included here were embedded within a larger survey, sometimes beginning with a distractor and some demographic questions and ending with manipulation checks and additional demographic questions. Participants were debriefed at the conclusion of experiments that included deception.

List of Scripts

1. Chapter 1: 2019 Gender Identity Attitudes Survey
2. Chapter 1: The Jack Reed Experiment (full scripts included)
3. Chapter 3: The Freedom and Safety Frames Experiment
4. Chapter 3: The Equality and Integrity (Mullen and Keisling) Experiment
5. Chapter 4: The Gender Identity Threat Experiment
6. Chapter 4: The Gender Identity Bolstering Experiment
7. Chapter 5: The Puppies and Spiders Experiment
8. Chapter 5: The Moral Elevation Experiment
9. Chapter 6: The Acknowledgment Experiment
10. Chapter 6: The Journey Story Experiment (full scripts included)

1. Chapter 1: 2019 Gender Identity Attitudes Survey

On the next few pages, we're going to ask you some questions about gender and sexuality.

We'd like to know your honest thoughts and feelings about these topics. Remember your answers are 100% confidential.

Please take your time and tell us what you really think. Your responses are very important to us!

Do you know the meaning of each of the following terms?
Heterosexual
Gay man
Lesbian
Bisexual
Cisgender
Transgender
Non-binary gender
[Possible responses for each gender identity: Yes, definitely; I think so; No, not at all; Don't know]

How comfortable would you be with [**heterosexual people**] in each of the following situations?
[Question repeated for other gender identities: **gay men, bisexual men, lesbians, bisexual women, transgender men, transgender women, people with non-binary gender**]
As part of your family
As one of your friends
As one of your work colleagues
As one of the people you play sports with
Becoming parents
As your doctor
As your representative in Congress
As the star of your favorite sports team
As the President of the United States
[Possible responses for each situation: Very comfortable; Somewhat comfortable; Somewhat uncomfortable; Very uncomfortable]

2. The Jack Reed Experiment

[RANDOMIZATION PLACES RESPONDENTS INTO EITHER THE REPUBLICAN, DEMOCRATIC, OR VETERAN CONDITIONS]

CONDITIONS 1 AND 2: REPUBLICAN & DEMOCRAT

1. Generally speaking, do you consider yourself to be a Republican, a Democrat, or something else? [Republican; Democrat; Independent; Something else]

[RANDOMIZATION AFFECTS QUESTION 2: REED IS EITHER (FALSELY) IDENTIFIED AS A REPUBLICAN OR AS A DEMOCRAT]

2. [**Republican/Democratic**] U.S. Senator Jack Reed recently cosponsored legislation in favor of transgender Americans serving in the U.S. Armed Forces. He also tweeted about the bill.

What about you? Do you support or oppose transgender Americans serving openly in the U.S. Armed Forces? [Strongly support; somewhat support; somewhat oppose; strongly oppose]

Please tell us how much you agree or disagree with each statement below.

3. I would not mind if my neighbor was transgender. [Agree; Somewhat agree; Somewhat disagree; Disagree]

4. Transgender people violate the traditions of American culture. [Agree; Somewhat agree; Somewhat disagree; Disagree]

5. Congress should pass laws to protect transgender people from discrimination in public places like housing, restaurants, and other public places. [Agree; Somewhat agree; Somewhat disagree; Disagree]

6. Congress should pass laws to protect transgender people from job discrimination. [Agree; Somewhat agree; Somewhat disagree; Disagree]

7. Businesses should be able to refuse services to transgender people. [Agree; Somewhat agree; Somewhat disagree; Disagree]

8. The idea of someone changing their sex disgusts me. [Agree; Somewhat agree; Somewhat disagree; Disagree]

9. Transgender people should be able to change the sex listed on their driver's license or state ID card. [Agree; Somewhat agree; Somewhat disagree; Disagree]

10. Transgender people should have to use the public restroom that corresponds to their gender as assigned at birth. [Agree; Somewhat agree; Somewhat disagree; Disagree]

11. Transgender people deserve health insurance that covers all transgender-related health issues. [Agree; Somewhat agree; Somewhat disagree; Disagree]

12. Are you currently serving in (or are you a veteran of) the U.S. Armed Forces or as a National Guard or Reserves enlistee? [Yes; No]

13. What is your gender? [Male; Female; Other (open-ended)]

14. What is your sexual orientation? [Straight; Gay/lesbian/queer; Other (open-ended)]

15. Do you personally know a person who is transgender or gender nonconforming? [Yes; No]

CONDITION 3: VETERAN

1. Are you currently serving in (or are you a veteran of) the U.S. Armed Forces or as a National Guard or Reserves enlistee? [Yes; No]

2. **U.S. Army Veteran** U.S. Senator Jack Reed recently cosponsored legislation in favor of transgender Americans serving in the U.S. Armed Forces. He also tweeted about the bill.

What about you? Do you support or oppose transgender Americans serving openly in the U.S. Armed Forces? [Strongly support; somewhat support; somewhat oppose; strongly oppose]

Please tell us how much you agree or disagree with each statement below.

3. I would not mind if my neighbor was transgender. [Agree; Somewhat agree; Somewhat disagree; Disagree]

4. Transgender people violate the traditions of American culture. [Agree; Somewhat agree; Somewhat disagree; Disagree]

5. Congress should pass laws to protect transgender people from discrimination in public places like housing, restaurants, and other public places. [Agree; Somewhat agree; Somewhat disagree; Disagree]

6. Congress should pass laws to protect transgender people from job discrimination. [Agree; Somewhat agree; Somewhat disagree; Disagree]

7. Businesses should be able to refuse services to transgender people. [Agree; Somewhat agree; Somewhat disagree; Disagree]

8. The idea of someone changing their sex disgusts me. [Agree; Somewhat agree; Somewhat disagree; Disagree]

9. Transgender people should be able to change the sex listed on their driver's license or state ID card. [Agree; Somewhat agree; Somewhat disagree; Disagree]

10. Transgender people should have to use the public restroom that corresponds to their gender as assigned at birth. [Agree; Somewhat agree; Somewhat disagree; Disagree]

11. Transgender people deserve health insurance that covers all transgender-related health issues. [Agree; Somewhat agree; Somewhat disagree; Disagree]

12. Generally speaking, do you consider yourself to be a Republican, a Democrat, or something else? [Republican; Democrat; Independent; Something else]

13. What is your gender? [Male; Female; Other (open-ended)]

14. What is your sexual orientation? [Straight; Gay/lesbian/queer; Other (open-ended)]

15. Do you personally know a person who is transgender or gender nonconforming? [Yes; No]

16. If you had to guess, would you say Senator Reed is a Republican or a Democrat? [Republican; Democrat]

3. The Freedom and Safety Frames Experiment

CONDITION 1: POSITIVE/SAFETY

Keeping kids safe means allowing them to use the restroom without worrying about getting attacked or harassed. To do this, we need to allow transgender youth to use the restroom of their choice.

Keep kids safe. Allow kids to use the restroom they prefer.

CONDITION 2: NEGATIVE/SAFETY

Keeping kids safe means allowing them to use the restroom without worrying about getting attacked or harassed. To do this, we need to keep men who say they are transgender out of women's restrooms.

Keep kids safe. Keep men out of the ladies room.

CONDITION 3: POSITIVE/FREEDOM

Transgender people should have the freedom to use the bathroom of their choice. No one should be forced to go into a bathroom they don't want to use.

It's all about freedom. Allow everyone to choose the restroom they prefer.

CONDITION 4: NEGATIVE/FREEDOM

Men and women should have the freedom to use a bathroom just for them, just for men or just for women.

It's all about freedom. Allow everyone to choose the restroom that is just for them.

CONDITION 5: PLACEBO

Using fewer paper towels when you use the restroom helps save trees and protect our planet.

Protect our trees. Protect the world. Use fewer paper towels.

4. The Equality and Integrity (Mullen and Keisling) Experiment

CONDITION 1: MULLEN/INTEGRITY

Ex Joint Chiefs Chairman Supports Transgender Troops
BY REBECCA NORTON - 05/4/18

Admiral Mike Mullen, former Chairman of the Joint Chiefs of Staff, is calling on Congress not to ban openly transgender service members from the military.

Mullen, who was the highest-ranking military officer in the country from 2007 to 2011, released a statement yesterday as Congress began debate on a new effort to ban transgender troops.

"No matter how I look at the issue, I cannot escape being troubled by the fact that Congress is considering a policy which forces young men and women to lie about who they are in order to defend their fellow citizens," Mullen said.

"Thousands of transgender Americans are currently serving in uniform and there is no reason to single out these brave men and women," he continued. "It comes down to integrity—theirs as individuals and ours as an institution."

In late March, the Pentagon requested that transgender troops no longer be able to serve in the United States military. The policy recommendation is currently being debated in Congress, with a vote expected later this month.

CONDITION 2: KEISLING/INTEGRITY

Transgender Equality Activist Supports Transgender Troops
BY REBECCA NORTON - 05/4/18

Mara Keisling, founder and executive director of the National Center for Transgender Equality, is calling on Congress not to ban openly transgender service members from the military.

Keisling, a national leader in the fight for transgender equality, released a statement yesterday as Congress began debate on a new effort to ban transgender troops.

"No matter how I look at the issue, I cannot escape being troubled by the fact that Congress is considering a policy which forces young men and women to lie about who they are in order to defend their fellow citizens," Keisling said.

"Thousands of transgender Americans are currently serving in uniform and there is no reason to single out these brave men and women," she continued. "It comes down to integrity—theirs as individuals and ours as an institution."

In late March, the Pentagon requested that transgender troops no longer be able to serve in the United States military. The policy recommendation is currently being debated in Congress, with a vote expected later this month.

CONDITION 3: MULLEN/EQUALITY

Ex Joint Chiefs Chairman Supports Transgender Troops
BY REBECCA NORTON - 05/4/18

Admiral Mike Mullen, former Chairman of the Joint Chiefs of Staff, is calling on Congress not to ban openly transgender service members from the military.

Mullen, who was the highest-ranking military officer in the country from 2007 to 2011, released a statement yesterday as Congress began debate on a new effort to ban transgender troops.

"Efforts to ban transgender servicemembers from serving in our nation's military are unconstitutional and violate the equal opportunity rights of transgender Americans," Mullen said.

Mullen continued, "On this day and every day, I continue to stand with transgender people of all backgrounds—from service members and students, to workers and parents—in celebration of their lives and with unwavering commitment for the fight for full equality."

In late March, the Pentagon requested that transgender troops no longer be able to serve in the United States military. The policy recommendation is currently being debated in Congress, with a vote expected later this month.

CONDITION 4: KEISLING/EQUALITY

Transgender Equality Activist Supports Transgender Troops
BY REBECCA NORTON - 05/4/18

Mara Keisling, founder and executive director of the National Center for Transgender Equality, is calling on Congress not to ban openly transgender service members from the military.

Keisling, a national leader in the fight for transgender equality, released a statement yesterday as Congress began debate on a new effort to ban transgender troops.

"Efforts to ban transgender servicemembers from serving in our nation's military are unconstitutional and violate the equal opportunity rights of transgender Americans," Keisling said.

Keisling continued, "On this day and every day, I continue to stand with transgender people of all backgrounds—from service members and students, to workers and parents—in celebration of their lives and with unwavering commitment for the fight for full equality."

In late March, the Pentagon requested that transgender troops no longer be able to serve in the United States military. The policy recommendation is currently being debated in Congress, with a vote expected later this month.

5. The Gender Identity Threat Experiment

Please tell us your gender [Male; Female; Other]

This study is being administered to students at universities across the United States.

[SURVEY SPLITS INTO CONDITIONS HERE]
Condition 1: Bem, male consonant
Condition 2: Bem, male dissonant
Condition 3: Big 5 (men)
Condition 4: Bem, female consonant
Condition 5: Bem, female dissonant
Condition 6: Big 5 (women)

In conditions 1, 2, 4, and 5, respondents answered the Bem Sex Role Inventory (BSRI), a 60-question test. The test is formatted with 60 different personality traits on which participants rate themselves based on a 7-point Likert scale. Traits are evenly dispersed: 20 masculine, 20 feminine, and 20 filler traits thought to be gender neutral.

In conditions 3 and 6, respondents answered the Big 5 Personality Test. The test consists of 50 items that participants rate on how true they are about themselves on a 5-point scale where 1 = Disagree, 3 = Neutral, and 5 = Agree.

Bem Sex Role Inventory (BSRI)
Instructions: Please rate yourself on each item below. It is on a 1-7 scale, from 1 (never or almost never true) to 7 (almost always true), with neutral in the middle (3, 4, or 5). Please push the button for each item.

Warm
Solemn
Willing to take a stand
Tender
Friendly
Aggressive
Gullible
Inefficient
Acts like a leader
Childlike
Adaptable
Individualistic
Does not use harsh language
Unsystematic
Competitive
Loves children
Tactful
Ambitious
Gentle

Conventional
Self-reliant
Yielding
Helpful
Defends own beliefs
Cheerful
Moody
Independent
Shy
Conscientious
Athletic
Affectionate
Theatrical
Assertive
Flatterable
Happy
Strong personality
Loyal
Unpredictable
Forceful
Feminine
Reliable
Analytical
Sympathetic
Jealous
Leadership ability
Sensitive to others' needs
Truthful
Willing to take risks
Understanding
Secretive
Makes decisions easily
Compassionate
Sincere
Self-sufficient
Eager to soothe hurt feelings
Conceited
Dominant
Soft-spoken
Likeable
Masculine

Respondents were presented (false) results, depending on their condition.

CONDITION 1 and CONDITION 5: Bem Scale, Male Consonant OR Female Dissonant

Test results are on a 0 to 50 scale of possible scores on the gender identity survey (see below). The range from 0 to 25 is the masculine half of the scale and 26-50 the feminine half. In the middle of each range, brackets indicate the "average male range" and "average female range," respectively.

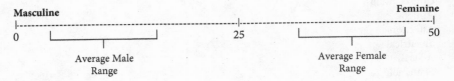

Click to the next screen to get your score.

YOUR SCORE: 11. Based on your responses, your score is within the MASCULINE range of responses.

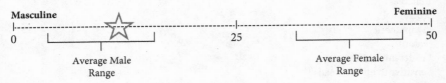

CONDITION 2 and CONDITION 4: Bem Scale,
Male Dissonant OR Female Consonant

Test results are on a 0 to 50 scale of possible scores on the gender identity survey (see below). The range from 0 to 25 is the masculine half of the scale and 26-50 the feminine half. In the middle of each range, brackets indicate the "average male range" and "average female range," respectively.

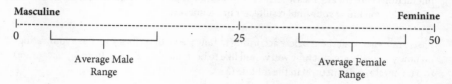

Click to the next screen to get your score.

YOUR SCORE: 32. Based on your responses, your score is within the FEMININE range of responses.

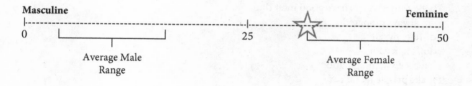

CONDITION 3 and CONDITION 6: Big 5, Male OR Female

The Big Five personality dimensions provide a very broad overview of someone's personality. These have been gathered through the result of decades' worth of psychological research into personality. While they don't capture the idiosyncrasies of everyone's personality, it is a theoretical framework in which to understand general components of our personality that seem to be the most important in our social and interpersonal interactions with others. Please answer the questions carefully on the next several screens. We will let you know your final result later in the survey.

Please rate each statement below according to how well it describes you. Base your ratings on how you really are, not how you would like to be. It is on a 1-5 scale, from 1 (inaccurate) to 5 (accurate), with neutral in the middle (3).

I often feel blue
I feel comfortable around people
I believe in the importance of art
I have a good word for everyone
I am often down in the dumps
I make friends easily
I tend to vote for liberal political candidates
I believe that others have good intentions
I am always prepared
I dislike myself
I don't talk a lot
I have a vivid imagination
I make people feel at ease
I pay attention to details
I have frequent mood swings
I am skilled in handling social situations
I carry the conversation to a higher level
I respect others
I get chores done right away
I panic easily
I am the life of the party
I enjoy hearing new ideas
I accept people as they are
I carry out my plans
I rarely get irritated
I know how to captivate people
I am not interested in abstract ideas
I have a sharp tongue
I make plans and stick to them
I seldom feel blue
I have little to say
I do not like art
I shirk my duties
I cut others to pieces

I waste my time
I feel comfortable with myself
I keep in the background
I avoid philosophical discussion
I suspect hidden motives in others
I find it difficult to get down to work
I am not easily bothered by things
I would describe my experiences as somewhat dull
I do not enjoy going to art museums
I get back at others
I do just enough work to get by
I am very pleased with myself
I don't like to draw attention to myself
I tend to vote for conservative political candidates
I insult people
I don't see things through

Click to the next screen to see your score.

Decades of research on personality has uncovered five broad dimensions of personality. These are not "types" of personalities but dimensions of personality. So someone's personality is the combination of each of their Big Five personality characteristics. For example, someone may be very sociable (high Extraversion), not very friendly (low Agreeableness), hard working (high Conscientiousness), easily stressed (low Emotional Stability), and extremely creative (high Intellect).

YOUR RESULTS:
1. Extraversion (your level of sociability and enthusiasm): 38% (moderate)
2. Agreeableness (your level of friendliness and kindness): 29% (moderate)
3. Conscientiousness (your level of organization and work ethic): 42% (moderate–above average)
4. Emotional Stability (your level of calmness and tranquility): 40% (moderate)
5. Intellect (your level of creativity and curiosity): 50% (moderate–above average)

[SURVEY MERGES AGAIN HERE]

DEPENDENT VARIABLES

As you may know, transgender people are those who identify as a gender different from the one from when they were born. Some think that bathrooms should be organized by sex; others think that people should be able to choose which bathroom or locker room fits their gender identity. What about you? Do you think people who are transgender should: (1) be allowed to use the bathrooms and locker rooms of their preferred gender or (2) have to use the bathrooms and locker rooms of the gender they were born?

　How strongly do you feel about the answer you just gave? [Very strongly; Somewhat strongly; Not very strongly]

Do you favor or oppose laws to protect transgender people against job discrimination? [Favor; Oppose; Don't know]

　Do you favor such laws strongly or not strongly? [Strongly; Not strongly]

Some people feel that the government in Washington should make every effort to improve the social and economic position of people who are transgender or who do not conform to a gender. (Suppose these people are at one end of a scale, at point 1.) Others feel that the government should not make any special effort to help these groups because they should help themselves. (Suppose these people are at the other end, at point 7.) And, of course, some other people have opinions somewhere in between, at points 2, 3, 4, 5, or 6. What about you? Do you feel that government should help to improve the social and economic position of transgender people?

Many minority groups, including gay, lesbian, and bisexual people, overcame prejudice and worked their way up on their own. Transgender people should do the same without any special favors. Would you say you agree strongly, agree somewhat, neither agree nor disagree, disagree somewhat, or disagree strongly with this statement?

How often have you felt sympathy for transgender people? Would you say very often, fairly often, not often, or never?

How much do transgender people have in common with your own beliefs? Would you say a great deal, a lot, a moderate amount, a little, or nothing at all?

Among your immediate family members, relatives, neighbors, co-workers, or close friends, are any of them transgender or gender non-conforming? [Yes; No]

How serious a problem is discrimination against transgender people in the United States? Would you say not a problem at all, a minor problem, a moderately serious problem, a very serious problem, or an extremely serious problem?

When employers make decisions about hiring and promotion, how often do you think they discriminate against transgender people? Would you say never, some of time, most of the time, or always?

Suppose your state had a ballot initiative in an upcoming election where you could vote on a law that would require public bathrooms and locker rooms to be divided in the traditional way, male or female. This law would require transgender people to use the bathroom of the sex they were assigned at birth, not the one with which they currently identify. How would you vote on such a measure? Note: a "yes" vote would mean requiring bathrooms divided by male and female; a "no" vote would mean allowing transgender people to choose which bathroom they want to use.

[Definitely vote yes; Probably vote yes; Undecided; Probably vote no; Definitely vote no]

Would you be willing to receive ONE email about how to sign a petition to encourage lawmakers to pass a transgender anti-discrimination law? Your email address will never be sold or shared with anyone and the information will be completely anonymous. [Yes; No]

[If YES]: Please enter your e-mail to receive ONE email about how to sign a petition for laws to protect transgender people from discrimination. Again, it will never be sold or shared with anyone and the information is completely anonymous.

PLEASE READ THE FOLLOWING CAREFULLY:

The survey you just completed contained deception. Your reported score on the test was randomly assigned to you regardless of your answers on the survey. Thus, your responses do NOT match the score you received and were manipulated as an element of the research design to measure your responses to later questions in the survey. The purpose of the deception was to test the effect of the perceptions of gender on political and social attitudes. This study (Study number STU00202691) was approved by the Institutional Review Board at Northwestern University. If you have any questions about this study, you may contact Brian Harrison at Brian.Harrison@northwestern.edu. If you have any questions about your rights as a research subject, you may call the Institutional Review Board Office of Northwestern University at telephone number (847) 467-1723. Please click the button below to move forward in the survey to indicate you understand the paragraph above.

o Yes, I have read the paragraph and understand the information provided.

6. The Gender Identity Bolstering Experiment

Please tell us your gender [Male; Female; Other]

Next, we'd like you to answer a series of questions that are a part of a large national study.

The scale is being administered nationally to large numbers of people to investigate and to measure individual differences in masculinity and femininity.

[SURVEY SPLITS INTO CONDITIONS HERE]

CONDITION 1 and CONDITION 2:
Men, with score OR Men, no score

Please indicate the degree to which you agree or disagree with each of the following questions.
[Strongly agree; Disagree; Somewhat disagree; Neither agree nor disagree; Somewhat agree; agree; Strongly agree]

Men should be the leader in any group.
Men should watch football games instead of soap operas.
Men should have some home improvement skills.
Men should be able to fix most things around the house.
A man should prefer watching action movies to reading romantic novels.
Men should always like to have sex.
Boys should prefer to play with trucks rather than dolls.
A man should always be the boss.
A man should not turn down sex.
A man should know how to repair his car if it should break down.
A man should never admit when others hurt his feelings.
Men should be detached in emotionally charged situations.
It is important for a man to take risks, even if he might get hurt.
A man should always be ready for sex.
Nobody respects a man very much who frequently talks about his worries, fears, and problems. A real man enjoys a bit of danger now and then.
A man should never back down in the face of trouble.
A man should always try to project an air of confidence, even if he doesn't really feel confident inside.
Men should not be too quick to tell others that they care about them.
When the going gets tough, men should get tough.
I think a young man should be physically tough, even if he's not big.
When a man is feeling a little pain, he should try not to let it show very much.

[SURVEY SPLITS HERE: Only men assigned to Condition 1 see the next set of items prior to the conditions merging together again.]

Test results are on a 0 to 50 scale of possible scores on the gender identity survey (see below). The range from 0 to 25 is the masculine half of the scale and 26-50 the feminine half.

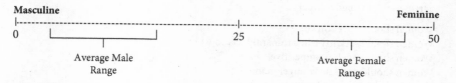

NOTE: People who have scores between 0 and 15 on the scale tend to be very masculine.

Click to the next screen to get your score. It may take a few seconds for your score to be calculated.

YOUR SCORE: 6. Based on your responses, your score is within the VERY MASCULINE range of responses.

Your score is at the high end of the scale, suggesting that you are <u>very masculine compared to most college-aged men.</u>

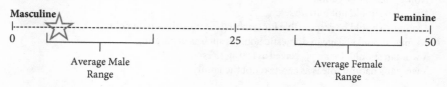

Extensive research shows that masculine men tend to be different in important ways that affect future professional success and personal relationship quality.

CONDITION 3 and CONDITION 4:
Women, with score OR Women, no score

Please indicate the degree to which you agree or disagree with each of the following questions.
[Strongly agree; Disagree; Somewhat disagree; Neither agree nor disagree; Somewhat agree; Agree; Strongly agree]

Women should have soft voices.
Women should seek to be in a romantic relationship.
Women should not be competitive.
Women should not date younger men.
Women should not tell dirty jokes.
Women should let other people know they are special.
Women should take care to keep in touch with friends.
Women should not show anger.
Women should downplay their accomplishments.
Women should enjoy taking care of children.
Women should enjoy spending time making their living space look nice.
Women should not brag about their achievements.
Women should be ashamed if they are thought of as mean.
Women should try to look physically attractive in public.
When someone's feelings are hurt, women should try to make them feel better.
A woman should know how people are feeling.
Women should be gentle.
A woman should not initiate sex.
A woman should be responsible for teaching family values to her children.
Women should engage in domestic hobbies such as decorating.
A woman should not be perceived as too aggressive.
A woman's natural role is as caretaker of the family.

[SURVEY SPLITS HERE: Only women assigned to Condition 3 see the next set of items prior to the conditions merging together again.]

Test results are on a 0 to 50 scale of possible scores on the gender identity survey (see below). The range from 0 to 25 is the masculine half of the scale and 26-50 the feminine half.

NOTE: People who have scores between 35 and 50 on the scale tend to be very feminine.

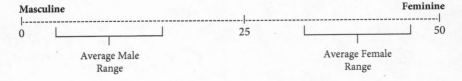

Click to the next screen to get your score. It may take a few seconds for your score to be calculated.

YOUR SCORE: 39. Based on your responses, your score is within the VERY FEMININE range of responses.

Your score is at the high end of the scale, suggesting that you are very feminine compared to most college-aged women. Extensive research shows that feminine women tend to be different in important ways that affect future professional success and personal relationship quality.

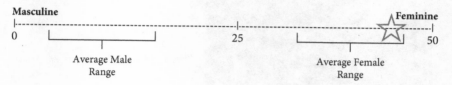

[SURVEY MERGES AGAIN HERE]

Now we'd like to move on to a different topic. We're also interested in how people think about various issues going on right now in American politics.

As with the previous set of questions, these are being administered nationally to large numbers of students to investigate and to measure individual differences in political interest and attitudes.

The next two questions will ask you how you're feeling right now. Please read them carefully.

On a scale of 1 (extremely unhappy) to 7 (extremely happy), how do you feel right now? [Extremely unhappy; Moderately unhappy; Slightly unhappy; Neither happy nor unhappy; Slightly happy; Moderately happy; Extremely happy]

On a scale of 1 (extremely bad) to 7 (extremely good), how do you feel right now? [Extremely bad; Moderately bad; Slightly bad; Neither good nor bad; Slightly good; Moderately good; Extremely good]

DEPENDENT VARIABLES

Policy makers have recently debated whether transgender people should be allowed to serve openly in the U.S. military, including people like U.S. Air Force Staff Sgt. Logan Ireland (pictured below).

What do you think? Do you agree or disagree with a policy allowing transgender people to serve in the military?
[Strongly disagree; Disagree; Somewhat disagree; Neither agree nor disagree; Somewhat agree; Agree; Strongly agree]

Suppose your state had a ballot initiative in an upcoming election where you could vote on whether transgender people serve in the military. How would you vote on such a measure?
Note: a "yes" vote means allowing transgender people to serve in the military; a "no" vote means not allowing transgender people to serve in the military.
[Definitely vote no; Probably vote no; Probably vote yes; Definitely vote yes]

Below are a few statements about transgender people.

Please read each statement carefully and check whether you strongly agree, somewhat agree, somewhat disagree, or strongly disagree.

I would not mind if my neighbor was transgender.
Transgender people violate the traditions of American culture.
Businesses should be able to refuse services to transgender people.
The idea of someone changing their sex disgusts me.
Transgender people are sick and need help from a mental health professional.
Transgender people deserve health insurance that covers all transgender-related issues.
Congress should pass laws to protest transgender people from discrimination in housing, restaurants, and other public places.

Would you be willing to sign a petition urging lawmakers to allow transgender people to serve in the military?

If yes, enter your full name and we will add you to the petition. [Full name; I do not wish to sign the petition]
    [If full name entered: What is your current zip code (e.g., 12345)?]

<u>PLEASE READ THE FOLLOWING CAREFULLY:</u>

The survey you just completed contained deception.

Your reported score on the test was randomly assigned to you regardless of your answers on the survey. Thus, your responses do NOT match the score you received and were manipulated as an element of the research design to measure your responses to later questions in the survey. The purpose of the deception was to test the effect of the perceptions of gender on political and social attitudes.

This study was approved by the Institutional Review Board at Menlo College. If you have any questions about this study, you may contact Melissa Michelson at Melissa.Michelson@menlo.edu. If you have any questions about your rights as a research subject, you may call the Institutional Review Board Office of Menlo College at 650-543-3859.

Please click the button below to move forward in the survey to indicate you understand the paragraph above.
    o Yes, I have read the paragraph and understand the information provided.

Thank you very much for your participation in this survey! We truly value your time and appreciate your help. If you have any questions, please contact Melissa.Michelson@menlo.edu. Thank you!

7. The Puppies and Spiders Experiment

SPIDERS CONDITION

We are studying the effects of different emotions on attitudes and thoughts.

In this particular study, we're interested in FEAR and things that people find scary or frightening. We're going to show you a series of photos and we'd like you to rate each on a scale of 1 (not very scary) to 5 (extremely scary).

[PHOTOS OF SPIDERS SHOWN HERE]

PUPPIES CONDITION

We are studying the effects of different emotions on attitudes and thoughts.

For this study, we're interested in the effect of happiness or joy and things that people find cute or endearing.

We're going to show you a series of photos and we'd like you to rate each on a scale of 1 (not very cute) to 5 (extremely cute).

[PHOTOS OF SPIDERS SHOWN HERE]

[SURVEY MERGES HERE]

The next two questions will ask you how you're feeling right now. Please read them carefully.

On a scale of 1 (extremely bad) to 7 (extremely good), how do you feel right now?
[Extremely bad; Moderately bad; Slightly bad; Neither good nor bad; Slightly good; Moderately good; Extremely good]

On a scale of 1 (extremely unhappy) to 7 (extremely happy), how do you feel right now?
[Extremely unhappy; Moderately unhappy; Slightly unhappy; Neither happy nor unhappy; Slightly happy; Moderately happy; Extremely happy]

Thanks for completing that survey!

There is one other set of questions we'd like you to answer. It shouldn't take more than a few minutes. Please read the questions closely and answer the best you can.

Suppose your state had a ballot initiative in an upcoming election where you could vote on whether transgender people should be able to use the bathroom of their choice. How would you vote on such a measure?

Note: a "yes" vote means allowing transgender people to choose the bathroom or locker room they want to use; a "no" vote means not allowing transgender people to use the bathroom they want to use.

[Definitely vote no; Probably vote no; Probably vote yes; Definitely vote yes]

Below are a few statements about transgender people.

Please read each statement carefully and check whether you strongly agree, somewhat agree, somewhat disagree, or strongly disagree.

I would not mind if my neighbor was transgender.
Transgender people violate the traditions of American culture.
Business should be able to refuse services to transgender people.
The idea of someone changing their sex disgusts me.
Transgender people are sick and need help from a mental health professional.
Transgender people deserve health insurance that covers all transgender related issues.
Congress should pass laws to protect transgender people from discrimination in housing, restaurants, and other public places.

Would you be willing to sign a petition urging lawmakers to support transgender people by passing laws that protect their rights?

If yes, enter your full name and we will add you to the petition. [Full name; I do not wish to sign the petition]

   [If full name entered: What is your current zip code (e.g., 12345)?]

8. The Moral Elevation Experiment

Please watch the following video carefully. After it's finished, we'll ask you some questions about it.

Please note: you will not be able to move forward in the survey until the video is completely finished.

[*RANDOM ASSIGNMENT TO MORAL ELEVATION, AMUSEMENT, OR CONTROL VIDEO HERE*]

In your own words, please briefly describe what happened in the video you just watched. Note: please don't tell us what you thought about the video; just what happened in the video.

The next few pages have some statements about transgender people.

Please read each statement carefully; then, check whether you strongly agree, somewhat agree, somewhat disagree, or strongly disagree.

I would not mind if my neighbor were transgender.
Transgender people violate the traditions of American culture.
Congress should pass laws to protect transgender people from discrimination in housing, restaurants, and other public places.
Congress should pass laws to protect transgender people from job discrimination.
Businesses should be able to refuse services to transgender people.
The idea of someone changing their sex disgusts me.
Transgender people are sick and need help from a mental health professional.
Transgender people deserve the same rights and protections as other Americans.
Transgender people should be able to serve openly in the U.S. military.
Transgender people should be able to change the sex listed on their driver's license or state ID card.
Transgender people should not be able to adopt children.
Transgender people should have to use the public restrooms that are consistent with the gender they were assigned at birth.
Transgender people deserve health insurance that covers all transgender-related issues.
Insurance companies should not be required to pay for medical treatment related to transgender health issues.

Suppose your state had a ballot initiative in an upcoming election where you could vote on whether transgender people should be able to use the bathroom of their choice. How would you vote on such a measure?
Note: a "yes" vote means allowing transgender people to choose the bathroom or locker room they want to use; a "no" vote means not allowing transgender people to use the bathroom they want to use.
[Definitely vote no; Probably vote no; Probably vote yes; Definitely vote yes]

Would you be willing to sign a petition urging lawmakers to support transgender people by passing laws that guarantee them the same rights as other Americans?

If yes, enter your full name and we will add you to the petition. [Full name; I do not wish to sign the petition]
    [If full name entered: What is your current zip code (e.g., 12345)?]

9. Acknowledgment Experiment

FEMALE (KATHY) CONTROL CONDITION

"Hi, my name is Kathy. It can be hard to understand what it means to recycle, especially if you've never recycled before. Recycling means taking things that would otherwise be thrown away and using them for something new.

In many places, it's legal to have only public trashcans but no public recycling bins, including in public restrooms, which means many people throw away items like bottles, cans, and paper towels that could easily be recycled.

It's important to pass laws that make it easier to recycle to give the environment the protection it deserves."

MALE (KARL) CONTROL CONDITION

"Hi, my name is Karl. It can be hard to understand what it means to recycle, especially if you've never recycled before. Recycling means taking things that would otherwise be thrown away and using them for something new.

In many places, it's legal to have only public trashcans but no public recycling bins, including in public restrooms, which means many people throw away items like bottles, cans, and paper towels that could easily be recycled.

It's important to pass laws that make it easier to recycle to give the environment the protection it deserves."

FEMALE (KATHY) TREATMENT CONDITIONS

"Hi, my name is Kathy, and I am transgender. It can be hard to understand what it means to be transgender, especially if you've never met a transgender person before.

Being transgender means that I know myself to be a different gender than what people thought I was when I was born. When I was growing up, people thought I was a man, but I knew that I was a woman.

In many places, the law allows people to treat transgender people like me unfairly, including when they are trying to find a job or even when trying to use a public restroom. I can even be fired just for being who I am.

STIGMA SCRIPT ADDS:
There are many unfair and untrue ideas and assumptions about transgender people. We are often treated differently just because of who we are or how we look.

DISCOMFORT SCRIPT ADDS:
Some people feel uncomfortable thinking about what it means to be transgender, or who belongs in what space. But you don't have to be comfortable to know that everyone should be treated fairly.

It's important to pass laws that give transgender people like me the equal protection we deserve."

MALE (KARL) TREATMENT CONDITIONS

"Hi, my name is Karl, and I am transgender. It can be hard to understand what it means to be transgender, especially if you've never met a transgender person before.

Being transgender means that I know myself to be a different gender than what people thought I were when I was born. When I was growing up, people thought that I was a woman, but I knew that I was a man.

In many places, the law allows people to treat transgender people like me unfairly, including when they are trying to find a job or even when trying to use a public restroom. I can even be fired just for being who I am.

STIGMA SCRIPT ADDS:
There are many unfair and untrue ideas and assumptions about transgender people. We are often treated differently just because of who we are or how we look.

DISCOMFORT SCRIPT ADDS:
Some people feel uncomfortable thinking about what it means to be transgender, or who belongs in what space. But you don't have to be comfortable to know that everyone should be treated fairly.

It's important to pass laws that give transgender people like me the equal protection we deserve."

10. The Journey Story Experiment

TREATMENT SCRIPT/ENGLISH

California Halloween 2018 Survey

Being transgender means that you know yourself to be a different gender than what people thought you were when you were born. For example, a person who was thought to be male and raised as a boy but who knows herself to be a woman might call herself transgender.

Kimberly Shappley used to think people who said they were transgender were confused or mentally ill. Then she realized, and gradually accepted, that her child was transgender. Identified as a boy at birth, Kai was most definitely a girl. "She knows who she is," Kimberly says.

Even if you have not supported transgender people in the past, it's okay to change your mind and support transgender rights.

Are you, personally, comfortable or uncomfortable when you are around someone who is transgender? [Comfortable; Somewhat comfortable; Somewhat uncomfortable; Uncomfortable]

Thinking about people that identify as transgender, which comes closer to your view? [People are born that way; People choose to live that way; People are that way because of how they are raised]

Please tell us how much you agree or disagree with each statement below.

3. Legal protections that apply to gay and lesbian people should also apply to transgender people. [Agree; Somewhat agree; Somewhat disagree; Disagree]

4. Transgender people are sick and need help from a mental health professional. [Agree; Somewhat agree; Somewhat disagree; Disagree]

5. Congress should pass laws to protect transgender people from job discrimination. [Agree; Somewhat agree; Somewhat disagree; Disagree]

6. Congress should pass laws to protect transgender people from discrimination in public accommodations like restaurants and movie theaters. [Agree; Somewhat agree; Somewhat disagree; Disagree]

7. Transgender people should have to use the public restroom that corresponds to their gender as assigned at birth. [Agree; Somewhat agree; Somewhat disagree; Disagree]

8. Business owners should be able to refuse services to transgender people if it conflicts with their religious beliefs. [Agree; Somewhat agree; Somewhat disagree; Disagree]

Thank you for your time! Please return this completed survey to the person who gave it to you.

TREATMENT SCRIPT/SPANISH

California Halloween 2018 Encuesta

Ser transgénero significa que sabes que eres un género diferente al que la gente pensaba que eras cuando naciste. Por ejemplo, una persona que pensaba que era un hombre y crió niño, pero que sabe que es una mujer, podría llamarse transgénero.

Kimberly Shappley solía pensar que las personas que decían que eran transgénero estaban confundidas o mentalmente enfermas. Entonces se dio cuenta, y gradualmente aceptó, que su hijo era transgénero. Identificado como niño al nacer, Kai era definitivamente una niña. "Ella sabe quién es ella," dice Kimberly.

Incluso si no ha apoyado a personas transgénero en el pasado, está bien cambiar de opinión y respaldar los derechos de las personas transgénero.

1 ¿Está usted personalmente cómodo o incómodo cuando está cerca de alguien que es transgénero? [Cómodo; Algo cómodo; Algo incómodo; Incómodo]

2. Pensando en las personas que se identifican como transgénero, ¿cuál se acerca más a su punto de vista? [La gente nace así; La gente elige vivir de esa manera; Las personas son así por la forma en que son criados]

Díganos cuánto está de acuerdo o en desacuerdo con cada una de las siguientes declaraciones.

3. Las protecciones legales que se aplican a las gays y lesbianas también deben aplicarse a las personas transgénero. [De acuerdo; Algo de acuerdo; Algo en desacuerdo; Desacuerdo]

4. Las personas transgénero están enfermas y necesitan la ayuda de un profesional de salud mental. [De acuerdo; Algo de acuerdo; Algo en desacuerdo; Desacuerdo]

5. El congreso debe aprobar leyes para proteger a las personas transgénero de la discriminación laboral. [De acuerdo; Algo de acuerdo; Algo en desacuerdo; Desacuerdo]

6. El congreso debe aprobar leyes para proteger a las personas transgénero de la discriminación en lugares públicos como restaurantes y cines. [De acuerdo; Algo de acuerdo; Algo en desacuerdo; Desacuerdo]

7. Las personas transgénero deben tener que usar el baño público que corresponda a su género según lo asignado al nacer. [De acuerdo; Algo de acuerdo; Algo en desacuerdo; Desacuerdo]

8. Los dueños de negocios deberían poder rechazar los servicios a personas transgénero si entran en conflicto con sus creencias religiosas. [De acuerdo; Algo de acuerdo; Algo en desacuerdo; Desacuerdo]

¡Gracias por tu tiempo! Por favor devuelva esta encuesta completada a la persona que se la entregó.

CONTROL SCRIPT/ENGLISH

California Halloween 2018 Survey

Being transgender means that you know yourself to be a different gender than what people thought you were when you were born. For example, a person who was thought to be male and raised as a boy but who knows herself to be a woman might call herself transgender.

Are you, personally, comfortable or uncomfortable when you are around someone who is transgender? [Comfortable; Somewhat comfortable; Somewhat uncomfortable; Uncomfortable]

Thinking about people that identify as transgender, which comes closer to your view? [People are born that way; People choose to live that way; People are that way because of how they are raised]

Please tell us how much you agree or disagree with each statement below.

3. Legal protections that apply to gay and lesbian people should also apply to transgender people. [Agree; Somewhat agree; Somewhat disagree; Disagree]

4. Transgender people are sick and need help from a mental health professional. [Agree; Somewhat agree; Somewhat disagree; Disagree]

5. Congress should pass laws to protect transgender people from job discrimination. [Agree; Somewhat agree; Somewhat disagree; Disagree]

6. Congress should pass laws to protect transgender people from discrimination in public accommodations like restaurants and movie theaters. [Agree; Somewhat agree; Somewhat disagree; Disagree]

7. Transgender people should have to use the public restroom that corresponds to their gender as assigned at birth. [Agree; Somewhat agree; Somewhat disagree; Disagree]

8. Business owners should be able to refuse services to transgender people if it conflicts with their religious beliefs. [Agree; Somewhat agree; Somewhat disagree; Disagree]

Thank you for your time! Please return this completed survey to the person who gave it to you.

CONTROL SCRIPT/SPANISH

California Halloween 2018 Encuesta

Ser transgénero significa que sabes que eres un género diferente al que la gente pensaba que eras cuando naciste. Por ejemplo, una persona que pensaba que era un hombre y crió niño, pero que sabe que es una mujer, podría llamarse transgénero.

Incluso si no ha apoyado a personas transgénero en el pasado, está bien cambiar de opinión y respaldar los derechos de las personas transgénero.

1 ¿Está usted personalmente cómodo o incómodo cuando está cerca de alguien que es transgénero? [Cómodo; Algo cómodo; Algo incómodo; Incómodo]

2. Pensando en las personas que se identifican como transgénero, ¿cuál se acerca más a su punto de vista? [La gente nace así; La gente elige vivir de esa manera; Las personas son así por la forma en que son criados]

Díganos cuánto está de acuerdo o en desacuerdo con cada una de las siguientes declaraciones.

3. Las protecciones legales que se aplican a las gays y lesbianas también deben aplicarse a las personas transgénero. [De acuerdo; Algo de acuerdo; Algo en desacuerdo; Desacuerdo]

4. Las personas transgénero están enfermas y necesitan la ayuda de un profesional de salud mental. [De acuerdo; Algo de acuerdo; Algo en desacuerdo; Desacuerdo]

5. El congreso debe aprobar leyes para proteger a las personas transgénero de la discriminación laboral. [De acuerdo; Algo de acuerdo; Algo en desacuerdo; Desacuerdo]

6. El congreso debe aprobar leyes para proteger a las personas transgénero de la discriminación en lugares públicos como restaurantes y cines. [De acuerdo; Algo de acuerdo; Algo en desacuerdo; Desacuerdo]

7. Las personas transgénero deben tener que usar el baño público que corresponda a su género según lo asignado al nacer. [De acuerdo; Algo de acuerdo; Algo en desacuerdo; Desacuerdo]

8. Los dueños de negocios deberían poder rechazar los servicios a personas transgénero si entran en conflicto con sus creencias religiosas. [De acuerdo; Algo de acuerdo; Algo en desacuerdo; Desacuerdo]

¡Gracias por tu tiempo! Por favor devuelva esta encuesta completada a la persona que se la entregó.

Notes

Chapter 1

1. Another popular acronym is LGBTQ, adding Q for queer (or, less frequently, questioning). Both are considered inclusive terms to refer to members of the community.
2. Bisexual people also lack visibility, an issue explored by other scholars, but attitudes toward bisexuals are improving (Herek 2002; Israel and Mohr 2008; Rubinstein, Makov, and Sarel 2013; Helms and Waters 2016; Matsick and Rubin 2018; Dyar and Feinstein 2018).
3. Many of the same issues apply to gender nonconforming people and other groups within the LGBT umbrella (e.g., genderqueer, genderfluid, and pangender people). While our focus here is on transgender people, we expect that our theory of attitudinal change would also apply to other stigmatized groups, including these other identities.
4. *Passing* generally refers to the degree to which a transgender person conforms to traditional expectations of one's gender, such as whether a transgender man appears to be masculine or to conform to traditional male or masculine stereotypes. Passing is a problematic concept because it implies a degree of success or failure in one's gender presentation, rather than acknowledging that everyone expresses their gender differently. Civil rights and liberties should not be predicated on a person's adherence to gender or sex stereotypes.
5. Randomized experiments are a powerful method of determining causality that have become a standard tool in social science research over the past two decades. Taking a cue from medical research, a standard experiment randomizes a pool of potential people or groups into treatment and control groups, much like medical tests expose treatment patients to new drugs or procedures while retaining a control group that receives no treatment or perhaps a sugar pill with no active ingredients. The next step is to compare any changes in health or survival between the two groups. Similarly, social science researchers conducting an experiment will apply an intervention to the treatment group and either no intervention or a placebo intervention to the control group and then compare the outcome variable for the two groups. For example, a group of respondents to a survey could be randomly divided into a treatment group that receives a message in favor of transgender rights while a control group receives a message in favor of recycling. Respondents in both groups are then asked their attitudes about transgender rights. If the randomization was done properly, any difference in those attitudes can be attributed to the different messages to which the two groups were exposed.

Chapter 2

1. The names used are pseudonyms.
2. The Lucid Marketplace is an automated marketplace that connects researchers with willing online research participants. For more information, see https://support.lucidhq.com/s/article/Working-with-Lucid-Audience.
3. Norton and Herek conducted a poll on attitudes toward transgender rights in 2005, but results were not published until 2013.
4. As with all of the experiments in this book, prior to collecting data, we obtained institutional review board (IRB) approval through Menlo College. The undergraduate lab experiment described in chapter 4 was also approved by the IRB at Northwestern University.
5. Only the differences for Democrats are statistically significant, reflecting the larger number of Democratic participants. These results are *not* consistent with the Theory of Dissonant Identity Priming; in fact, they are contrary to what we would expect if that theory were at play. Looking specifically at the 156 participants in the veteran condition who offered a guess as to Senator Reed's partisanship, a much larger proportion of those who identified him as a Democrat were strong supporters of transgender troops (81.1%, 90/111) compared to those guessing him to be a Republican (66.7%, 30/45); again, this result reflects the larger number of Democratic respondents in our sample. Of the 18 Republicans who answered this question, 4 of 6 who guessed that Reed was a Republican support transgender troops. Among the 12 who identified Reed as a Democrat, 10 support transgender troops. Among the 80 Democrats who answered this question, 58 of 59 who identified Reed as a Democrat also support transgender troops, as do all 21 who identified him as a Republican. Neither of these differences is statistically significant, again failing to support the Theory of Dissonant Identity Priming.

Chapter 3

1. Opponents of transgender rights often dismiss transgender women as confused men in drag, not just when debating bathroom access. In 2012, True the Vote targeted transgender people as potentially engaging in voter fraud if their gender expression did not match their identification, sending out an advertisement that included cartoon images of a hairy man in a dress and the message "Prevent voter fraud!" across the top (Paschall 2016).
2. https://www.youtube.com/watch?time_continue=32&v=D7thOvSvC4E
3. The compromise over repeal was controversial, in part because it created a moratorium on local nondiscrimination ordinances through 2020. The American Civil Liberties Union and Lambda Legal called the compromise a "fake" repeal bill that "keeps in place the most harmful parts of the law," while the Human Rights Campaign and other gay rights groups called the deal "shameful." On the other side of the issue, religious and cultural conservatives denounced the removal of transgender bathroom provisions.

4. See https://www.mafamily.org/profamilyevent/vote-no-on-question-3/
5. Berinsky, Huber, and Lenz (2012) found that while MTurk workers are younger and more ideologically liberal than the general public, the tool is a valid low-cost method of conducting experiments (also see Levay, Freese, and Druckman 2016; Coppock 2019).
6. As an aside, a contemporary Department of Defense analysis found that the military spent $84 million in 2014 on erectile dysfunction prescriptions—roughly $42 million on the drug Viagra alone (see Kime 2015).

Chapter 4

1. Randomization checks confirmed that men and women had the same average BSRI scores in the threatening and nonthreatening conditions and did not vary by political ideology across all three conditions (threatening, nonthreatening, and placebo).
2. See Appendix Table A4.1.

Chapter 5

1. For more details about the Lucid platform, see chapter 2.
2. http://www.lgbtmap.org/effective-messaging/restaurant-ad
3. http://openscienceframework.org/project/fG5xB/. For more details see Lai, Haidt, and Nosek (2014: 783).
4. For more details about the Lucid platform, see chapter 2.

Chapter 6

1. https://www.youtube.com/watch?v=6s3Fx0lq9Ws
2. http://www.lgbtmap.org/effective-messaging/restaurant-ad
3. http://lgbtmap.org/file/talking-about-transgender-people-and-restrooms.pdf
4. This experiment, including the photo pretest, was conducted in collaboration with Dr. Logan Casey, then a researcher at the Harvard Research Opinion Program at the Harvard T. H. Chan School of Public Health and currently policy researcher for the Movement Advancement Project (MAP).
5. For more details about MTurk and the quality of MTurk data, see chapter 3.
6. http://www.lgbtmap.org/effective-messaging/restaurant-ad
7. For more details about MTurk and the quality of MTurk data, see chapter 3.
8. While the possible scale of the index ranged from 6 to 24, no one scored lower than 12.

Chapter 7

1. https://www.youtube.com/watch?time_continue=1&v=w519kGUAIhI

References

Adams, Henry E., Lester W. Wright Jr., and Bethany Lohr. 1996. "Is Homophobia Associated with Homosexual Arousal?" *Journal of Abnormal Psychology* 105, 3: 440–445.

Adams, Nick, Arielle Gordon, M. J. Okma, and Sue Yacka-Bible. 2018. *More Than a Number: Shifting the Media Narrative on Transgender Homicides.* GLAAD Media Institute, March 28, 2018. https://www.glaad.org/publications/more-than-a-number

Ahmed, Sara. 2004. *The Cultural Politics of Emotion.* New York: Routledge.

Akerlof, George A., and Rachel E. Kranton. 2000. "Economics and Identity." *Quarterly Journal of Economics* 115, 3: 715–753.

Albertson, Bethany, and Shana B. Gadarian. 2015. *Anxious Politics: Democratic Citizenship in a Threatening World.* New York: Cambridge University Press.

Algoe, Sara B., and Jonathan Haidt. 2009. "Witnessing Excellence in Action: The 'Other-Praising' Emotions of Elevation, Gratitude, and Admiration." *Journal of Positive Psychology* 4, 2: 105–127.

Allen, Karma. 2019. "Allies Need to Focus Specifically on Transgender Issues in Wake of Violence: Activists." *ABC News*, June 21, 2019. https://abcnews.go.com/US/allies-focus-specifically-transgender-issues-wake-violence-activists/story?id=63689763

Allport, Gordon W. 1954. *The Nature of Prejudice.* New York: Doubleday.

Associated Press. 2017. "How AP Tallied the Cost of North Carolina's 'Bathroom Bill.'" *Associated Press*, March 27, 2017. https://apnews.com/ec6e9845827f47e89f40f33bb7024f61

Ayoub, Phillip M. 2016. *When States 'Come Out': Europe's Sexual Minorities and the Politics of Visibility.* New York: Cambridge University Press.

Ayoub, Phillip, and Jeremiah Garretson. 2017. "Getting the Message Out: Media Context and Global Changes in Attitudes toward Homosexuality." *Comparative Political Studies* 50, 8: 1055–1085.

Barron, Laura G., Michelle Hebl, and Eden B. King. 2011. "Effects of Manifest Ethnic Identification on Employment Discrimination." *Cultural Diversity and Ethnic Minority Psychology* 17, 1: 23–30.

Barth, Jay L., Marvin Overby, and Scott H. Huffmon. 2009. "Community Context, Personal Contact, and Support for an Anti-Gay Rights Referendum." *Political Research Quarterly* 62, 2: 355–365.

Berg, Alex. "How 'Toxic Masculinity' Fuels Transgender Victimization." *NBCnews.com*, August 4, 2017. https://www.nbcnews.com/think/nbc-out/analysis-how-toxic-masculinity-fuels-transgender-victimization-ncna789621

Berinsky, Adam J., Gregory A. Huber, and Gabriel S. Lenz. 2012. "Evaluating Online Labor Markets for Experimental Research: Amazon.com's Mechanical Turk." *Political Analysis* 20, 3: 351–368.

Bernritter, Stefan F., Iris van Ooijen, and Barbara C. N. Müller. 2017. "Self-Persuasion as Marketing Technique: The Role of Consumers' Involvement. *European Journal of Marketing* 51, 5–6: 1075–1090.

Bettcher, Talia Mae. 2013. "Trans Women and Interpretive Intimacy: Some Initial Reflections." In D. Castenada, ed., *The Essential Handbook of Women's Sexuality*. Santa Barbara, CA: Prager, pp. 51–68.

Boren, Michael. 2018. "Why a Transgender Woman Was Sent to a Men's Prison in Philadelphia." *Philadelphia Inquirer*, June 13, 2018. https://www.inquirer.com/philly/news/transgender-prison-inmates-philadelphia-police-policy-reeanna-segin-20180612.html

Boyd, Nan Alamilla. 2006. "Bodies in Motion: Lesbian and Transsexual Histories." In Susan Stryker and Stephen Whittle, eds., *The Transgender Studies Reader*. New York: Routledge, pp. 420–433.

Brader, Ted. 2005. "Striking a Responsive Chord: How Political Ads Motivate and Persuade Voters by Appealing to Emotions." *American Journal of Political Science* 49, 2: 388–405.

Brader, Ted. 2006. *Campaigning for Hearts and Minds: How Emotional Appeals in Political Ads Work*. Chicago: University of Chicago Press.

Brassel, Sheila T., and Veanne N. Anderson. 2019. "Who Thinks Outside the Gender Box? Feminism, Gender Self-Esteem, and Attitudes toward Trans People." *Sex Roles*. https://doi.org/10.1007/s11199-019-01066-4

Brewer, Marilynn B., and Rupert J. Brown. 1998. *Intergroup Relations*. New York: McGraw-Hill.

Brewer, Marilynn B., and Layton N. Lui. 1989. "The Primacy of Age and Sex in the Structure of Person Categories." *Social Cognition* 7, 3: 262–274.

Bridges, Tristan, and Tara Leigh Tober. 2017. "Masculinity & Violence, and the Violence of Masculinity." *Huffington Post*, November 16, 2017. https://www.huffingtonpost.com/entry/masculinity-violence-and-the-violence-of-masculinity_us_5a0d2d59e4b023a796fed40c

Bromwich, Jonah Engel. 2017. "How U.S. Military Policy on Transgender Personnel Changed Under Obama." *New York Times*, July 26, 2017. https://www.nytimes.com/2017/07/26/us/politics/trans-military-trump-timeline.html

Broockman, David, and Joshua Kalla. 2016. "Durably Reducing Transphobia: A Field Experiment on Door-to-Door Canvassing." *Science* 352, 6282: 220–224.

Brough, Aaron R., James E. B. Wilkie, Jinjing Ma, Mathew S. Isaac, and David Gal. 2016. "Is Eco-Friendly Unmanly? The Green-Feminine Stereotype and Its Effect on Sustainable Consumption." *Journal of Consumer Research* 43, 4: 567–582.

Brown, Anna. 2017. "Republicans, Democrats Have Starkly Different Views on Transgender Issues." *Pew Research Center*, November 8, 2017. https://www.pewresearch.org/fact-tank/2017/11/08/transgender-issues-divide-republicans-and-democrats/

Brown, George R. 2006. "Transsexuals in the Military: Flight into Hypermasculinity." In Susan Stryker and Stephen Whittle, eds., *The Transgender Studies Reader*. New York: Routledge, pp. 537–544.

Burdge, Barb J. 2007. "Bending Gender, Ending Gender: Theoretical Foundations for Social Work Practice with the Transgender Community." *Social Work* 52, 3: 243–250.

Burke, Peter J. 1991. "Identity Processes and Social Stress." *American Sociological Review* 56, 6: 836–849.

Burke, Peter J., and Jan E. Stets. 2009. *Identity Theory*. New York: Oxford University Press.

Butler, Judith. 1990. *Gender Trouble: Feminism and the Subversion of Identity*. New York: Routledge.

Camp, Bayliss J. 2008. "Mobilizing the Base and Embarrassing the Opposition: Defense of Marriage Referenda and Cross-Cutting Electoral Cleavages." *Sociological Perspectives* 51, 4: 713–733.

Campbell, Donald T. 1965. "Ethnocentric and Other Altruistic Motives." In David Levine, ed., *Nebraska Symposium on Motivation*, v. 13. Lincoln: University of Nebraska Press, pp. 283–311.

Campbell, David E., and J. Quin Monson. 2008. "The Religion Card: Gay Marriage and the 2004 Presidential Election." *Public Opinion Quarterly* 72, 3: 399–419.

Casey, Logan S. 2016. "The Politics of Disgust: Public Opinion Toward LGBTQ People and Policies." PhD Dissertation, University of Michigan.

Cavanaugh, Sheila L. 2010. *Queering Bathrooms: Gender, Sexuality, and the Hygienic Imagination*. Toronto: University of Toronto Press.

Cavanaugh, Sheila L. 2013. "Touching Gender: Abjection and the Hygienic Imagination." In Susan Stryker and Aren Z. Aizura, eds., *The Transgender Studies Reader 2*. New York: Routledge, pp. 426–442.

Charlesworth, Tessa E. S., and Mahzarin R. Banaji. 2019. "Patterns of Implicit and Explicit Attitudes, Vol. I: Long-Term Change and Stability from 2007 to 2016." *Psychological Science* 30, 2: 174–192.

Charlotte Observer. 2016. "McCrory Looks to Legislature for Help to Repeal Charlotte's Non-Discrimination Ordinance." *Charlotte Observer*, February 24, 2016. https://www.charlotteobserver.com/news/politics-government/article62053587.html

Chong, Dennis, and James N. Druckman. 2007. "Framing Theory." *Annual Review of Political Science* 10: 103–126.

Christensen, Jen. 2019. "Killings of Transgender People in the US Saw Another High Year." *CNN.com*, January 26, 2019. https://www.cnn.com/2019/01/16/health/transgender-deaths-2018/index.html

Citrin, Jack, and Matthew Wright. 2009. "Defining the Circle of We: American Identity and Immigration Policy." *The Forum* 7, 3: article 6.

Clifford, Scott, and Dane G. Wendell. 2015. "How Disgust Influences Health Purity Attitudes." *Political Behavior* 38, 1: 155–178.

Clifford, Scott, and Jennifer Jerit. 2018. "Disgust, Anxiety, and Political Learning in the Face of Threat." *American Journal of Political Science* 62, 2: 266–279.

Clifford, Scott, Jennifer Jerit, Carlislee Rainey, and Matt Motyl. 2015. "Moral Concerns and Policy Attitudes: Investigating the Influence of Elite Rhetoric." *Political Communication* 32, 2: 229–248.

Cohen, Geoffrey L., and David K. Sherman. 2014. "The Psychology of Change: Self-Affirmation and Social Psychological Intervention." *Annual Review of Psychology* 65: 333–371.

Cohen, Geoffrey L., David K. Sherman, Anthony Bastardi, Lillian Hsu, Michelle McGoey, and Lee Ross. 2007. "Bridging the Partisan Divide: Self-Affirmation Reduces Ideological Closed-Mindedness and Inflexibility in Negotiation." *Journal of Personality and Social Psychology* 93, 3: 415–430.

Conover, Pamela Johnston. 1988. "The Role of Social Groups in Political Thinking." *British Journal of Political Science* 18, 1: 51–76.

Coppock, Alexander. 2019. "Generalizing from Survey Experiments Conducted on Mechanical Turk: A Replication Approach." *Political Science Research and Methods* 7, 3: 613–628.

Coppock, Alexander E., and Oliver A. McClellan. 2019. "Validating the Demographic, Political, Psychological, and Experimental Results Obtained from a New Source of Online Survey Respondents." *Research & Politics.* https://doi.org/10.1177/2053168018822174

Cosmides, Leda, and John Tooby. 2000. "Evolutionary Psychology and the Emotions." *Handbook of Emotions* 2, 2: 91–115.

CRS. 2016a. "Law Enforcement and the Transgender Community - CRS Roll Call Training Video." United States Department of Justice, Community Relations Service, July 20, 2016. https://www.justice.gov/crs/video/law-enforcement-and-transgender-community-crs-roll-call-training-video

CRS. 2016b. "Respecting Identity | Law Enforcement Training and the Transgender Community." United States Department of Justice, Community Relations Service, November 29, 2016. https://www.justice.gov/crs/video/respecting-identity-law-enforcement-training-and-transgender-community

Cunningham, Emily, Catherine A. Forestell, and Cheryl L. Dickter. 2013. "Induced Disgust Affects Implicit and Explicit Responses toward Gay Men and Lesbians." *European Journal of Social Psychology* 43, 5: 362–369.

Currah, Paisley, and Lisa Lean Moore. 2013. "'We Won't Know Who You Are': Contesting Sex Designations in New York City Birth Certificates." In Susan Stryker and Aren Z. Aizura, eds., *Transgender Studies Reader 2.* New York: Routledge, pp. 607–622.

Dann, Carrie. 2019. "Most Americans Are A-OK With a Gay Presidential Candidate. That's a Big Shift in Less Than 15 Years." *NBC News,* April 1, 2019. https://www.nbcnews.com/card/most-americans-are-ok-gay-presidential-candidate-s-big-shift-n989541

Davis, Fred. 1961. "Deviance Disavowal: The Management of Strained Interaction by the Visibly Handicapped." *Social Problems* 9, 2: 120–132.

Davis, Heath Fogg. 2017. *Beyond Trans: Does Gender Matter?* New York: New York University Press.

Department of Defense. 2018. "2016 Demographics: Profile of the Military Community." http://download.militaryonesource.mil/12038/MOS/Reports/2016-Demographics-Report.pdf

Doherty, Carroll, Jocelyn Kiley, and Rachel Weisel. 2015. "Support for Same-Sex Marriage at Record High, but Key Segments Remain Opposed: 72% Say Legal Recognition is 'Inevitable.'" *Pew Research Center,* June 8, 2015. https://www.pewresearch.org/wp-content/uploads/sites/4/2015/06/6-8-15-Same-sex-marriage-release1.pdf

Domonoske, Camila. 2017. "17-Year-Old Transgender Boy Wins Texas Girls' Wrestling Championship." *National Public Radio,* February 27, 2017. http://www.npr.org/sections/thetwo-way/2017/02/27/517491492/17-year-old-transgender-boy-wins-texas-girls-wrestling-championship

Downs, Anthony. 1957. *An Economic Theory of Democracy.* New York: Harper and Row.

Druckman, James N. 2004. "Political Preference Formation: Competition, Deliberation, and the (Ir)relevance of Framing Effects." *American Political Science Review* 98, 4: 671–686.

Dyar, Christina, and Brian A. Feinstein. 2018. "Binegativity: Attitudes Toward and Stereotypes About Bisexual Individuals." In D. Joye Swan and Shani Habibi, eds., *Bisexuality: Theories, Research, and Recommendations for the Invisible Sexuality.* Cham, Switzerland: Springer, pp. 95–111.

Eagly, Alice H., and Shelly Chaiken. 1993. *The Psychology of Attitudes.* Orlando, FL: Harcourt Brace Jovanovich College Publishers.

Egan, Patrick J. 2013. "Analyzing the Evidence: Contact with Gay People and Attitudes about Gay Rights." In Theodore Lowi, Benjamin Ginsberg, Kenneth Shepsle, and Stephen Ansolabehere, eds., *American Government: Power and Purpose* (13th ed.). New York: W. W. Norton.

Ehrlich, Gaven, and Richard H. Gramzow. 2015. "The Politics of Affirmation Theory: When Group-Affirmation Leads to Greater Ingroup Bias." *Personality and Social Psychology Bulletin* 41, 8: 1110–1122.

Elephant. 2019. "How Advertisers Woke Up to the Aesthetic of New Masculinity." *Elephant.art*, March 6, 2019. https://elephant.art/advertising-and-the-aesthetic-of-new-masculinity/

Ely, Robin J. 1995. "The Power in Demography: Women's Social Constructions of Gender Identity at Work." *Academy of Management Journal* 38, 3: 589–634.

Engel, Stephen M. 2016. *Fragmented Citizens: The Changing Landscape of Gay and Lesbian Lives.* New York: New York University Press.

Enloe, Cynthia. 2017. *Exposing and Challenging the Persistence of Patriarchy.* Berkeley: University of California Press.

Enten, Harry. 2017. "Republican Senators Aren't Embracing Trump's Transgender Military Ban." *FiveThirtyEight*, July 26, 2017. https://fivethirtyeight.com/features/republican-senators-arent-embracing-trumps-transgender-military-ban/

Erikson, Robert S., and Kent L Tedin. 2015. *American Public Opinion: Its Origins, Content and Impact* (9th ed.). New York: Routledge.

Fasteau, Marc F. 1974. *The Male Machine.* New York: McGraw-Hill.

Ferdman, Soraya. 2018. "One Year After Trump Tweeted He'd Ban Transgender Troops, the Fight to Stop Him Continues." *Mashable*, July 26, 2018. https://mashable.com/2018/07/26/trump-transgender-military-ban/#_cqM5xsMGaqZ

Festinger, Leon. 1957. *A Theory of Cognitive Dissonance.* Stanford, CA: Stanford University Press.

Fiske, Susan T., and Shelley E. Taylor. 1991. *Social Cognition* (2nd ed.). New York: McGraw-Hill.

Flores, Andrew. 2015. "Attitudes toward Transgender Rights: Perceived Knowledge and Secondary Interpersonal Contact." *Politics, Groups, and Identities* 3, 3: 398–416.

Flores, Andrew R., and Scott Barclay. 2016. "Backlash, Consensus, Legitimacy, or Polarization: The Effect of Same-Sex Marriage Policy on Mass Attitudes." *Political Research Quarterly* 69, 1: 43–56.

Flores, Andrew R., Donald P. Haider-Markel, Daniel C. Lewis, Patrick R. Miller, Barry L. Tadlock, and Jami K. Taylor. 2017. "Challenged Expectations: Mere Exposure Effects on Attitudes About Transgender People and Rights." *Political Psychology* 39, 1: 197–216.

Flores, Andrew R., Donald P. Haider-Markel, Daniel C. Lewis, Patrick R. Miller, Barry L. Tadlock, and Jami K. Taylor. 2018. "Transgender Prejudice Reduction and Opinions on Transgender Rights: Results from a Mediation Analysis on Experimental Data." *Research & Politics.* doi:10.1177/2053168018764945.

Flores, Andrew R., Jody L. Herman, Gary J. Gates, and Taylor N. T. Brown. 2016. "How Many Adults Identify as Transgender in the United States?" *Williams Institute*, June 2016. https://williamsinstitute.law.ucla.edu/wp-content/uploads/How-Many-Adults-Identify-as-Transgender-in-the-United-States.pdf

Focus on the Family. 2015. "Transgenderism: Our Position." http://www.focusonthefamily.com/socialissues/sexuality/transgenderism/transgenderism-our-position

Furedi, Frank. 1997. *Culture of Fear.* London: Cassell.

Gadarian, Shana K., and Eric Van der Vort. 2017. "The Gag Reflex: Disgust Rhetoric and Gay Rights in American Politics." *Political Behavior* 40, 2: 521–543.

Gal, David and James Wilkie. 2010. "Real Men Don't Eat Quiche: Regulation of Gender-Expressive Choices by Men." *Social Psychological and Personality Science,* 1, 4: 291-301.

Gallup. 2019. "Gay and Lesbian Rights." *Gallup.com.* http://www.gallup.com/poll/1651/gay-lesbian-rights.aspx

Garretson, Jeremiah. 2018. *The Path to Gay Rights: How Activism and Coming Out Changed Public Opinion.* New York: New York University Press.

Gates, Gary J., and Jody L. Herman. 2014. "Transgender Military Service in the United States." Williams Institute, UCLA School of Law.

Gemmill, Allie. 2018. "Janet Mock Wrote and Directed an Episode of 'Pose' and Made TV History." *Teen Vogue,* July 9, 2018. https://www.teenvogue.com/story/janet-mock-wrote-directed-episode-of-pose-made-tv-history

Gender Equal NZ. 2018. "Gender Attitudes Survey: Full Results 2017." National Council of Women of New Zealand. Wellington, New Zealand.

Giddens, Anthony. 1990. *The Consequences of Modernity.* Stanford, CA: Stanford University Press.

Gillig, Traci K., and Sheila T. Murphy. 2016. "Fostering Support for LGBTQ Youth? The Effects of a Gay Adolescent Media Portrayal on Young Viewers." *International Journal of Communication* 10: 3828–3850.

Gillig, Traci K., Erica L. Rosenthal, Sheila T. Murphy, and Kate Langrall Folb. 2018. "More Than a Media Moment: The Influence of Televised Storylines on Viewers' Attitudes Toward Transgender People and Policies." *Sex Roles* 78, 7–8: 515–527.

GLAAD. 2012. "Victims or Villains: Examining Ten Years of Transgender Images on Television." *GLAAD,* November 20, 2012. https://www.glaad.org/publications/victims-or-villains-examining-ten-years-transgender-images-television

GLAAD. 2015. "Number of Americans Who Report Knowing a Transgender Person Doubles in Seven Years, According to New GLAAD Survey." *GLAAD,* September 17, 2015. http://www.glaad.org/releases/number-americans-who-report-knowing-transgender-person-doubles-seven-years-according-new

Glick, Peter, Candice Gangl, Samantha Gibb, Susan Klumpner, and Emily Weinberg. 2007. "Defensive Reactions to Masculinity Threat: More Negative Affect Toward Effeminate (but Not Masculine) Gay Men." *Sex Roles* 57, 1–2: 55–59.

Glotfelder, Michael Ann. 2012. "Undergraduate Students' Gender Self-Esteem and Attitudes Towards Transmen, Transwomen, Gay Men, and Lesbian Women." PhD Dissertation, Indiana State University. http://hdl.handle.net/10484/4592

Goldberg, Lesley. 2017. "Ryan Murphy Makes History With Largest Cast of Transgender Actors for FX's 'Pose.'" *Hollywood Reporter,* October 25, 2017. https://www.hollywoodreporter.com/live-feed/ryan-murphy-makes-history-largest-cast-transgender-actors-fxs-pose-1051877

Goldberg, Lewis R. 1993. "The Structure of Phenotypic Personality Traits." *American Psychologist* 48, 1: 26–34.

Green, Emma. 2019. "America Moved On From Its Gay-Rights Moment—And Left a Legal Mess Behind." *TheAtlantic.com,* August 17, 2019. https://www.theatlantic.com/politics/archive/2019/08/lgbtq-rights-america-arent-resolved/596287/

Haider-Markel, Donald, Patrick R. Miller, Andrew Flores, Daniel C. Lewis, Barry Tadlock, and Jami K. Taylor. 2017. "Bringing 'T' to the Table: Understanding Individual

Support of Transgender Candidates for Public Office." *Politics, Groups, and Identities* 5, 3: 399–417.

Haidt, Jonathan. 2003a. "The Moral Emotions." In Richard J. Davidson, Klaus R. Scherer, and H. Hill Goldsmith, eds., *Handbook of Affective Sciences*. New York: Oxford University Press, pp. 852–870.

Haidt, Jonathan. 2003b. "Elevation and the Positive Psychology of Morality." In Corey L. M. Keyes and Jonathan Haidt, eds., *Flourishing: Positive Psychology and the Life Well-Lived*. Washington, DC: American Psychological Association, pp. 275–289.

Haidt, Jonathan. 2006. *The Happiness Hypothesis: Finding Modern Truth in Ancient Wisdom*. New York: Basic Books.

Haines, Elizabeth L., and Laura J. Kray. 2005. "Self-Power Associations: The Possession of Power Impacts Women's Self-Concepts." *European Journal of Social Psychology* 35, 5: 643–662.

Halberstam, Judith. 1998. *Female Masculinity*. Durham, NC: Duke University Press.

Harbin, Ami, Brenda Beagan, and Lisa Goldberg. 2012. "Discomfort, Judgment, and Health Care for Queers." *Bioethical Inquiry* 9, 2: 149–160.

Harrison, Brian F. 2020. *A Change is Gonna Come: How to Have Effective Political Conversations in a Divided America*. New York: Oxford University Press.

Harrison, Brian F., and Melissa R. Michelson. 2012. "Not That There's Anything Wrong with That: The Effect of Personalized Appeals on Marriage Equality Campaigns." *Political Behavior* 34, 2: 325–344.

Harrison, Brian F., and Melissa R. Michelson. 2015. "God and Marriage: The Impact of Religious Identity Priming on Attitudes toward Same-Sex Marriage." *Social Science Quarterly* 96, 5: 1411–1423.

Harrison, Brian F., and Melissa R. Michelson. 2016. "More than a Game: Football Fans and Marriage Equality." *PS: Political Science & Politics* 49, 4: 782–787.

Harrison, Brian F., and Melissa R. Michelson. 2017a. *Listen, We Need to Talk: How to Change Attitudes about LGBT Rights*. New York: Oxford University Press.

Harrison, Brian F., and Melissa R. Michelson. 2017b. "Using Experiments to Understand Public Attitudes towards Transgender Rights." *Politics, Groups, and Identities* 5, 1: 152–160.

Harrison, Brian F., and Melissa R. Michelson. 2019. "Gender, Masculinity Threat, and Support for Transgender Rights: An Experimental Study." *Sex Roles* 80, 1–2: 63–75.

Hastorf, Albert H., Jeffrey Wildfogel, and Ted Cassman. 1979. "Acknowledgement of Handicap as a Tactic in Social Interaction." *Journal of Personality and Social Psychology* 37, 10: 1790–1797.

Hebl, Michelle R., and Robert E. Kleck. 2002. "Acknowledging One's Stigma in the Interview Setting: Effective Strategy or Liability?" *Journal of Applied Social Psychology* 32, 2: 223–249.

Hebl, Michelle R., and Jeanine L. Skorinko. 2005. "Acknowledging One's Physical Disability in the Interview: Does 'When' Make a Difference?" *Journal of Applied Social Psychology* 35, 12: 2477–2492.

Heise, David R. 2007. *Expressive Order: Confirming Sentiments in Social Actions*. New York: Springer.

Helms, Jeffrey L., and Ashley M. Waters. 2016. "Attitudes Toward Bisexual Men and Women." *Journal of Bisexuality* 16, 4: 454–467.

Herek, Gregory M. 2002. "Heterosexuals' Attitudes Toward Bisexual Men and Women in the United States." *Journal of Sex Research* 39, 4: 264–274.

Herek, Gregory M., and John P. Capitanio. 1996. "Some of my Best Friends: Intergroup Contact, Concealable Stigma, and Heterosexuals' Attitudes toward Gay Men and Lesbians." *Personality and Social Psychology Bulletin* 22, 4: 412–424.

Herek, Gregory M., and Eric K. Glunt. 1993. "Interpersonal Contact and Heterosexual's Attitudes Toward Gay Men: Results from a National Survey." *Journal of Sex Research* 30, 3: 239–244.

Herek, Gregory M., and Kevin A. McLemore. 2013. "Sexual Prejudice." *Annual Review of Psychology* 64: 309–333.

Hewstone, Miles, Mark Rubin, and Hazel Willis. 2002. "Intergroup Bias." *Annual Review of Psychology* 53: 575–604.

Hillygus, Sunshine D., and Todd G. Shields. 2005. "Moral Issues and Voter Decision Making in the 2004 Presidential Election." *PS: Political Science & Politics* 38, 2: 201–209.

Hoffarth, Mark Romeo, and Gordon Hodson. 2018. "When Intergroup Contact Is Uncommon and Bias Is Strong: The Case of Anti-Transgender Bias." *Psychology & Sexuality* 9, 3: 237–250.

Hogg, Michael A., and Dominic Abrams. 1988. *Social Identifications: A Social Psychology of Intergroup Relations and Group Processes*. New York: Routledge.

Hogg, Michael A., and Dominic Abrams. 1990. *Social Identity Theory: Constructive and Critical Advances*. New York: Springer-Verlag Publishing.

Holbrook, Morris B., and John O'Shaughnessy. 1984. "The Role of Emotion in Advertising." *Psychology and Marketing* 1, 2: 45–64.

Holden, Dominic. 2018. "We Made a List of All the Anti-LGBT Stuff Trump Has Done as President." *Buzzfeed News*, June 30, 2018. https://www.buzzfeednews.com/article/dominicholden/trump-lgbt-anti-actions-administration-pride-month

Huebner, Andrew J. 2018. "Gee! I Wish I Were a Man: Gender and the Great War." In Kara Dixon Vuic, ed., *The Routledge History of Gender, War, and the U.S. Military*. New York: Routledge, pp. 68–86.

Huetteman, Emmarie. 2019. "Trump Administration Rule Would Undo Health Care Protections for LGBTQ Patients." *Salon.com*, July 1, 2019. https://www.salon.com/2019/06/30/trump-administration-rule-would-undo-health-care-protections-for-lgbtq-patients_partner/

Human Rights Campaign Foundation. 2018. "Epidemic of Violence: Fatal Anti-Transgender Violence in America in 2018." *Human Rights Campaign*, November 19, 2018. https://assets2.hrc.org/files/assets/resources/AntiTransViolence-2018Report-Final.pdf

Inbar, Yoel., David A. Pizarro, Joshua Knobe, and Paul Bloom. 2009. "Disgust Sensitivity Predicts Intuitive Disapproval of Gays." *Emotion* 9, 3: 435–439.

Inbar, Yoel, David Pizarro, Ravi Iyer, and Jonathan Haidt. 2012. "Disgust Sensitivity, Political Conservativism, and Voting." *Social Psychological and Personality Science* 3, 5: 537–544.

Inbar, Yoel, and David Pizarro. 2014. "Disgust, Politics, and Responses to Threat." *Behavioral and Brain Sciences* 37, 3: 315–316.

Israel, Tania, and Jonathan J. Mohr. 2008. "Attitudes Toward Bisexual Women and Men." *Journal of Bisexuality* 4, 1–2: 117–134.

Jackman, Mary. 1994. *The Velvet Glove: Paternalism and Conflict in Gender, Class, and Race Relations*. Berkeley: University of California Press.

Jackson, Richard. 2011. "Culture, Identity, and Hegemony: Continuity and (the Lack of) Change in US Counterterrorism Policy from Bush to Obama. *International Politics* 48, 2–3: 390–411.

James, Sandy E., Jody L. Herman, Susan Rankin, Mara Keisling, Lisa Mottet, and Ma'ayan Anafi. 2016. *The Report of the 2015 U.S. Transgender Survey.* Washington, DC: National Center for Transgender Equality.

Jeffreys, Sheila. 2014. "The Politics of the Toilet: A Feminist Response to the Campaign to 'Degender' a Women's Space." *Women's Studies International Forum* 45: 42–51.

Johnson, David K. 2004. *The Lavender Scare: The Cold War Persecution of Gays and Lesbians in the Federal Government.* Chicago: University of Chicago Press.

Jones, Bryan, and Howard Rachlin. 2006. "Social Discounting." *Psychological Science* 17, 4: 283–286.

Jones, Jeffrey M. 2017. "In U.S., 10.2% of LGBT Adults Now Married to Same-Sex Spouse." *Gallup*, June 22, 2017. https://news.gallup.com/poll/212702/lgbt-adults-married-sex-spouse.aspx

Jones, Philip Edward, and Paul R. Brewer. 2018. "Elite Cues and Public Polarization on Transgender Rights." *Politics, Groups, and Identities.* doi:10.1080/21565503.2018.1441722.

Jones, Philip Edward, and Paul R. Brewer. 2019. "Gender Identity as a Political Cue: Voter Responses to Transgender Candidates." *Journal of Politics* 81, 2: 697–701.

Jones, Philip Edward, Paul R. Brewer, Dannagal G. Young, Jennifer L. Lambe, and Lindsay H. Hoffman. 2018. "Explaining Public Opinion toward Transgender People, Rights, and Candidates." *Public Opinion Quarterly* 82, 2: 252–278.

Jones, Robert P., Natalie Jackson, Maxine Najle, Oyindamola Bola, and Daniel Greenberg. 2019. "America's Growing Support for Transgender Rights." *PRRI*, June 10, 2019. https://www.prri.org/research/americas-growing-support-for-transgender-rights

Juang, Richard M. 2006. "Transgendering the Politics of Recognition." In Paisley Currah, Richard M. Juang, and Shannon Price Minter, eds., *Transgender Rights.* Minneapolis: University of Minnesota Press, pp. 242–261.

Kam, Cindy D., and Beth A. Estes. 2016. "Disgust Sensitivity and Public Demand for Protection." *Journal of Politics* 78, 2: 481–496.

Karner, Tracy. 1996. "Fathers, Sons, and Vietnam: Masculinity and Betrayal in the Life Narratives of Vietnam Veterans with Post Traumatic Stress Disorder." *American Studies* 37, 1: 63–94.

Keltner, Dacher, and Jonathan Haidt. 2003. "Approaching Awe, a Moral, Spiritual, and Aesthetic Emotion." *Cognition & Emotion* 17, 2: 297–314.

Kime, Patricia. 2015. "DoD Spends $84M a Year on Viagra, Similar Meds." *MilitaryTimes*, February 13, 2015. https://www.militarytimes.com/pay-benefits/military-benefits/health-care/2015/02/13/dod-spends-84m-a-year-on-viagra-similar-meds/

Kimmel, Michael S. 1996. *Manhood in America: A Cultural History.* New York: Free Press.

Kimmel, Michael. 2012. "Masculinity, Mental Illness, and Guns: A Lethal Equation?" *CNN.com*, December 19, 2012. http://www.cnn.com/2012/12/19/living/men-guns-violence/

King, Mark E., Sam Winter, and Beverly Webster. 2009. "Contact Reduces Transprejudice: A Study on Attitudes towards Transgenderism and Transgender Civil Rights in Hong Kong." *International Journal of Sexual Health* 21, 1: 17–34.

Klar, Samara. 2013. "The Influence of Competing Identity Primes on Political Preferences." *Journal of Politics* 75, 4: 1108–1124.

Knaff, Donna B. 2018. "Homos, Whores, Rapists, and the Clap: American Military Sexuality Since the Revolutionary War." In Kara Dixon Vuic, ed., *The Routledge History of Gender, War, and the U.S. Military.* New York: Routledge, pp. 269–286.

Kristof, Nicholas. 2018. "It's Time to Talk About the N.R.A." *New York Times,* October 29, 2018. https://www.nytimes.com/interactive/2018/10/29/opinion/nra-mass-shootings-pittsburgh.html

Lai, Calvin K., Jonathan Haidt, and Brian A. Nosek. 2014. "Moral Elevation Reduces Prejudice against Gay Men." *Cognition and Emotion* 28, 5: 781–794.

Lang, Nico. 2016. "Record Number of Americans Say Firing Someone for Being LGBT Should Be Illegal." *The Advocate,* October 12, 2016. http://www.advocate.com/politics/2016/10/12/record-number-americans-say-firing-someone-being-lgbt-should-be-illegal

Lauber, Christopher, Carlos Nordt, Luis Falcato, and Wulf Rössler. 2004. "Factors Influencing Social Distance Toward People with Mental Illness." *Community Mental Health Journal* 40, 3: 265–274.

Lazarsfeld, Paul F., Bernard Berelson, and Hazel Gaudet. 1948. *The People's Choice: How the Voter Makes Up His Mind in a Presidential Campaign* (2nd ed.). New York: Columbia University Press.

Lee, Cynthia, and Peter Kwan. 2014. "The Trans Panic Defense: Masculinity, Heteronormativity, and the Murder of Transgender Women." *Hastings Law Journal* 66, 1: 77–132.

Lehmiller, Justin J., Alvin T. Law, and Teceta Thomas Tormala. 2010. "The Effect of Self-Affirmation on Sexual Prejudice." *Journal of Experimental Social Psychology* 46, 2: 276–285.

Levant, Ronald F., Rosalie J. Hall, and Thomas J. Rankin. 2013. "Male Role Norms Inventory–Short Form (MRNI-SF): Development, Confirmatory Factor Analytic Investigation of Structure, and Measurement Invariance across Gender." *Journal of Counseling Psychology* 60, 2: 228–238.

Levay, Kevin E., Jeremy Freese, and James N. Druckman. 2016. "The Demographic and Political Composition of Mechanical Turk Samples." *SAGE Open* 6, 1. doi:10.1177/2158244016636433

Levi, Jennifer L., and Bennett H. Klein. 2006. "Pursuing Protection for Transgender People Through Disability Laws." In Paisley Currah, Richard M. Juang, and Shannon Price Minter, eds., *Transgender Rights.* Minneapolis: University of Minnesota Press, pp. 74–92.

Lewis, Daniel C., Andrew R. Flores, Donald P. Haider-Markel, Patrick R. Miller, Barry L. Tadlock, and Jami K. Taylor. 2017. "Degrees of Acceptance: Variation in Public Attitudes Toward Segments of the LGBT Community." *Political Research Quarterly* 70, 4: 861–875.

Lewis, Daniel C., Jami K. Taylor, Brian DiSarro, and Matthew L. Jacobsmeier. 2015. "Is Transgender Policy Different? Policy Complexity, Policy Diffusion, and LGBT Nondiscrimination Law." In Jami K. Taylor and Donald P. Haider-Markel, eds., *Transgender Rights and Politics: Groups, Issue Framing, & Policy Adoption.* Ann Arbor: University of Michigan Press, pp. 155–188.

Lewis, Gregory B. 2005. "Same-Sex Marriage and the 2004 Presidential Election." *PS: Political Science & Politics* 38, 2: 195–199.

Lewis, Gregory P. 2007. "Personal Relationships and Support for Gay Rights." *Andrew Young School of Policy Studies, Georgia State University, Research Paper Series, Working Paper 07-10*, March 2007. http://aysps.gsu.edu/publications/2007/index.htm

Loewenstein, George, and Deborah Small. 2007. "The Scarecrow and the Tin Man: The Vicissitudes of Human Sympathy and Caring." *Review of General Psychology* 11, 2: 112–126.

Lopez, German. 2019. "The House Just Passed a Sweeping LGBTQ Rights Bill." *Vox. com*, May 17, 2019. https://www.vox.com/policy-and-politics/2019/5/17/18627771/equality-act-house-congress-lgbtq-rights-discrimination

Lorde, Audre. 1978. "A Litany for Survival." In *The Collected Poems of Audre Lorde*. New York: W. W. Norton.

Lyons, Brent J., Larry R. Martinez, Enrica N. Ruggs, Michelle R. Hebl, Ann Marie Ryan, Katherine R. O'Brien, and Adam Roebuck. 2018. "To Say or Not to Say: Different Strategies of Acknowledging a Visible Disability." *Journal of Management* 44, 5: 1980–2007.

Maass, Anne, Mara Cadinu, Gaia Guarnieri, and Annalisa Grasselli. 2003. "Sexual Harassment Under Social Identity Threat: The Computer Harassment Paradigm." *Journal of Personality and Social Psychology* 85, 5: 853–870.

Macmillan, Ross, and Rosemary Gartner. 1999. "When She Brings Home the Bacon: Labor-Force Participation and the Risk of Spousal Violence Against Women." *Journal of Marriage and the Family* 61, 4: 947–958.

Marcus, George EE. 2003. "The Psychology of Emotion and Politics." In David O. Sears, Leonie Huddy, and Robert Jervis, eds., *Oxford Handbook of Political Psychology*. New York: Oxford University Press: pp. 182–221.

Marcus, George, W. Russell Neuman, and Michael MacKuen. 2000. *Affective Intelligence and Political Judgment*. Chicago: University of Chicago Press.

Margolin, Emma. 2016. "With Transgender Military Ban Lifted, Obama Cements Historic LGBT Rights Legacy." *NBC News*, June 30, 2016. https://www.nbcnews.com/feature/nbc-out/transgender-military-ban-lifted-obama-cements-historic-lgbt-rights-legacy-n600541

Martin, Carol Lynn, and Diane N. Ruble. 2010. "Patterns of Gender Development." *Annual Review of Psychology* 61: 353–381.

Martínez, Carmen, Carolina Vázquez, and Juan Manuel Falomir-Pichastor. 2015. "Perceived Similarity with Gay Men Mediates the Effect of Antifemininity on Heterosexual Men's Antigay Prejudice." *Journal of Homosexuality* 62, 11: 1560–1575.

Mason, Liliana. 2018. *Uncivil Agreement: How Politics Became Our Identity*. Chicago: University of Chicago Press.

Matsick, Jes L., and Jennifer D. Rubin. 2018. "Bisexual prejudice among lesbian and gay people: Examining the roles of gender and perceived sexual orientation." *Psychology of Sexual Orientation and Gender Diversity* 5, 2: 143–155.

McCall, Cade, and Nilanjana Dasgupta. 2007. "The Malleability of Men's Gender Self-Concept." *Self and Identity* 6, 2–3: 173–188.

McClosky, Herbert, and Alida Brill. 1983. *The Dimensions of Tolerance: What Americans Believe About Civil Liberties*. New York: Russell Sage Foundation.

McDermott, Monika L. 2016. *Masculinity, Femininity, and American Political Behavior*. New York: Oxford University Press.

McGuire, William J. 1985. "Attitudes and Attitude Change." In Gardner Lindzey and Elliot Aronson, eds., *Handbook of Social Psychology* (3rd ed., Vol. 2). New York: Random House, pp. 233–346.

Meadows, Tey. 2018. *Trans Kids: Being Gendered in the Twenty-First Century.* Berkeley: University of California Press.

Meier, Stacey Colton, and Christine M. Labuski. 2013. "The Demographics of the Transgender Population." In Amanda K. Baumle, ed., *International Handbook on the Demography of Sexuality.* New York: Springer, pp. 289–327.

Michelson, Melissa R., and Elizabeth JoAnn Schmitt. 2019. "Party Politics in the U.S." In Donald P. Haider-Markel, ed., *Oxford Encyclopedia of LGBT Politics and Policy.* New York: Oxford University Press.

Milk, Harvey. 1978. "That's What America Is." Speech given at Gay Freedom Day Parade of June 25, 1978, San Francisco, CA. Transcript provided in Schilts, Randy. 1982. *The Mayor of Castro Street: The Life and Times of Harvey Milk.* New York: St. Martin's Press.

Miller, Patrick R., Andrew R. Flores, Donald P. Haider-Markel, Daniel C. Lewis, Barry L. Tadlock, and Jami K. Taylor. 2017. "Transgender Politics as Body Politics: Effects of Disgust Sensitivity and Authoritarianism on Transgender Rights Attitudes." *Politics, Groups, and Identities* 5, 1: 4–24.

Mills, Judson, Faye Z. Belgrave, and Kathy M. Boyer. 1984. "Reducing Avoidance of Social Interaction with a Physically Disabled Person by Mentioning the Disability Following a Request for Aid." *Journal of Applied Social Psychology* 14, 1: 1–11.

Monro, Surya. 2005. "Beyond Male and Female: Poststructuralism and the Spectrum of Gender." *International Journal of Transgenderism* 8, 1: 3–22.

Monro, Surya. 2019. "Non-Binary and Genderqueer: An Overview of the Field." *International Journal of Transgenderism* 20, 2–3: 126–131.

Mooijman, Marlon, and Chadly Stern. 2016. "When Perspective Taking Creates a Motivational Threat: The Case of Conservatism, Same-Sex Sexual Behavior, and Anti-Gay Attitudes." *Personality and Social Psychology Bulletin* 42, 6: 738–754.

Moyer, Justin Wm. 2015. "Why Houston's Gay Rights Ordinance Failed: Fear of Men in Women's Bathrooms." *Washington Post,* November 3, 2015. https://www.washingtonpost.com/news/morning-mix/wp/2015/11/03/why-houstons-gay-rights-ordinance-failed-bathrooms/

Mucciaroni, Gary. 2008. *Same Sex, Different Politics: Success & Failure in the Struggles Over Gay Rights.* Chicago: University of Chicago Press.

Murib, Zein. 2019. "Administering Biology: How 'Bathroom Bills' Criminalize and Stigmatize Trans and Gender Nonconforming People in Public Space." *Administrative Theory & Praxis.* doi: 10.1080/10841806.2019.1659048

Myers, Sarah Parry. 2018. "'The Women Behind the Men Behind the Gun': Gendered Identities and Militarization in the Second World War." In Kara Dixon Vuic, ed., *The Routledge History of Gender, War, and the U.S. Military.* New York: Routledge, pp. 87–102.

Nagoshi, Julie L., Katherine A. Adams, Heather K. Terrell, Eric D. Hill, Stephanie Brzuzy, and Craig T. Nagoshi. 2008. "Gender Differences in Correlates of Homophobia and Transphobia." *Sex Roles* 59, 7–8: 521–531.

National Center for Transgender Equality (NCTE). 2016a. "Frequently Asked Questions About Transgender People." *National Center for Transgender Equality,* July 9, 2016. http://www.transequality.org/issues/resources/frequently-asked-questions-about-transgender-people

National Center for Transgender Equality (NCTE). 2016b. "An Introduction to Transgender People." *National Center for Transgender Equality,* July 11, 2016. https://www.youtube.com/watch?v=YSuJ70OMo3I

New York Times. 2018. "A Growing Problem for the Military Transgender Ban: Facts." *New York Times*, April 29, 2018. https://www.nytimes.com/2018/04/29/opinion/military-transgender-ban.html

Noble, Greg. 2005. "The Discomfort of Strangers: Racism, Incivility and Ontological Security in a Relaxed and Comfortable Nation." *Journal of Intercultural Studies* 26, 1: 107–120.

Norton, Aaron T., and Gregory M. Herek. 2013. "Heterosexuals' Attitudes Toward Transgender People: Findings from a National Probability Sample of U.S. Adults." *Sex Roles* 68, 11–12: 738–753.

Nussbaum, Martha. 2010. *From Disgust to Humanity: Sexual Orientation and Constitutional Law*. New York: Oxford University Press.

Oaks, Penelope J., S. Alexander Haslam, and John C. Turner. 1994. *Stereotyping and Social Reality*. Cambridge, MA: Wiley-Blackwell.

Panagopoulos, Costas. 2011. "Thank You for Voting: Gratitude Expression and Voter Mobilization." *Journal of Politics* 73, 3: 707–717.

Paschall, Patrick A. 2016. "Transgender Voters." In Kyle L. Kreider and Thomas J. Baldino, eds., *Minority Voting in the United States* (Vol. 2). Santa Barbara, CA: Praeger, pp. 408–430.

Payne, Elizabethe, and Melissa Smith. 2014. "The Big Freak Out: Educator Fear in Response to the Presence of Transgender Elementary School Students." *Journal of Homosexuality* 61, 3: 399–418.

Pell, Samantha. 2019. "Girls Say Connecticut's Transgender Athlete Policy Violates Title IX, File Federal Complaint." *Washington Post*, June 19, 2019. https://www.washingtonpost.com/sports/2019/06/19/girls-say-connecticuts-transgender-athlete-policy-violates-title-ix-file-federal-complaint/

Petty, Richard E., and John T. Cacioppo. 1981. *Attitudes and Persuasion: Classic and Contemporary Approaches*. Dubuque, IA: William C. Brown.

Petty, Richard E., and John T. Cacioppo. 1986. "The Elaboration Likelihood Model of Persuasion." *Advances in Experimental Social Psychology* 19: 124–181.

Pew Research Center. 2012. "More Support for Gun Rights, Gay Marriage Than in 2008, 2004." *Pew Research Center*, April 25, 2012. https://www.pewresearch.org/wp-content/uploads/sites/4/legacy-pdf/4-25-12-Social-Issues.pdf

Pew Research Center. 2015. "Support for Same-Sex Marriage at Record High, but Key Segments Remain Opposed." *Pew Research Center*, June 8, 2015. https://www.pewresearch.org/wp-content/uploads/sites/4/2015/06/6-8-15-Same-sex-marriage-release1.pdf

Pew Research Center. 2016. "Vast Majority of Americans Know Someone Who Is Gay, Fewer Know Someone Who Is Transgender." *Pew Research Center*, September 28, 2016. https://www.pewforum.org/2016/09/28/5-vast-majority-of-americans-know-someone-who-is-gay-fewer-know-someone-who-is-transgender/

Pew Research Center. 2017. "The Partisan Divide on Political Values Grows Even Wider." *Pew Research Center*, October 5, 2017. https://www.people-press.org/2017/10/05/the-partisan-divide-on-political-values-grows-even-wider/

Plutchik, Robert. 1980. *Emotion: A Psychoevolutionary Synthesis*. New York: Harper and Row.

Plutchik, Robert. 2001. "The Nature of Emotions: Human Emotions Have Deep Evolutionary Roots, a Fact That May Explain Their Complexity and Provide Tools for Clinical Practice." *American Scientist* 89, 4: 344–350.

Poteat, Tonia, Danielle German, and Deanna Kerrigan. 2013. "Managing Uncertainty: A Grounded Theory of Stigma in Transgender Health Care Encounters." *Social Science & Medicine* 84: 22–29.

Pride on Screen. 2019. "Pride on Screen: Trans Visibility." *Crooked Minis*, June 26, 2019. https://crooked.com/podcast/pride-on-screen-trans-visibility/

Rasinski, Kenneth A. 1989. "The Effect of Question Wording on Public Support for Government Spending." *Public Opinion Quarterly* 53, 3: 388–394.

Raymond, Janice. 1979. *The Transsexual Empire: The Making of the She-Male*. Boston: Beacon Press.

Redlawsk, David P. 2006. "Feeling Politics: New Research into Emotion and Politics." In David P. Redlawsk, ed., *Feeling Politics: Emotion in Political Information Processing*. New York: Palgrave Macmillan, pp. 1–10.

Rimmerman, Craig A. 2015. *The Lesbian and Gay Movements: Assimilation or Liberation?* (2nd ed). Boulder, CO: Westview Press.

Rivera, Luis M., and Nilanjana Dasgupta. 2018. "The Detrimental Effect of Affirming Masculinity on Judgments of Gay Men." *Psychology of Men & Masculinity* 19, 1: 102–116.

Robinson, Grant. 2018. "Grainger Co. Shop Owner That Made Headlines for 'No Gays Allowed' Sign Calls SCOTUS Ruling a Win." *WBIR.com*, June 4, 2019. https://www.wbir.com/article/news/local/grainger-co-shop-owner-that-made-headlines-for-no-gays-allowed-sign-calls-scotus-ruling-a-win/51-561483750

Rosentiel, Tom. 2007. "Four-in-Ten Americans Have Close Friends or Relatives Who are Gay." *Pew Research Center*, May 22, 2007. https://www.pewresearch.org/2007/05/22/fourinten-americans-have-close-friends-or-relatives-who-are-gay/

Roughgarden, Joan. 2013. *Evolution's Rainbow: Diversity, Gender, and Sexuality in Nature and People*. Berkeley: University of California Press.

Rubin, Mark, and Miles Hewstone. 1998. "Social Identity Theory's Self-Esteem Hypothesis: A Review and Some Suggestions for Clarification." *Personality and Social Psychology Review* 2, 1: 4–62.

Rubinstein, Tanya, Shiri Makov, and Ayelet Sarel. 2013. "Don't Bi-Negative: Reduction of Negative Attitudes Toward Bisexuals by Blurring the Gender Dichotomy." *Journal of Bisexuality* 13, 3: 356–373.

Rudman, Laurie A., and Julie E. Phelan. 2010. "The Effect of Priming Gender Roles on Women's Implicit Gender Beliefs and Career Aspirations." *Social Psychology* 41, 3: 192–202.

Sachdev, Itesh, and Richard Y. Bourhis. 1987. "Status Differentials and Intergroup Behaviour." *European Journal of Social Psychology* 17, 3: 277–293.

Safer, Joshua D., and Vin Tangpricha. 2019. "Care of the Transgender Patient." *Annals of Internal Medicine In the Clinic*. 171,1; ITC1–ITC16.

Sarup, Gian, Robert W. Suchner, and Gitanjali Gaylord. 1991. "Contrast Effects and Attitude Change: A Test of the Two-Stage Hypothesis of Social Judgment Theory." *Social Psychology Quarterly* 54, 4: 364–372.

Schaefer, Agnes Gereben, Radha Iyengar Plumb, Srikanth Kadiyala, Jennifer Kavanagh, Charles C. Engel, Kayla M. Williams, and Amii M. Kress. 2016. *Assessing the Implications of Allowing Transgender Personnel to Serve Openly*. Santa Monica, CA: RAND Corporation. https://www.rand.org/pubs/research_reports/RR1530.html

Scherer, Klaus R. 2000. "Psychological Models of Emotion." In Joan C. Borod, ed., *The Neuropsychology of Emotion*. New York: Oxford University Press: pp. 137–162.

Scheve, Kenneth, and David Stasavage. 2006. "Religion and Preferences for Social Insurance." *Quarterly Journal of Political Science* 1, 3: 255–286.

Schiappa, Edward, Peter B. Gregg, and Dean E. Hewes. 2005. "The Parasocial Contact Hypothesis." *Communication Monographs* 72, 1: 92–115.

Schilt, Kristen, and Laurel Westbrook. 2015. "Bathroom Battlegrounds and Penis Panics." *Contexts* 14, 3: 26–31.

Schnall, Simone, and Jean Roper. 2012. "Elevation Puts Moral Values Into Action." *Social Psychological and Personality Science* 3, 3: 373–378.

Schnall, Simone, Jean Roper, and Daniel M. T. Fessler. 2010. "Elevation Leads to Altruistic Behavior." *Psychological Science* 21, 3: 315–320.

Schneider, Anne, and Helen Ingram. 1993. "Social Construction of Target Populations: Implications for Politics and Policy." *American Political Science Review* 87, 2: 334–347.

Schwarz, Norbert, and Gerd Bohner. 2001. "The Construction of Attitudes." In Abraham Tesser and Norbert Schwarz, eds., *Blackwell Handbook of Social Psychology: Intraindividual Processes*. Malden, MA: Blackwell Publishing, pp. 436–457.

Serano, Julia. 2013. "Skirt Chasers: Why the Media Depicts the Trans Revolution in Lipstick and Heels." In Susan Stryker and Aren Z. Aizura, eds., *The Transgender Studies Reader 2*. New York: Routledge, pp. 226–233.

Sherif, Carolyn W., Muzafer Sharif, and Roger E. Nebergall. 1965. *Attitude and Attitude Change: The Social Judgment-Involvement Approach*. Philadelphia: Saunders.

Silver, Nate. 2015. "Change Doesn't Usually Come This Fast." *FiveThirtyEight.com*, June 26, 2015. https://fivethirtyeight.com/features/change-doesnt-usually-come-this-fast/

Sinclair, Stacey, Curtis D. Hardin, and Brian S. Lowery. 2006. "Self-Stereotyping in the Context of Multiple Social Identities." *Journal of Personality and Social Psychology* 90, 4: 529–542.

Singletary, Sarah L., and Michelle R. Hebl. 2009. "Compensatory Strategies for Reducing Interpersonal Discrimination: The Effectiveness of Acknowledgments, Increased Positivity, and Individuating Information." *Journal of Applied Psychology* 94, 3: 797–805.

Skipworth, Sue Ann, Andrew Garner, and Bryan Dettrey. 2010. "Limitations of the Contact Hypothesis: Heterogeneity in the Contact Effect on Attitudes Toward Gay Rights." *Politics & Policy* 38, 5: 887–906.

Smith, Daniel A., Matthew DeSantis, and Jason Kassel. 2006. "Same-Sex Marriage Ballot Measures and the 2004 Presidential Election." *State and Local Government Review* 38, 2: 78–91.

Smith, Rachel A. 2007. "Language of the Lost: An Explication of Stigma Communication." *Communication Theory* 17, 4: 462–485.

Smith, Sara, Amber Axelton, and Donald Saucier. 2009. "The Effects of Contact on Sexual Prejudice: A Meta-Analysis." *Sex Roles* 61, 3: 178–191.

Sniderman, Paul M., and Sean M. Theriault. 2004. "The Structure of Political Argument and the Logic of Issue Framing." In Willem E. Saris and Paul M. Sniderman, eds., *Studies in Public Opinion*. Princeton, NJ: Princeton University Press, pp. 133–165.

Solomon, Marc. 2014. *Winning Marriage: The Inside Story of How Same-Sex Couples Took on the Politicians and Pundits—and Won*. New York: ForeEdge Publishers.

Starr, Christine R., and Eileen L. Zurbriggen. 2017. "Sandra Bem's Gender Schema Theory After 34 Years: A Review of its Reach and Impact." *Sex Roles* 76, 9–10: 566–578.

Steinmetz, Katy. 2019. "Why Federal Laws Don't Explicitly Ban Discrimination Against LGBT Americans." *Time.com*, March 21, 2019. https://time.com/5554531/equality-act-lgbt-rights-trump/

Stone, Amy. 2012. *Gay Rights at the Ballot Box*. Minneapolis: University of Minnesota Press.

Stone, Jeff, Jessica Whitehead, Toni Schmader, and Elizabeth Focella. 2011. "Thanks for Asking: Self-Affirming Questions Reduce Backlash when Stigmatized Targets Confront Prejudice." *Journal of Experimental Social Psychology* 47, 3: 589–598.

Tadlock, Barry L., Andrew R. Flores, Donald P. Haider-Markel, Daniel C. Lewis, Patrick R. Miller, and Jami K. Taylor. 2017. "Testing Contact Theory and Attitudes on Transgender Rights." *Public Opinion Quarterly* 81, 4: 956–972.

Tajfel, Henri. 1979. *Studies in the Social Psychology of Intergroup Relations*. London: European Monographs in Social Psychology.

Tajfel, Henri. 1981. *Human Groups and Social Categories: Studies in Human Psychology*. Cambridge University Press.

Tajfel, Henri, and John C. Turner. 1979. "An Integrative Theory of Intergroup Conflict." In William G. Austin and Stephen Worchel, eds., *The Social Psychology of Intergroup Relations*. Monterey, CA: Brooks/Cole, pp. 7–24.

Tajfel, Henri, and John C. Turner. 1986. "The Social Identity Theory of Intergroup Relations." In Stephen Worchel and William G. Austin, eds., *Psychology of Intergroup Relations*. Chicago: Nelson-Hall, pp. 7–24.

Taylor, Jami K., and Daniel C. Lewis. 2015. "The Advocacy Coalition Framework and Transgender Inclusion in LGBT Rights Activism." In Jami K. Taylor and Donald P. Haider-Markel, eds., *Transgender Rights and Politics: Groups, Issue Framing, & Policy Adoption*. Ann Arbor: University of Michigan Press, pp. 108–132.

Taylor, Jami K., Daniel C. Lewis, and Donald P. Haider-Markel. 2018. *The Remarkable Rise of Transgender Rights*. Ann Arbor: University of Michigan Press.

Taylor, Jami K., Barry L. Tadlock, Sarah J. Poggione, and Brian DiSarro. 2014. "Transgender-Inclusive Ordinances in Cities." In Jami K. Taylor and Donald P. Haider-Markel, eds., *Transgender Rights and Politics: Groups, Issue Framing, & Policy Adoption*. Ann Arbor: University of Michigan Press, pp. 135–154.

Tee, Nicola, and Peter Hegarty. 2006. "Predicting Opposition to the Civil Rights of Trans Persons in the United Kingdom." *Journal of Community & Applied Social Psychology* 16, 1: 70–80.

Terrizzi Jr., John A., Natalie J. Shook, and W. Larry Ventis. 2010. "Disgust: A Predictor of Social Conservativism and Prejudicial Attitudes toward Homosexuals." *Personality and Individual Differences* 49, 6: 587–592.

Theisen, Lauren. 2019. "Purple-Haired Lesbian Goddess Flattens France Like a Crêpe." *Deadspin*, June 28, 2019. https://deadspin.com/purple-haired-lesbian-goddess-flattens-france-like-a-cr-1835954827

Thorbecke, Catherine. 2018. "Transgender Athletes Speak Out as Parents Petition to Change Policy That Allows Them to Compete as Girls." *Good Morning America, ABC News*, June 22, 2018. https://abcnews.go.com/GMA/News/transgender-athletes-speak-parents-petition-change-policy-compete/story?id=56071191

Tobin, Desiree D., Meenakshi Menon, Madhavi Menon, Brooke C. Spatta, Ernest Hodges, and David G. Perry. 2010. "The Intrapsychics of Gender: A Model of Self-Socialization." *Psychological Review* 117, 2: 601–622.

Tompkins, Avery. 2014. "Asterisk." *Transgender Studies Quarterly* 1, 1–2: 26–27.

Tourjée, Diana. 2015. "Why Do Men Kill Trans Women? Gender Theorist Judith Butler Explains." *Broadly, Vice.com,* December 16, 2015. https://www.vice.com/en_us/article/ z4jd7y/why-do-men-kill-trans-women-gender-theorist-judith-butler-explains

Townsend, Megan. 2014. "GLAAD's Third Annual Trans Images on TV Report Finds Some Improvement." *GLAAD,* November 18, 2014. https://www.glaad.org/blog/ glaads-third-annual-trans-images-tv-report-finds-some-improvement

Tropiano, Stephen. 2002. *The Prime Time Closet: A History of Gays and Lesbians on TV.* New York: Hal Leonard Corporation.

Tupes, Ernest C., and Raymond E. Christal. 1961. "Recurrent Personality Factors Based on Trait Ratings." No. ASD-TR-61-97. Personal Research Lab, Lackland AFB, Texas. http://www.dtic.mil/get-tr-doc/pdf?AD=AD0267778

Vakratsas, Demetrios, and Tim Ambler. 1999. "How Advertising Works: What Do We Really Know?" *Journal of Marketing* 63, 1: 26–43.

Van de Vyver, Julie, and Dominic Abrams. 2017. "Is Moral Elevation an Approach-Oriented Emotion?" *The Journal of Positive Psychology* 12, 2: 178–185.

Villicana, Adrian, Luis M. Rivera, and Donna M. Garcia. 2018. "When One's Group is Beneficial: The Effect of Group-Affirmation and Subjective Group Identification on Prejudice." *Group Processes & Intergroup Relations* 21, 6: 962–976.

Vincent, Wilson, Dominic J. Parrott, and John L. Peterson. 2011. "Effects of Traditional Gender Role Norms and Religious Fundamentalism on Self-Identified Heterosexual Men's Attitudes, Anger, and Aggression Toward Gay Men and Lesbians." *Psychology of Men & Masculinity* 12, 4: 383–400.

Vokey, Megan, Bruce Tefft, and Chris Tysiaczny. 2013. "An Analysis of Hyper-Masculinity in Magazine Advertisements." *Sex Roles* 68, 9–10: 562–576.

Wade, Lisa. 2016. "The Hypermasculine Violence of Omar Mateen and Brock Turner." *New Republic,* June 14, 2016. https://newrepublic.com/article/134270/ hypermasculine-violence-omar-mateen-brock-turner

Weinstein, Netta, William S. Ryan, Cody R. DeHaan, Andrew K. Przybylski, Nicole Legate, and Richard M. Ryan. 2012. "Parental Autonomy Support and Discrepancies Between Implicit and Explicit Sexual Identities: Dynamics of Self-Acceptance and Defense." *Journal of Personality and Social Psychology* 102, 4: 815–832.

Westbrook, Laurel, and Kristen Schilt. 2014. "Doing Gender, Determining Gender: Transgender People, Gender Panics, and the Maintenance of the Sex/Gender/ Sexuality System." *Gender & Society* 28, 1: 32–57.

Where We Are on TV. 2019. "Where We Are on TV: 2018–2019." *GLAAD.org,* May 30, 2019. https://www.arcusfoundation.org/wp-content/uploads/2019/05/ GLAAD-Where-We-Are-on-TV.pdf

White, Judith B., and Wendy L. Gardner. 2009. "Think Women, Think Warm: Stereotype Content Activation in Women with a Salient Gender Identity, Using a Modified Stroop Task." *Sex Roles* 60, 3: 247–260.

Wilchins, Riki Anne, 1997. *Read My Lips: Sexual Subversion and the End of Gender.* Ithaca, NY: Firebrand Books.

Wilkinson, Wayne. 2004. "Authoritarian Hegemony, Dimensions of Masculinity, and Male Antigay Attitudes." *Psychology of Men & Masculinity* 5, 2: 121–131.

Willer, Robb, Christabel Rogalin, Bridget Conlon, and Michael T. Wojnowicz. 2013. "Overdoing Gender: A Test of the Masculine Overcompensation Thesis." *American Journal of Sociology* 118, 4: 980–1022.

Wood, Wendy P. Niels Christensen, Michelle R. Hebl, and Hank Rothgerber. 1997. "Conformity to Sex-Typed Norms, Affect, and the Self-Concept." *Journal of Personality and Social Psychology* 73, 3: 523–535.

Worthen, Meredith G. F. 2013. "An Argument for Separate Analyses of Attitudes Toward Lesbian, Gay, Bisexual Men, Bisexual Women, MtF and FtM Transgender Individuals." *Sex Roles* 68, 11–12: 703–723.

Zaller, John. 1992. *The Nature and Origins of Mass Opinion*. New York: Cambridge University Press.

Index

Tables and figures are indicated by *t* and *f* following the page number